For the Love of Hockey

W9-BGW-659

For the Love of HOCKEY

Hockey Stars' Personal Stories

COMPILED BY CHRIS McDONELL

Foreword by John Davidson

FIREFLY BOOKS

A FIREFLY BOOK

Copyright © 2001 Firefly Books

All rights reserved. No part of this publication may be reproduced, stored in a retrieval system or transmitted in any form or by any means, electronic, mechanical, photocopying, recording or otherwise, without the prior written permission of the Publisher.

First paperback edition 2001

U.S. Cataloguing-in-Publication Data
(Library of Congress Standards)

McDonell, Chris.
    For the love of hockey / Chris McDonell – revised and updated edition
[200] p. : col. ill. (some col.) ; cm.
Originally published, 1997.
ISBN 1-55209-606-8
1. Hockey – Biography.   2. National Hockey League.   I. Title.
796.962 / 0922   21   2001   CIP

National Library of Canada Cataloguing in Publication Data

Main entry under title:

For the love of hockey : hockey stars' personal stories

Rev. and updated.
ISBN 1-55209-606-8

1. Hockey – Anecdotes.   2. National Hockey League – Anecdotes.
3. Hockey players – Anecdotes.   I. McDonell, Chris.

GV848.5.A1F67 2001   796.962'092'2   C2001-930478-1

Published in the United States in 2001 by
Firefly Books (U.S.) Inc.
P.O. Box 1338, Ellicott Station
Buffalo, New York 14205

Produced by
Bookmakers Press Inc.
12 Pine Street
Kingston, Ontario K7K 1W1
(613) 549-4347
tcread@sympatico.ca

Design by
Ulrike Bender
Studio Eye

Color separations by
Friesens, Altona, Manitoba

Printed and bound in Canada by
Friesens, Altona, Manitoba

Printed on acid-free paper

The Publisher acknowledges the financial support of the Government of Canada through the Book Publishing Industry Development Program for its publishing activities.

Published in Canada in 2001 by
Firefly Books Ltd.
3680 Victoria Park Avenue
Willowdale, Ontario M2H 3K1

Front cover:
Mario Lemieux raises his arm in triumph as he completes his hat trick in a 1996 game against the St. Louis Blues. Photograph © Doug MacLellan/Hockey Hall of Fame.

Page 7:
Bobby Orr, playing for the NHL All-Stars against the defending Stanley Cup champion Toronto Maple Leafs, fires a shot on net in the 1968 NHL All-Star game. Photograph © Graphic Artists/Hockey Hall of Fame.

Page 198:
In a classic confrontation between two National Hockey League legends, Montreal's Jean Beliveau is in all alone against Toronto's Johnny Bower. Photograph © Frank Prazak/Hockey Hall of Fame.

Back cover:
Wayne Gretzky, early in his career with the Edmonton Oilers. Photograph © Doug MacLellan/Hockey Hall of Fame.

To Quinn, Tara and Isaac McDonell-Gordon,

who helped me learn to play again,

and to Sue Gordon,

my partner and my love

CONTENTS

Foreword

There's still nothing I enjoy more than going into an arena the morning of a game. The players arrive for a short skate, some of their family members watch proudly, reporters are gathered and buzzing with rumors, kids are hanging around looking for autographs, and the sound of pucks hitting the boards and the glass reverberates through the building. It is the calm before the storm. By 4:30 in the afternoon, the tension starts to mount, the coaches have less to say, and the players turn inward, tightening the circle around them.

Many of the stories in this book point to the importance and special quality of team camaraderie. I agree. In the locker room preparing for a game, you have the feeling of going into battle, and all around you are those who will be in the foxhole with you. There's nothing better than being in the trenches with your teammates.

When I was growing up in Canada, I lived for hockey. I loved playing net the first time I tried it, and I had some success. I was always drawing goalies instead of listening to my teachers. I could hardly wait to watch *Hockey Night in Canada* on Saturday nights. Television was as close as most of us got to our passion for the NHL, so when I made it to the St. Louis Blues in 1973, I could not believe my good fortune. I played against legends such as Gordie Howe, Bobby Hull, Bobby Orr and, later, Wayne Gretzky. In fact, I played with or against 41 of the men in this book.

Standing on the ice with players I had looked up to as a kid and as a fan was initially an experience that felt larger than life. That changed once I got to know them and I discovered we shared a common language: hockey. *For the Love of Hockey* speaks that language fluently. The kinds of stories and information in the book are what I look for in my work as a broadcaster. It's hard to find fresh material about players who have been interviewed hundreds if not thousands of times, but I found so many anecdotes here that I had not heard before. For a hockey or sports fan, these stories allow you to get to know an absolutely remarkable group of players from a number of decades, including dozens of Hall of Famers, future Hall of Famers and young stars. Every position on the ice is covered. Different cultures are here. French- and English-Canadians, Americans, Russians, Slovakians, Czechs, Swedes, Finns—the cross section is wonderful.

In the first game I played in the Montreal Forum, we lost 2–1, but I stopped "The Pocket Rocket," Henri Richard, on a breakaway. I'll never forget that. It's the kind of memory that stirs in me when I read *For the Love of Hockey*. I was on the bench in my NHL rookie year as the backup goalie when Frank Mahovlich skated by and I shouted at him, as players often do at the opposition. Barclay Plager, our captain, turned around and tore a strip off me. "Don't yell at 'The Big M'! Don't get him mad!" I learned that lesson in a hurry.

I grew up a Bobby Orr fan and remained one even after playing against him. The first time I faced Boston, he killed about a minute and a half of a two-minute penalty single-handedly, with our whole team chasing him around the ice. He would not give up the puck, and it was one of the most amazing performances I have ever witnessed.

Every story in this book triggers a similar recollection for me, because each man here has contributed to the game of hockey. I met Glenn Hall when I was broadcasting for Calgary. He was goaltending coach for the Flames at the time and is still a remarkable man, but when you look deeply at his career, you see his greatness. I was a goaltender at Bobby Hull's last training camp. His shoulders were bad, worn out from all those years of firing the puck and hitting, and he wasn't shooting well. But his shot came back to him toward the end of camp. He nailed me right in the chest, and I had trouble breathing. Seeing Bobby, Brett and Dennis Hull together is unique. Dennis Hull is famous for his wit and is a rarity in that he has become more legendary since he retired as a player.

We all know that these guys scored goals and many of them won championships. But getting inside them and hearing what they have to say makes this book so interesting and shows me why the hockey fan is—in my opinion—the most passionate fan in all of sports. Hockey is a lifeline for people all over the world. Peter Stastny's passion comes through, as strongly felt as that of any Canadian, clearly showing that it's the game that brings this out, independent of a national culture.

I've had the opportunity to work with Wayne Gretzky in New York for a full season now. I've witnessed his genuine love of the game. He wants to know what's going on in the rest of the league, he knows the standings, who's where in the scoring race and what team is in trouble or on a roll. He doesn't need to, but he pays attention to those things.

Seeing Lanny McDonald in this book stirs up vivid

John Davidson began his broadcasting career while recuperating from knee surgery during the 1981-82 season. When injuries permanently ended his playing days after the 1983-84 season, he moved behind the mike full-time. (Opposite) Davidson was traded to the New York Rangers in the summer of 1975 and helped lead the team to the 1979 Stanley Cup finals.

memories for me. I played for the Lethbridge Sugar Kings with Lanny when I was 16 years old in what is now called Tier Two Junior in Alberta. We were losing a playoff game 2–1 when, 19 seconds into the third period, the Lethbridge arena caught fire. A beyond-capacity crowd of almost 1,800 people was almost literally hanging from the rafters, but everyone marched out of the rink in an orderly way, including the players. We stood across the street still in our skates and watched the building burn right down to the ground in 90 minutes.

I was playing for the New York Rangers in 1979 when we upset Los Angeles, the Islanders and Philadelphia before losing the Stanley Cup finals against Montreal. That Canadiens team was one of the greatest in NHL history. Guy Lafleur alone had 13 shots in one game— most of them pegged for the top corner on my glove-hand side—but we beat them 4–1 in the opening game and gave them a bit of a scare. Getting that far was the highlight of my career, but it's also haunting to have come that close to winning a championship. We were three games away from a Stanley Cup win, but we *didn't* win. Whenever I broadcast the final game of the season, I am reminded of what it feels like to be on the other side of the victory. It is not a good feeling.

The nicest compliment I ever received in hockey came from Mike Bossy, a guy who could put the puck through the eye of a needle—sideways if he needed to. Mike said I was the toughest goaltender he ever played against. But my second career as a broad-caster has been much more successful. I did not get what I should have as a player, partly because of injuries and perhaps because my dedication to the sport was not what it could have been. I was the first goaltender to play in the NHL directly out of junior hockey, and I should have taken some time to mature in the minors. I certainly wish I possessed then the work habits I have now! I could have avoided some injuries (I had two operations on my back and six on my knees) and been a better goalie when I did play, not just the decent playoff goaltender that I believe I was. When I look at the players in this book, I see their dedication and understand why they are the great ones.

In my playing days, 1973 to 1983, a lot of players took a similar approach to mine, and there are some guys in this book who were even a little wacko at times. Yet their talent level was enormously high. Rick Middleton, for example, was always an outstanding hockey player but was so reckless away from the rink when he was a New York Ranger. We called him "Silky" because he was so smooth on the ice. He was like a slinky toy, snaking and winding his way through and around guys, and it was pitiful to face him on a breakaway. Not content merely to shoot the puck, he would bend a goalie backwards and twist him around before he scored.

I was glad to see Slava Fetisov included here. North American hockey fans were robbed by not seeing him play very often while he was in his prime. His accomplishments are almost folklore in his homeland. Not enough people here know his story, and it is as compelling as any in the book.

Broadcasting hockey is similar to playing in some respects—thankfully without the threat of injuries! It's a team effort, and the pressure, although different, is still there. I'm thankful I found a way to stay connected to the game I love. Hockey has given me so much, even the chance to get to know the many great young stars in this book who arrived in the NHL after I retired as a player.

Injuries ended my playing days, but the fire inside has never gone out. I probably have more of a passion for hockey now then I did when I was a goalie. I have some concerns about the business side of hockey today, but I trust that everyone involved with the game—the new fans in new cities, the players and the owners— will never take hockey for granted. The tradition, speed, skill, toughness and entertainment that hockey pro-vides took decades to cultivate and need to be nurtured. The players in *For the Love of Hockey* represent those facets of the game at its highest level, and the more we hear such players speak, the better off will be the game of hockey.

—*John Davidson*

(**Opposite**) *Davidson was the first-round draft choice of the St. Louis Blues in 1973 and became the first NHL goalie to successfully jump to the league directly from junior hockey.*

Andy Bathgate

My brother Frank, a top prospect with the New York Rangers organization, was sent to Guelph to play junior in 1949. I decided to follow him. I wanted to help my mother financially, and the Winnipeg junior team had offered me only $200 for the entire season. My father had suffered with cancer for two years before he died when I was 13, leaving us almost penniless.

Though uninvited, I went to training camp with Frank. The coach ordered me off the ice on first sight. In that case, my brother said, he was leaving too. Windsor

had offered me a tryout, so my brother and I were at the train station ready to leave when the Guelph people had a change of heart. I made the team and scored 21 goals in 40 games. The next year, we won the Memorial Cup, with seven future NHLers on the team.

The Rangers forced me to turn pro before I wanted to. I had had a serious knee operation, with plates inserted, and I hadn't had a chance to test it yet. I even had to take a $1,500 pay cut. After some fierce negotiations with Guelph, my contract recognized that I was looking after my mother. The people of Guelph were so good to us. It was a wonderful place and time to grow up. The crowds were big for the games, and there was great community spirit. If we were out late, management heard of it the next day, because the whole town knew we had an 11 o'clock curfew.

New York was an unbelievable contrast, and the first two years were the loneliest of my life. I was sent to play for Vancouver, where I was teamed up with Larry Popein. The Rangers seemed to have no plans for Larry, so I declared that if Larry didn't get invited to training camp for the Rangers, I wasn't going either. It was a bit of a wedge to get something better for both of us, but Larry was invited to camp and became my center for seven years in New York on a line with Dean Prentice. His skating and speed created openings so that we got some points and were noticed. We improved every year, as did the team, and we had some success.

I was only ever as good as my linemates, not able to overpower opponents like Howe and Hull and do it on my own. I had a career year when I won the Hart Trophy as league MVP in 1959. To win it over Gordie Howe when our team didn't even make the playoffs made it very special. I think the award was recognition for producing under adverse conditions.

In the late 1950s, spearing in the NHL was really getting bad. One night, Red Sullivan got stuck with a stick in a game against Montreal. Down he went. Winded, we thought. In the dressing room, it became obvious that he needed serious medical attention. He passed out and was rushed to emergency. When Red's wife, my wife and I got to the hospital after the game, the doctor said, "We've lost him." Miraculously, another doctor put a large needle into his heart and revived him. It turned out Red had a ruptured spleen.

I was very upset and wrote an article in a major sports magazine. I identified five of the biggest names in the game as perpetrators, signing my name to a piece entitled "Atrocities on Ice." This made headlines in all the newspapers. As an NHL MVP, I hoped my concerns would be listened to. Instead, NHL President Clarence Campbell fined me. I told him that I went to the media because complaining within the league accomplished nothing. I would have been told to be a man, to go out and fight. I argued that this practice of spearing had to get cleaned up before someone was killed, but I got little public or private support.

At the end of the year, I did receive a letter from Frank Selke, Sr., of the Montreal Canadiens. He acknowledged my contribution in bringing this serious problem to league attention. A much stiffer rule was adopted for the next season. I heard years later that it was Mr. Selke who nominated me to the Hockey Hall of Fame.

When I was traded to Toronto in 1964, I knew my purpose—score goals. The Leafs were in fifth place then, but we went on to win the Cup. I contributed with some important goals, including the game-tying goal late in game six of the finals to avoid defeat. I crossed the blue line and let go one of the best shots of my career, picking the top right-hand corner over Terry Sawchuk's shoulder. Bobby Baun went on to score in overtime.

I gave us the lead in game seven on a breakaway from our own blue line. I went in on Sawchuk and tucked the puck into the top corner of the net, knowing that Terry couldn't lift his left arm very high. We eventually won 4–0.

Winning the Stanley Cup was my most satisfying achievement. Still, it would have been sweeter to win with New York. The Rangers are still in my blood.

Andy Bathgate

Andy Bathgate, Hart Trophy winner and three-time All-Star with the New York Rangers, was team captain when he was traded late in the 1963-64 season. (OPPOSITE) Bathgate scored several critical goals for the Leafs in Toronto's surge for a third consecutive championship and in 1964 was able to sip champagne from the Stanley Cup.

Jean Beliveau

Montreal had a great team when I signed with them in 1953. Even so, we lost to Detroit two years in a row in seven-game Stanley Cup finals. Toe Blake gave a brief speech shortly after he was named coach in 1955. "I have great hockey players here," he said. "But if we want to win anything, we have to find a way to become a unit." That was a turning point for the club. We adjusted our game so that the team came first and individual success second. Five Stanley Cups in a row followed.

In my early years, the press was on me to play rougher, but I'd grown up close to the church and it wasn't really in me. Still, I came out in my third year determined to throw my weight around a little more. I got a lot of penalties—for boarding and some hard hitting—and I got a lot more respect when it was seen that I could play a belligerent game if I wanted to. I set a club record for penalties that was broken only by John Ferguson six or seven years later, which makes for a good trivia question. I also won the scoring championship and the MVP. Despite that success, I enjoyed playing the game most in my own style, according to the rules.

You don't get tired of winning the Stanley Cup, but it does get more difficult. I think the team kept improving until it peaked with an incredibly balanced squad in 1958, though we won two more Cups after that. Bert Olmstead and Bernie Geoffrion were my wingers, and Bert was always on us to do better, work harder. He was great in the corners and would give me hell if I came in to help him, telling me to get back in front of the net. I thank him, because I played my best hockey in those years.

One set play we had was for me to pull back just before a face-off in the other team's end. I'd look to see where the defensemen were placing themselves. If they were wide apart, I'd give Bernie a subtle glance. He'd then know to go straight to the net, and I'd try to flip the puck to him. Of course, it didn't always work, but we got some quick goals that way. I watch today to see whether the centers look at their opponents setting up, and most often they don't. The game is one of improvisation—that's the beauty of it—but there are times when you can make it easier for yourself.

My teammates voted me captain in 1961, which was an honor I treasure. Before that, I was not even an alternate captain, so it came as something of a shock. There was a secret vote, and Bernie Geoffrion and I were tied after the first round. A second vote was taken, and Toe Blake came, shook my hand and said, "Boys, here's your new captain." Bernie, an alternate captain, had been on the team longer and was upset about this for a few days. I went to Mr. Selke and suggested I give up the "C" to bring peace to the team. He refused the offer, since the players themselves had made the decision. Bernie and I roomed together for 11 years, and warm feelings were soon restored.

In the 1960s, Toe used to have all the new members of the team play with me. I told them to stick to their game and play their strengths, and I would make the adjustments needed. I hope that I'm remembered as a player who could score, but I enjoyed making a good play as much as scoring. I particularly loved to see the youngsters net their share of goals.

I miss the action on the ice and the satisfaction of winning the Stanley Cup, but above all, I miss the family atmosphere, the spirit and togetherness of the team. I enjoyed the long time we spent on trains. If someone was going through a tough time, there was opportunity to talk. After a game on the road, it was normal for 14 or 15 of us to go out for a beer. We had our usual haunts, and pretty much everyone would drop in. These things are good for a team.

I've always believed that a public person should retire early rather than too late. I understand that some are not in a position to do this, but 1971 provided me with a perfect time to retire. I had an excellent season, was top scorer on the team, and we won the Stanley Cup for my tenth time. I had wanted to retire the previous season, but Sam Pollock asked me to play another year to help the team through a transition to younger players. I haven't been the type to hang up my skates and still grasp for the glory and publicity that comes with being a player, but working for Molson, owner of the Montreal Canadiens, has kept me close to the team. My credo has been "Be there when they need you," and I've tried to live this on and off the ice.

*Montreal finally succeeded in 1953 in signing Jean Beliveau, already a young star for several seasons in the Quebec Senior League. (*Opposite*) Perhaps the quintessential Canadiens captain, Beliveau creates some open ice against Jim Dorey and Brian Glennie (right) of the Toronto Maple Leafs.*

Leo Boivin

My goal from the time I was a kid was to play in the National Hockey League. Although everybody always said I was too small—I only grew to be 5 feet 7½ inches —I had pretty good weight and skated very well, so I kept plugging away. As a junior, I used to hit a lot. Maybe I was trying to prove that although I wasn't as tall as the other guys, I was just as tough. Not that I tried to hurt anybody, but it was an important part of my game. I used to *get* hit a lot too; it wasn't all one way. But I enjoyed the body check.

I belonged to Boston as a junior, but when I was 19, Boston and Toronto made a deal; I was the amateur thrown in. I was playing for the Maple Leafs farm team

in Pittsburgh in the 1951-52 season. Fernie Flaman got a broken jaw, so I was called up. I had never even been in Maple Leaf Gardens before. It struck me as a great honor to come in and wear the Leafs sweater.

We were playing a home-and-home pair of games against Detroit. I lined up for the opening face-off, and Detroit started with Gordie Howe, Sid Abel and Ted Lindsay. On that first shift, I knocked Howe down. What a sensation! That really felt good. We won the game that night but went back to Detroit and lost, and then I returned to Pittsburgh for the rest of the season.

The next year I was back up with the Leafs to stay. When I broke in with Toronto, they had a system where the defense stood right up and took the man. It was always, "Take the man." Hap Day, the general manager, was the most knowledgeable hockey person I ever encountered. He always said: "You have a job to do, so do it well. If the other guy can't do his job, we'll replace him." You had to come to play every night, and when you got hurt, you didn't want to be out of the lineup very long, because somebody would come in and take your place.

I was with the Toronto Maple Leafs for 2½ years before being traded to Boston, where I played for 11½ years. With the system we used in Boston, I had great opportunities for open-ice hitting. Sometimes I hit with the shoulder, but mainly I used the hip. I went into whoever had his head down.

We ended up in the finals for the Stanley Cup two years in a row against Montreal. One night, Rocket Richard scored four goals on us—everything he shot

went in. He was such a great competitor. He had one thing in mind, and it was to put the puck in the net. From the red line in, he'd go around you, through you or over you. He had a terrific shot. One of us would often have an ankle in a pail of ice on the train ride home.

In the 1957 Stanley Cup finals in Montreal, I caught the Rocket with a beautiful hip check. He went really high and over me. Red Storey was the referee and gave me a penalty. Oh, was I mad! He called me for kneeing, but I had no knee at all in that hit. In the films we saw later that summer, they showed that check as a highlight. Lynn Patrick, our general manager, was furious at the call. Storey might have been looking the other way and just saw Richard going through the air.

When I first broke into the league and I'd hit the Rocket like that, he'd always swing his stick when he got into the air. After getting about 15 stitches in the head and over the eye, I learned to grab his stick.

All the players played tough, so when you made a big hit on someone, you really needed to keep your wits about you for the rest of the game, because someone was certainly going to retaliate. But everybody hit pretty clean.

One time I hit Stan Mikita in Chicago, and he went right up in the air. When he came down, his skate caught the back of my neck. I didn't even know I was cut until I put my hand over my neck and went to the bench. The gash took 40 stitches to close—20 inside and 20 outside.

I was captain in Boston for four years, and those were hard times as a player. One year, we started 11 rookies. It was too much, and we didn't get out of the cellar for quite a while. In those days, each team would generally change only one or two men a season. There was a tight bond among the players because we played together for a long time—they didn't move people the way they do today. When you played, you took care of each other. If you didn't, you were told about it. We'd go on three-week road trips, and we got to be like a family.

Leo Boivin

Leo Boivin was known as one of the NHL's hardest-hitting bodycheckers in a 19-year Hall of Fame career that included a stop in Pittsburgh for their inaugural 1967-68 NHL season. (Opposite) A Boston Bruin from late 1954 until 1966, Boivin is shown muscling Frank Mahovlich off the puck while Fern Flaman looks on.

Peter Bondra

I was born in the Ukraine but grew up in Czecho-slovakia. That's why I had no international experience until I was well into my twenties. I held Russian citizen-ship, even though I had moved to Czechoslovakia when I was 3 years old. Denied the chance to play for any national teams, I always cheered for Czechoslovakia and in my heart belonged there. With the country's recent political changes, I became a Slovakian citizen, giving me a chance to play for my homeland in the 1996 World Cup. Most people don't even know where Slovakia is, so

it was great to show the world that we can play hockey. The highlight for me was when we almost beat Team Canada. Most of the guys on our team haven't had a chance to come to North America, let alone play hockey here, so it was a great experience for all of us. I'll proudly play for Slovakia whenever I possibly can.

I was about 8 before I started skating. My brother brought me to the rink, and I was really into it right away. I was a good enough hockey player to be selected to a class of fellow Czechoslovakian boys my age. We went to practice in the morning for a couple of hours, then went to classes together during regular school hours. We traveled all over the country to play games. Being on the ice every day was great for me. Hockey is big business now that I'm in the NHL, but even with all the travel, I love it as much now as I did then.

I was part of that class from grade five until grade eight. Then I joined the junior hockey team in my hometown of Obrutz. At age 17, I started to play for the town's professional team. After one year, I moved up to the elite league with a good team, Kosice, playing against Jaromir Jagr, Robert Reichel and other great players. The experience was excellent, and we won a couple of championships. I was pretty successful as I moved up the ladder in Czechoslovakia, with 30- and 35-goal seasons, but without international exposure, no one in the NHL really noticed.

In 1989, I met Jack Batten, who was scouting Richard Smehlik, a defenseman on the team I was playing against. The first game Jack saw me play, we won 4–2; I scored twice and had two assists. In our next match, Jack came specifically to see me. I scored again, and he asked to speak with me after the game. I went into his room, and he was sitting in a chair with his feet

up on the table. He told me he liked how I skated and scored and gave me my first inkling that I might be able to play in the NHL one day. Until then, it had never entered my mind.

We never saw NHL games, but I had seen great players like Wayne Gretzky, Mario Lemieux and Mark Messier in the Canada Cup tournaments. In the fall of 1990, I saw my first NHL game because I was playing in it! I was drafted in the eighth round by the Capitals in the spring of that year at age 22. I was chosen as the 156th pick overall, and no one really expected me to make it. But Washington put a contract on the table and I saw my chance.

I wasn't surprised to make the team, but I must say that Michal Pivonka was a great help on and off the ice. He's Czech, so he not only told me where to go on the ice but knew the help I'd need learning to pay my bills and find my way. That's really an agent's job, but an agent can spend only so much time with a player. Michal was there every day.

It wasn't easy to adjust to the North American game. Here you have to know what to do before you get the puck. At home, that wasn't part of the game; it was more about skating. I had reasonably good NHL seasons right from the start, but it took me a couple of years to get used to the differences.

After my first two seasons, I realized that I'd have to get stronger physically. I had good legs for skating, but I was too soft in the upper body. I had to be able to take more hits and not get knocked to my knees so often. I improved enough to score 37 goals in my third year with the Capitals, but my fourth season was dis-appointing, with only 24 goals. I was determined to get even stronger in the off-season. I led the league in goals the next year, but it was a season shortened by the lockout. I'd have to continue working to show it wasn't just luck. For that reason, breaking the 50-goal barrier the next year was especially meaningful to me. I've proved I belong.

Peter Bondra of the Washington Capitals led the NHL in goal scoring in the lockout-shortened 1994-95 season. (Opposite) Using the speed that is his greatest asset, Bondra moves into scoring range against a backpedaling Maple Leafs defense.

Mike Bossy

DESPITE MY GETTING MORE THAN 300 GOALS FOR LAVAL during my years in the Quebec junior league, in hindsight, it isn't too shocking that I only went fifteenth in the 1977 NHL entry draft. I wasn't even decent defensively as a junior, because no one asked me to do anything but get points and score goals. I have to admit that the Cleveland Barons, who had the fifth pick, had asked whether I would play for them if they drafted me. My agent and I dissuaded them by telling them I'd be asking for what was truly a ridiculous amount of money. I was surprised when the New York Islanders drafted me, but I knew right away that I was going into an ideal situation.

The Islanders had a lot of good young players and were a team on the rise. They told me there was a spot on the team for me if I wanted it. I responded by telling general manager Bill Torrey—more as a strategy than anything else—that if I played regularly, I could score more than 50 goals. I still remember the look on his face that said, "Who are you trying to kid?" I took success in stride as my rookie season progressed, and that bold prediction came true because of the guys I was playing with, the ice time I was getting and the confidence I had. But when the season was over, I looked back and was surprised to have scored 53 goals in my first NHL season.

I was on a line with Bryan Trottier and Clark Gillies right from the start. They were great guys—very intense about winning as a team and about doing well personally. That rubbed off on me as time went on. My favorite individual accomplishment is my nine consecutive 50-goal seasons. After my first campaign, I said, "Well, I scored 50 once. There's no reason why I can't do it every time." I went on a quest for at least 50 goals a year. My biggest disappointment came in my last season. Playing only 63 games with a painfully bad back (that eventually forced my retirement), I came up short with 39 goals.

One goal that stands out for me came in the Stanley Cup final against Vancouver in 1982. I still don't know how I got the shot off. My entire body was in midair, parallel to the ice, but I was able to backhand the puck through the legs of Richard Brodeur. For a split second, I didn't even know that I had scored. You don't have time to think in circumstances like that. The puck's there and the net's there, and instinct takes over.

I had a strong desire to score, there's no doubt about that. But from the point that the puck was on my stick to when it was in the net was always pure instinct. Scoring goals came to me in a natural and unexplainable way from the time I was a boy, but early in my career, I did discover one thing that worked: Shoot at the middle of the net. When most goalies were centered in the net, they'd guess I was going either left or right and leave the middle exposed, so I usually aimed for the five-hole. I also tried to release the puck sooner than the goalie expected. But if there was one thing I hated doing, it was missing the net with a shot. That seemed pretty stupid to me, so my main concern was at least to get every shot on net. If I wasn't able to beat the goalie, I knew there usually would be a rebound lying around for me or a teammate.

I learned to expect to have an opponent practically attached to me during games and to play through it. That was frustrating, but with success come some difficulties. What I got most upset about was the hitting from behind, the spearing and high sticking. One aspect of the game that has changed is the media attention to violence and a greater intolerance of it today. Things that weren't seen as violent when I was playing now are. Intentional fighting—when a team instructed a player to go after a more talented opponent—has been eliminated almost entirely from the game. I doubt you can ever take all fighting out of hockey, although I still completely disagree with it.

Our first Stanley Cup win was special because of being the first, but the others were also significant. You never forget that someone won the Stanley Cup. It's a nice stat to have beside your name, and four consecutive Cups is even better. I got so used to winning, I didn't think it was going to end. It was difficult to lose, but that brought me back down to earth by showing me we weren't invincible, and I got back to work right away.

I'm a stockbroker now, so I've certainly found something that gives me the same level of stress that I put myself under when I played hockey. I consider my clients part of my team. I'm a passionate person who takes pride in doing a job well, though I know you can't win all the time. But I enjoy what I do, and as in hockey, winning is definitely more fun.

Mike Bossy won 1978 Rookie of the Year honors with a record-breaking 53-goal season. He went on to cross the 50-goal mark nine years in a row. (OPPOSITE) Bossy, perhaps the premier sniper in NHL history, had a shot that made him a serious scoring threat from almost anywhere in the offensive zone.

Raymond Bourque

I WORE NUMBER 29 RIGHT THROUGH MY FIRST BRUINS training camp in 1979, but when I arrived for the first game of the season, Phil Esposito's old number seven was in my stall. I just put it on. Bobby Schmautz came up to me right before the game started and told me not to worry if I heard any hecklers. At that moment, I realized number seven might be a tough number to wear. But the fans were great, and I never heard anything about it from anyone other than the press. I always said that it wasn't a number I asked for, and if the Bruins ever wanted to retire Phil's sweater, I'd have no objections.

Nothing was ever said about that until late 1987 when Terry O'Reilly called me on behalf of Harry Sinden at 1:30 in the afternoon the day they raised Phil's sweater into the rafters of the Boston Garden. I readily agreed to change numbers, and because it was so last-minute, only the trainer, Harry, Terry and I knew about it. It was a great surprise for everyone when I skated up to Phil, pulled off my number seven—I was wearing number 77 underneath—and handed the sweater to him. Phil was shocked and very appreciative, but I was pleased to help make Phil Esposito Night even sweeter for him. What Phil accomplished for the Bruins deserved to be fully acknowledged by having number seven elevated, not still worn on the ice. It was the right thing to do.

I grew up a Montreal Canadiens fan. I got spoiled seeing them win so many Stanley Cups, but they were great to watch while I dreamed of playing in the NHL. I was on the other side of the fence in a hurry when the Bruins, Montreal's great rival, drafted me. I wasn't a Canadiens fan for very long after I got here, that's for sure.

I came to the Bruins as a quiet guy who just wanted to make the team and establish himself as a good NHL hockey player. I knew I was a solid junior player, but you never know what's in store and how big the jump is going to be when you come to the NHL. The Bruins had lost to Montreal in overtime of the seventh game of the semifinals the year before and weren't really making a lot of changes. But I was welcomed with open arms by a great team of veterans. I felt as if I had touched "old-time" hockey when I joined players like Gerry Cheevers, Wayne Cashman and Jean Ratelle. Those guys had seen a lot of battles and a lot of success. Stepping into that atmosphere as an 18-year-old was unbelievably exciting. Things went well right away, but about all I had to say to the press for my first two years was, "I'm just glad to be here."

I guess now I'm helping to carry on the Bruins tradition. The Bruins have historically been a tight-knit family, and guys played together for a long time. You try to stay a unit and be a team, but there are obviously tremendous differences in the game today. With so many guys coming and going every year, it's tougher to really build on the feeling, the tradition, of being a Bruin, but I still try.

Whenever I go through contract negotiations, I think about what it might be like to be with another team. I went to arbitration in my last negotiations, and there were comments that if I had won my case, Harry Sinden might have traded me. I don't know about that. I'm in Boston because I want to be here. I love Boston. It's a great city to play hockey in, I'm established in the community, and it's all my kids know.

If I were ever to leave, it would have to be my call and only to win a Stanley Cup. A Stanley Cup would be unbelievable, but I always have hope here. We're no favorites by any means, but you never know. Some teams go through a year playing good solid hockey, "sleep" their way into the finals and win it all. That's the type of club we have. We're not going to blow out any teams, but hopefully, we'll be competitive and save our best until the last.

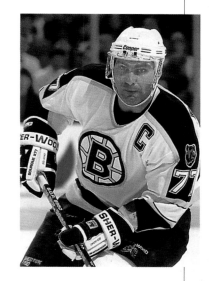

I've had a great relationship with the fans. We've had some terrific years here, and I've had some personal success. I think there's a mutual respect; they've been good to me, and I've been good to them. I've never stopped and really thought about all that's happened to me. I look at myself in the mirror, and I think that I still have something to prove. I don't know why, I don't know what it is, but that's a big reason why I'm the player I am. I respect the game, I love it. The only goal I have ever set is to go out and play as hard and as well as I can every day. It's been a great life in hockey, and I'm not ready to give it up yet.

After spending almost 20 stellar seasons on the Boston blue line, Ray Bourque requested a trade. In March 2000, he joined the Colorado Avalanche, and he was at last able to accomplish his mission by winning a Cup ring in June 2001. He retired the same month. (OPPOSITE) Bourque starts a rush in 1980, showing the poise that earned him his first of 19 All-Star berths and the Calder Trophy that year.

Johnny Bower

With only six NHL teams and six goalkeepers, you had to bide your time. I rode the buses for nine years before I was drafted by the New York Rangers in 1953. I played only one full season with them. Even though I posted a fine average, the Rangers sent me down to the minors again. Gump Worsley came up and played. One year was not satisfying. I felt I should have stayed longer, that I was as good as the other goalies. I got disheartened and it was a struggle at times, but I knew that if I kept working, something would give.

I was drafted by the Toronto Maple Leafs in 1958, the break I needed. By then, I had spent a total of 13 years in the minors. At age 34, I couldn't really figure out why

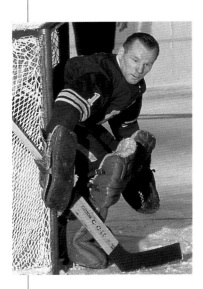

Toronto wanted me. Punch Imlach had coached an American League team that I played well against one year. I think he must have jotted my name in his book, because when he became the Leafs coach and general manager, he gave me a call. I admired Punch, although he was a very demanding person. He believed that what we did in practice, we'd do in a game, so I worked hard every time I was on the ice. The younger players wondered if we weren't leaving our game in practice, but we older guys—Allan Stanley, Timmy Horton, Al Arbour and I—agreed with Punch. We had a great blend of youth and experience.

I was scared, literally shaking in my boots, for my first game in Maple Leaf Gardens. My teammates knew it too. I had a good training camp, but it's different playing in front of 15,000 people. Punch grabbed me and told me that once the first period was over, I'd be fine. We won the game 3–1, and I was the happiest guy in the world. George Armstrong, our team captain, was my roommate. He'd roomed with goalies before and assured me, correctly, that after we'd done the circuit a couple of times, my nerves would settle down.

One year in the playoffs, Punch loosely piled about $12,000 in cash on a table in the middle of the dressing room. That money represented the bonus each of us would get for winning the Stanley Cup. It was part of his pep talk and it worked. I got along with Punch, although I got mad at him many times. Frank Mahovlich was the greatest left-winger we had, yet Punch would never give him a pat on the back. But Punch gave me an opportunity and said I'd be with the team as long as he was there. I outlasted him by

a few seasons, but we won four Stanley Cups together.

It was such a thrill to win the Cup. One year, I got so excited that at the end of the game, I threw my stick up in the air. I saw my teammates coming toward me to celebrate and realized I'd better get my stick. I looked up and—boom!—it came down on my forehead and cut me for seven stitches. I didn't feel a thing, bleeding all over the guys who were hugging me.

Charlie Rayner taught me the poke check when I first went to the Rangers. I practiced by lining up pucks in front of the net and diving out to poke them away. The timing had to be just right. We were once in double overtime and Yvan Cournoyer broke in with great speed, so if I'd missed, I would have lost the game in an embarrassing way. Well, I poke-checked the puck and sent it into the corner. George Armstrong head-manned the puck to Bobby Pulford, who scored.

Terry Sawchuk and I shared a Vezina Trophy one year. I learned to move better by watching him. He'd glide out to cut down a shooter's angle, whereas I had been more inclined to move out quickly and be off balance. Terry was a real loner. He was certainly a great competitor whose record speaks for itself, but I just couldn't talk to him. I asked him for help a couple of times, but he only reassured me without really offering any insight or assistance. One year, Punch told me that I'd start the season, but if I didn't play well, Terry would go in. Then Terry would start all the games until he didn't play well. I played about six games, but, maybe because of my age, I started to get a little tired. Punch put Terry in.

I worried that I might not play for a long time. After Terry played eight consecutive games, I was getting rusty, so I asked Eddie Shack to do me a favor in practice and take a good hard shot to Terry's glove side. Terry always was about the worst practice goalie I ever saw. Eddie had a heavy shot, and after he went in on Terry a couple of times, Terry wouldn't even try to stop him. Eddie got mad, and the next time he came in, he blasted one. Terry just waved his arm at it, but the puck hit his glove and broke his finger. I played the next 10 games. I still owe Eddie Shack a steak dinner for that.

Johnny Bower

Johnny Bower played goal on four Maple Leafs Stanley Cup-winning teams in the 1960s, finally retiring in 1970 at the age of 45. (Opposite) No goalie ever used the poke-check as effectively as Bower. Here, he strips the puck from the speedy Ken Wharram of the Blackhawks.

Johnny Bucyk

SCORING MY 500TH CAREER GOAL IN 1976, RIGHT IN BOSTON, was special. I have a tape of the game that I watch a lot and pictures hanging on a wall at home, but the best memento came from some of my teammates. We had five left-wingers and only three jobs on the team then. At the end of the season, the other four left-wingers, Wayne Cashman, Don Marcotte, Dave Forbes and Hank Nowak, presented me with a gold medal with "500" on it. That really touched me. I'm proud of that medal, and I wear it almost every day. It's not from the league or from the team but from

four guys who were fighting for my job. I'll never forget the gesture.

I grew up in the Detroit Red Wings organization and got my NHL call-up just before the 1955 playoffs. The Red Wings won, and though I never dressed for a game, they gave me a Stanley Cup ring. I didn't play much for the next two seasons either and scored only 11 goals, so I welcomed the trade for Terry Sawchuk that sent me to Boston. The Bruins told me of their plans to reunite me with my two linemates from minor pro hockey in Edmonton, Vic Stasiuk and Bronco Horvath. We became known as the Uke Line.

We went to the finals my first two years in Boston but then didn't make the playoffs for the next eight years. We battled the Rangers to see who would stay out of the basement; that was our Stanley Cup then. After our eight-year dry spell, things started to turn around. Milt Schmidt traded for Phil Esposito, Ken Hodge and Fred Stanfield from Chicago, and then Bobby Orr and Derek Sanderson arrived as rookies. You could see the wheels turning. We became an explosive hockey team and were dominant for about five years.

It had been exciting to watch the Red Wings in 1955, but winning the Stanley Cup in Boston in 1970 was a genuine thrill. I accepted the Cup as team captain and skated around the Boston Garden with it. That was something else. The fans had always been great to us, and they hadn't been able to celebrate a Cup win since 1941. More than a million people turned out for our victory parade. As fun as winning is, it wasn't really the same when we won in 1972, not near the experience.

We should have won four consecutive Stanley Cups from 1970 on. We had a terrific club in the 1970-71 season, probably our best team ever. The most satisfying moment for me turned out to be scoring my fiftieth

goal of the season, at the time becoming only the fifth player in history to reach that milestone. What made it even better was that I scored number 50 in Detroit. They'd traded me a lot of years before, but it still felt good to get it against them.

I also won my first of two Lady Byng trophies in 1971, which I'm very proud of. I played most of my career at 220 pounds, one of the heaviest players on the ice. I threw my weight around and always played a physical game. The other players respected me because they knew that if they left their head down, I'd hit them pretty hard. I just tried to stay out of the penalty box. Great goaltending by Ken Dryden ruined a wonderful year; Bernie Parent did the same in 1973.

Still, my biggest career disappointment was not being chosen to play for Team Canada in 1972. I would have loved to play the Russians. I heard that management believed I was a slow starter, which I dispute, but that was that. I decided to focus on my coming season with the Bruins and had a 40-goal year.

We lost some key players to expansion and the World Hockey Association in the summer of 1973, and the club started to fade a bit, but the chemistry was still great. Our team was always tight-knit, even in the lean years. We did everything as a group. That lasted until the late 1970s. You could see a change happening to all the teams then. With the big salaries came a lot of other commitments, and most players had little time to spend with their teammates.

Road trips were a lot more fun before expansion came. We traveled by train and really got to enjoy ourselves. When we went to New York, we'd spend three days there, so we could see the city, the museums, the Statue of Liberty or whatever. I saw the travel as my chance to get an education, since I'd left school at a young age. Now teams generally fly in the night before a game, or maybe the morning of a game, play and fly right out. It's strictly business.

I always wanted to play hockey more than anything. Just knowing that I'd be getting regular ice time had me excited to get to Boston from Detroit. Of course, my whole life changed as a result of that trade. I've now had 39 years in the Boston organization, 21 as a player. Now I work with the alumni and in community relations and do some broadcasting too. I've had the honor of seeing my number nine retired by the Bruins and raised into the rafters, and I've been elected into the Hockey Hall of Fame. Who could ask for more?

John Bucyk

Johnny Bucyk was a leader of the Boston Bruins for most of his Hall of Fame career. (OPPOSITE) All eyes are on the puck, but "The Chief" has an edge over Toronto's Larry Hillman (2) and Allan Stanley as he heads into the corner.

Pavel Bure

WE WERE IN DOUBLE OVERTIME IN THE SEVENTH AND deciding game of the 1994 conference quarterfinals. Mike Vernon was in the net for Calgary. I had scored a goal in the first period and assisted on our tying goal with four minutes left, but that would be quickly forgotten if we lost. Two minutes into the second overtime, Jeff Brown gave me a perfect pass and sent me in alone. I'll always remember that breakaway. I took the pass on my forehand and came straight in. I faked a backhand, and Mike made his move. When I quickly pulled the puck back to my forehand, I had an empty net to shoot at. I remember seeing the puck in the net, but the rest is a blur. I can't explain the feeling. I didn't know where to go or what to do, but I went a little crazy. That was the biggest goal I've ever scored.

My first game in the NHL was the best game of my life. I didn't score but played really well. I somehow slowed down right after that. I don't know why. It wasn't until the second half of the season that something clicked. I started to score a lot of goals and won the Calder Trophy. Then I got 60 goals in each of the following two seasons. What I do know is that no hockey player scores that many goals by himself. Perhaps something shifted on the team, because I give a lot of credit for those achievements to my teammates. It's a great feeling to score. That's my favorite part of the game. But if I scored only two or three goals in a season and we won the Stanley Cup, I'd be happy.

I first skated at age 6 on a small rink behind our apartment building in Moscow. I remember my very first time on the ice. It was dark, around seven or eight at night, and I surprised my family because I could skate immediately, without falling down. I started to play hockey right away, joined the Central Red Army club and worked my way up with them.

I had a lot of good coaches over the years, but my dad also worked with me. He was an Olympic swimmer when he was younger, not a hockey player. But he would come to all my practices and learn some tricks from the coaches there. Then he'd get me to work on specific drills for skating, shooting and conditioning.

I got a call-up to play a game for the elite-level team at age 16. It was a dream come true. I'd been watching guys like Sergei Makarov and Igor Larionov on television for years. They were really warm and supportive, giving me advice in a very kind way—where to go, how to get open, what to do with the puck, everything about the game. I was all ears! I joined the team as a regular member when I was 17.

Some of the coaches were worried about my small size, but I tried to reassure them that I'd be all right. They took a chance that I wouldn't get badly hurt, and I fit in pretty smoothly. It doesn't matter how fast you are, you have to be able to score. I was quick, but I got to play for the Red Army because I could put the puck in the net too.

The World Junior Championships in 1989 was my first crack at a world title. Playing with 19-year-olds Sergei Fedorov and Alexander Mogilny as linemates looked promising for me. We combined very effectively, and our team won the gold medal in a convincing way. Only 17, I was still just concentrating on doing well enough to move up to the Soviet national team from junior. Any future for our line quickly dissolved. Alex defected shortly after that tournament, and Sergei left for the NHL a year later.

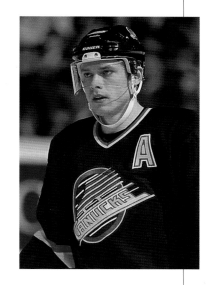

In the following season, I realized a huge dream and won a gold medal in the 1990 World Championships. Winning Olympic gold was the ultimate goal when I was growing up, though. I was always a little saddened to think that I'd never be able to compete in the Olympics once I joined the Vancouver Canucks. My dreams have changed a little because of my desire for a Stanley Cup, but still, that hope for an Olympic gold medal is there. I'm very happy that world politics and the NHL have changed enough that I may yet get a chance to go to the next Olympic games.

Pavel Bure, "The Russian Rocket," led the 1998 Olympics with 9 goals but had to settle for a silver medal. (OPPOSITE) Bure had two 60-goal seasons in Vancouver but requested a trade after the 1997-98 campaign. He joined the Florida Panthers in February 1999 and won the Richard Trophy both of the following two seasons.

Jim Carey

I NEVER WANTED TO PLAY NET. I ALWAYS WANTED TO PLAY forward. But since I was the only boy on my team who could skate backward, the coach kept putting me on defense. I *despised* defense at that age. I wanted to score goals like every other kid in "squirt" hockey. But the coach gave me the choice of playing defense or not playing at all. I hated it so much and complained so often that my mom suggested I should either quit or play net. When I decided to try goalie, right away my mom felt badly. She felt so worried and sorry about pushing me into the net that she stayed in the arena parking lot for most of my first game. But I played well and was able to make the A team.

I liked playing goal because I was good at it, but I've never lost my desire to score goals. Right through high school, I played forward in another league because I enjoyed it so much. To this day, I wonder what would have happened if I'd been able to stick with my favorite position. In college, we'd get a mandatory two weeks off at Christmas, and I'd get a chance to skate "out" for a couple of hours every day. I loved those times. Now that I'm in the NHL, there's an occasional day off but no shutdown time for that kind of fun.

Tom Barrasso, a local American kid, gave me a lot of personal inspiration. I was 9 years old when he made it to the NHL right out of high school. Tom's success gave me an it-can-be-done attitude; making the NHL became a more realistic goal. My mom encouraged me to be positive but not to put all my eggs in one basket. I went to a good high school and on to college for two years before I gave professional hockey a shot. My dream started to look more tangible when I reached college. I was Rookie of the Year as a freshman, playing guys I knew were going to the NHL. I had another good year as a sophomore and was then offered a chance to go to the Washington Capitals. At that point, my dream started to look very unrealistic! Everyone was so good.

I played one period in one exhibition game before being sent to the minors. I played for Portland in the American Hockey League, which was a great experience. I saw that I could play with the guys there, was called up to the Capitals and showed myself that I could play at that level. One of the turning points for me was my first game with Washington in the old Boston Garden. I'd had a lot of success in that building in high school, winning three state tournaments. It was about my third game up, and a lot of my family and friends were in the crowd. Ray Bourque scored on the first or second shot I faced, but I settled down and played well, and we beat the Bruins 3–1.

I don't think I fully realized that I was in the NHL until the following summer. You don't get much of a chance to savor the success you have, maybe not until you stop playing the game. I value being in the NHL most when I see how my parents respond. I saw the tears in their eyes when I was presented the Vezina Trophy at the NHL awards banquet in 1996. They appreciate seeing their son in the same spotlight that players such as Ken Dryden stood in. I'm so glad that they've been around to experience that. I hope that I feel the same way when I have kids.

Winning the Vezina and the First All-Star team selection in 1996 was exciting for me too. I'd like to think that I'd trade them in for a Stanley Cup, but they're the elite achievements for a goaltender. I never thought about awards during the season. The only individual trophy I ever coveted was the Calder in my rookie year of 1995. I was a lot more disappointed to come runner-up for the Calder than I was pleased to come in third that year for the Vezina. You only get one shot at Rookie of the Year. I wanted to win the Calder so badly that when I received another nomination for the Vezina in 1996, I hardly paid attention to it. I didn't want to get excited and then feel that letdown again.

When I look around the NHL, the best goalies, in my opinion, are around 30 years old. I look forward to that time of life. I feel better with every year of experience I get. My style works for me—I don't want to modify it much—so it's tough to explain what experience brings. I think it's just time spent in the game, seeing how you react to adversity, to different situations, to the team struggling. Hopefully, more games under my belt will pay dividends. Maybe that Stanley Cup won't come for two or three years. I know I'll look back and say I would *never* have won this if I hadn't had the experience.

At what turned out to be the peak of his career, in 1995-96, NHL sophomore Jim Carey won the Vezina Trophy and made the First All-Star team. (OPPOSITE) The Washington Capitals traded "Ace" to Boston in March 1997, but he failed to click with the Bruins. After a four-game stint with St. Louis in 1998-99, Carey retired from pro hockey.

Gerry Cheevers

I CAME BACK TO THE BOSTON BRUINS IN 1975 AFTER THE better part of four seasons in the WHA. I wasn't really ready to play, so I was scheduled to be Dave Reece's backup for the first week. Unfortunately, my first time on the bench was for the game in Maple Leaf Gardens when Darryl Sittler had his 10-point night. I never felt so badly for someone as I did for Dave, but with every goal that went in, I went farther down the aisle. It was bad to leave a nice guy like Dave in there so long, but I didn't want our coach, Don Cherry, to see me. Don knew I

wasn't ready, but if the Leafs had scored any more goals, I would have been hiding up in the stands with all my equipment on.

I served my goaltending apprenticeship with eight enjoyable years in the Toronto farm system. Maple Leafs goaltending was very solid but aging, with Johnny Bower, Terry Sawchuk and Don Simmons. I trusted that my day would come and was extremely disappointed when I was drafted by the Boston Bruins in 1965. Not only would I not get my chance with the Leafs, but the Bruins were a team going nowhere. It wasn't until "Number 4" showed up that I started to enjoy myself. I knew immediately that we were going to win a championship.

Eddie Johnston and I were buddies right from the start. We competed in a friendly manner, but more than anyone, he helped me to become a big-league goaltender. He had an uncanny knowledge of the game that he was willing to share. We're still the best of friends.

Winning the Stanley Cup in Boston was one of the greatest times of our lives. It's what everyone says it is: the ultimate. It had a lingering effect. It wasn't a day, a night or a week—it was happiness for an era. There was a love story happening between the team and the city for years. When you win the Cup, that love affair really matures. Believe me, it's fabulous.

I don't know how I got a reputation for being a "money" goaltender, because I probably lost almost as many big games as I won. Perhaps I'm remembered for playing well in some games that meant a lot to the team. If you aren't ready to perform well in a game that means elimination, then you shouldn't play professional hockey. I enjoyed those games, but you never win them all—no one does.

Circumstances dictated what I did. When a goal meant nothing to the outcome, I wouldn't always play the puck. My teammates laughed for a long time about one bouncing puck that I intentionally ignored. Although I saw it coming close to the net, I knew the approaching forward would have a tough time getting control of it, so I let it go. I heard it hit the post—closer to the net than I predicted—but I felt relieved that I'd played it properly. Unfortunately, it was the middle post that it hit.

I remember us killing a penalty late in a game against the Chicago Blackhawks. We had a big lead, and Bobby Hull wound up for a slap shot from in close. In short-handed situations, I had a deal with my defensemen: I'd take the large side of the net, and they'd take the short side. Well, my defenseman was doing what he was supposed to, but not me. I moved over right behind him, giving Bobby a yawning net to shoot into, and naturally, he scored. With nothing at stake, it didn't make much sense to take one off the shoulder, especially from Bobby. He was a dangerous shooter. Forget the embarrassment—I was fighting for my life.

I loved everything about hockey except practice. I was always trying to find ways out of it. One day, a puck flipped up and caught me just above the eye. It hit my mask and was such a feeble shot that it wouldn't have cut me even if I hadn't had the mask on. But I pretended that I was injured and went into the dressing room. Harry Sinden was coaching, and he came in after me. "You're not hurt," he said. "Get out there." My trainer, John Forristall, thought we should do something, so we painted a 12-stitch cut on my mask. Everyone laughed when I went back on the ice, but from then on, I decided to mark an honest estimation of the stitches I would have received if I hadn't been wearing a mask.

I don't think I knew a single player from my era who thought of playing *just* for the money. The money was good, the living was comfortable, but above all, we loved to play hockey. In fact, we were negligent about the financial side, which is being proven in some of the litigation you see today. The players in the game now are much more conscious of the money, and I think it's taken some of the fun out of the game.

Gerry Cheevers played without facial protection when he first joined the NHL, but he is remembered for his "stitch-mark" mask, which started as a joke but came to symbolize the hazards of goaltending. (OPPOSITE) *Cheevers moves out to snag a loose puck just outside his crease.*

Chris Chelios

THERE WAS A LOT OF PRESSURE ON OUR 1984 OLYMPIC TEAM because of the gold medal the U.S. won in 1980. We had such high expectations, because on paper, we had a good team, but we didn't peak at the right time. Everything went downhill after we lost an early game to Canada. I didn't really appreciate the experience until the week after the Olympics were over. Everything had happened so quickly: coming out of college, traveling around the country playing exhibition games, then going to Sarajevo. I was forced to take a break because of an ankle injury, and only then did I fully realize what a great honor it had been to compete for my country.

After playing in the Olympics, I joined the Montreal

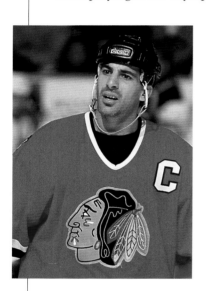

Canadiens for 12 games. I lined up against James Patrick in the second or third NHL game for both of us. We could each see the excitement that we felt being in NHL uniforms, because we had taken the same path to get there. We played against each other as juniors, in college and at the Olympics. I didn't know James very well, but we had built up a strong rivalry, and I still have a lot of respect for him. I didn't do very well at first and played with no confidence. We got into the playoffs, and as soon as I scored, everything was better. I don't know why it took a goal, but I was a different player after that. I surprised even myself when I came second to Mario Lemieux in the voting for the Calder Trophy the following season.

The highlight of my years in Montreal was winning the Stanley Cup in 1986 with guys like Bob Gainey, Larry Robinson and Guy Lafleur—legends of hockey when I grew up watching. There's nothing better than winning, especially in Montreal with their great history. I learned what hockey was all about in Canada. You sense the pride Canadians have in the game.

It took only about 15 seconds after talking on the phone with Canadiens general manager Serge Savard to realize that my trade to Chicago in 1991 was great news. If it had been any other city, I would have been disappointed. I love Montreal, and I'll never forget my time there. But I'm from Chicago, and it also has a great hockey tradition. I could have tested the free-agent market after the 1996-97 season, but money doesn't motivate me and I like how the Blackhawks organization treats me. I play hockey because I love it, and we have a great team here. I was fortunate to get back home and have my whole family together again. There aren't too many guys in the NHL who get to do that.

My leadership qualities are strongest on the ice. I'm not much of a talker, and sometimes I'm too emotional. Brent Sutter is my idea of a perfect leader. He's great in the dressing room, and he works hard on the ice. I'm more like Larry Robinson was. He set his example by the way he played during the game. In the dressing room, he acted like a kid, and that's the way I am, usually joking around. Sometimes I don't like the responsibility of being team captain. When things aren't going well, I want to concentrate on getting my own game on track and not worry about anyone else's. I've received a lot of help from Steve Smith and Brent Sutter—guys who have been there before—and I'm sure I'll get better at the job.

I felt lucky the first time I won the Norris Trophy, but after the second time, I wanted to win it again. It's something to aim for, but the Stanley Cup is what really motivates me. When a team does well, its players usually benefit by earning individual trophies anyway. There's nothing better than winning with the same group of guys you've played a long season with, although my experience in the 1996 World Cup surprised me in some ways.

Playing in the Olympics and the 1991 Canada Cup was exciting, but winning the World Cup was the biggest thrill I've had in international competition. I wanted to play, but it looked as if an injury I was nursing was going to keep me out of the lineup. I joined the team at the last minute and am so glad I did. It was the first time I was on the other end of the stick. I was used to watching Wayne Gretzky and Mark Messier carrying the trophies around. That victory was great for U.S. hockey, and it was even more special to win in Montreal.

Some of the guys I played with on the Canada Cup team I haven't talked to since. Winning the World Cup created a very different feeling on the team. We grew exceptionally close, especially because winning was something we didn't expect. That experience changed me in some ways, and I won't hit those guys quite as hard as I did when they weren't friends *except* when it comes down to a big game. When I'm fighting to make the playoffs or in playoff games, it doesn't matter who my opponent is! Winning is the best part of hockey, and I'll do whatever is necessary to accomplish that.

After almost nine seasons as a leader with his hometown Chicago Blackhawks, Chris Chelios agreed to a 1999 trade to the Detroit Red Wings. (OPPOSITE) Hard-nosed defenseman Chelios unloads his heavy slap shot, an important element of his strong offensive skills.

Dino Ciccarelli

It looked as if no team would ever take a chance on a kid who'd shattered his leg. I broke my femur badly enough in my second year of junior hockey that the doctors didn't give me much chance of ever being able to play professionally. I had scored 72 goals the previous season, but my injury wiped me off everyone's draft list in 1979. I wasn't going to let that stop me. I had to go through a year and a half of rehabilitation, but I was determined to do everything I could to live out my dream and play in the National Hockey League. I was totally frustrated when I recovered from the injury, scored 50 goals in my last season of junior and was passed on for the second time at the 1980 entry draft.

I don't blame anyone for not drafting me. Hockey is a business, and no one can afford to waste a pick on someone who might not be able to play. Lou Nanne of the Minnesota North Stars finally gave me an opportunity when he signed me as a free agent. He sent me to Oklahoma City to see how I'd fare in the minors. Things went well, and three-quarters of the way through the season, I was called up to Minnesota for a few games.

I've scored some special goals in my career, including overtime winners, but I'll always remember my first NHL goal with the most feeling. It came during my third time up with the North Stars. We were playing on Long Island, and I scored against Billy Smith on a shot from the slot. I'd imagined that moment so often during my time recovering from my broken leg. I still have that puck somewhere.

I had some immediate success, and my mindset changed. I wasn't content just to *get* to the NHL anymore. I wanted to make sure I *stayed* and had a good season. We had a bunch of young kids on our team, and we surprised everyone by getting to the Stanley Cup finals. It had nothing to do with the North Stars, but a gas-station chain was giving away Dino the Dinosaur dolls—a *Flintstones* cartoon character—with a fill-up. Some of the fans made a connection with my name, and before long, there were a lot of dinosaurs bobbing around in the crowd. That was a lot of fun for me at the time, and it seems even funnier now.

I have abilities that have allowed me to play only one style, and that's to be in front of the net. I need to look for goals on rebounds or deflections, because I've never been a gifted skater or capable of making pretty dekes.

My shot's not very hard either. I've worked hard to be consistent, whether we're playing a weak or a strong team, playing early in the season or late in the playoffs. My style benefits from that approach, and I've had pretty steady success.

I've been traded a few times, and that's always a shock. The feeling of rejection comes up first despite there being another team on the welcoming side. A trade is usually a bigger ordeal for the other family members than it is for the player. Playing hockey with a different bunch of guys isn't too difficult a transition, although moving from a contending team, such as the Detroit Red Wings, to one like Tampa Bay brings some frustrations. Our expectations were so high during my time in Detroit, and we came so close to winning the Stanley Cup that it's difficult to close that chapter of my career without actually having won.

I always try to keep things positive, and at my age, it's good to be playing more now than when I was in Detroit. I've joined a group of hardworking younger guys with the goal of making the playoffs. Once we do that, anything can happen. The Florida Panthers and the New Jersey Devils faced Detroit in my last years there with a less talented team on paper, but they won with a strong team effort.

Reaching the 500-goal milestone was special, and I'm proud of my personal accomplishments, but I'll reflect more upon those once I'm retired. Hockey is a team-oriented game, and everyone wants to reach the ultimate goal and win the Stanley Cup. I hope I've got a few more years left to try to win it, but if I don't, I'll be satisfied with the effort I've made.

When I miss a game now, I can feel how badly I'll miss the competition when I retire. Watching the game from the stands is exciting for the fans, but the real thrill for me is being with the guys and out on the ice. My success has always depended on my being hungry and aggressive in my approach to the game. The money's nice, but down deep, you have to love the game and the competition. I'll continue to play until that fire burns out.

Just before crossing the 600-career-goal mark, Dino Ciccarelli celebrates a 1996-97 tally for Tampa Bay. He completed his 19-season career in 1999 as a Florida Panther. (Opposite) Ciccarelli made a dramatic NHL entry in 1981 when he joined the Minnesota North Stars and helped them to their first Stanley Cup finals.

Paul Coffey

When I was a boy, a lot of my friends went to hockey school in the summer, where they'd be waterskiing, boating, canoeing and then playing hockey for an hour a day. I went to power-skating schools in Toronto, where we concentrated strictly on skating. I still try to do every drill in practice at full speed. Part of my skating ability is God-given, but to hone my skills, I work hard at skating every day. My skates are the most important part of my equipment. If my skates are not quite right, I feel very below average as a player. But if the fit is good, I feel as if I can do anything on the ice.

I played center when I was a kid. Dave Keon was my idol. My coach wanted to move me back to defense when I was playing on the tyke all-star team. I wasn't too happy, but my dad put it in simple terms for me: Playing defense equals more ice time. It wasn't a hard adjustment to make at the time.

I'll never be the type to reflect on past glories, but every Stanley Cup has been special. It was great to win in Pittsburgh with a super guy, Bob Johnson, as coach. It was also Mario Lemieux's first Cup, so it was huge for him. But nothing can take the place of *my* first Stanley Cup win with Edmonton—the older you are, the more you appreciate things. I had three Stanley Cups with the Oilers by the time I was 24 years old. I just figured that's what happens: You play hockey and you win a Cup. We didn't realize how lucky we were.

I scored 48 goals in the 1985-86 season, breaking Bobby Orr's record for defensemen. I wonder now how I did it. I had nine goals by Christmas but took off with four more on Boxing Day. It was pretty wild for the rest of the season. I had 48 with one game remaining, but I was such a kid that I wasn't even thinking of 50. I was so thrilled just to be mentioned in the same sentence as Bobby Orr.

One game that stands out for me was against the Russians for the 1984 Canada Cup. We were in sudden-death overtime, and I broke up a dangerous two-on-one. I poke-checked the pass and brought the puck back up the ice. I took a shot on net, the puck went into the corner, and John Tonelli did a great job getting the puck back to me again. Mike Bossy tipped in my wrist shot.

It hurts not to win, but I don't even think about the low points of my career. I've played with arguably the best players in the game. Guys such as Wayne Gretzky and Mario Lemieux like to play up high and get the puck hard on their stick, which was tailor-made for my passing game. Hockey has been very good to me, but it's a challenge every day. The game can knock you down and humble you very quickly if you don't keep your emotions in check and stay level. It also gets harder and harder to stay in the game because of the tremendous competition for jobs. The wolf is always at the door, with a couple of hundred kids every year trying for a spot. I think the easiest time in the league is a player's first two or three years. You get a little leeway when the coaches say, "He's young, he'll learn." Once you're through that babying stage, you'd better know what your job is, know that you have to be in shape and improving every game.

I enjoy being paired with a younger defenseman. Passing something on adds another little challenge. If something needs to be said, it is, but you have to let the younger guys develop their own personality and character. I can't be harping at them; who says what I think is right? I'm a hockey player, not a preacher. The last thing I want to do is start talking about "back when I won" or "when I was younger …"

I have always had a fear of failure, of not doing well, which has motivated me to play harder. When you're older, it's obvious that you're not playing for the money. We've done well enough financially over the years. We play for the competition and the love of the game. Getting out of bed after back-to-back games sometimes makes me wonder whether it's worth it, but as sore and tired as I am, I love to get to the rink. It's a privilege to play, and it's a lot of fun. I'm lucky enough to have won four Stanley Cups, which also keeps me in the game. I know how good that feels.

Hockey is a year-round job now. I take only a week or two off in the summer before I start training again. That pays dividends during the season, but unfortunately, it also takes time away from other important areas of my life. I'm married and have started a family now, so as I near the end of my hockey career, I'm starting to look forward to family time.

Three-time Norris Trophy winner and eight-time All-Star Paul Coffey began an injury-plagued downward spiral after his trade from Detroit in 1996. He spent time with five teams over the next five seasons. (Opposite) Coffey broke into the NHL as a teenager with the Edmonton Oilers and was an integral part of their first three Stanley Cup wins in the mid-1980s.

Yvan Cournoyer

When you're young, playing in the street, and you have a dream of being a Montreal Canadien, you're like every boy you know. We'd joke, "If I'm playing in the Forum, will you come and watch me?" I was always a fast skater, but I had to try a little harder because of my small size. I worked on my shot in the summers by shooting heavy pucks that my dad fabricated in his machine shop. They weighed between one and three pounds and really helped me. Developing a work ethic also paid off.

I remember my first goal as if it were yesterday. The Canadiens were in Detroit, had some injuries and had just lost several games. I was 19 when I was called up to the NHL, and I scored in my first game. I had a chance at a rebound and sent it into the top corner of the net. It was our seventh goal in a 7–3 victory. In those years, a player in my position could come up for only five games before the team had to "protect" him. I scored four goals in those five games, and we were winning. It was a promising start, and Frank Selke used to tell me that if he'd signed me that year, they would have won another Stanley Cup.

My game was to score goals. I'd go into the corner or wherever necessary for the puck, which is probably why I eventually had back surgery twice, broke several bones and suffered a concussion.

We were playing Detroit in my rookie year. I cut across the blue line and made a back pass. My teammate Dick Duff was following me, and Red Wings defenseman Doug Barkley was backing up. I looked behind, and Barkley changed direction and came toward me. As I turned around, he really hit me. That was the first shift of the third period; when I woke up, the game was over. I couldn't remember the play for two days. Then I gave Dick Duff hell, because I took that pounding and he hit the post!

I played only the power play for my first two years. Whenever I went in front of the Boston net, Ted Green would say, "I'm going to chop your head off." If you're going to play in the NHL, you have to ignore that kind of intimidation. The best way to counter threats was to score goals and keep on scoring goals.

The power play was even more important in the play-offs. My job was to make the other team really pay for taking a penalty. If opponents know that a penalty could likely mean a goal against, they adjust their game and become cautious. I used to plead jokingly with the others not to score until at least one minute into the power play so that I'd get some time on the ice.

The best reward for playing was the Stanley Cup. In the seventh game of the 1965 Stanley Cup final against Chicago, I was on the ice three times and got a goal and an assist; we won 4–0. Toe Blake always felt that if we won the Vezina Trophy, really a team trophy in those days, we'd win the Cup. I was an offensive player by nature, but by gradually breaking into the lineup, I improved defensively.

We had a great team in 1967 but learned a good lesson. We had the Cup final won before we played it and Toronto beat us. We lost but learned always to respect the other team. Every loss made us stronger, and I never went too many years without winning the Cup.

I had an excellent playoff in 1973 and won the Conn Smythe Trophy. It seemed as if my whole season had momentum from the 1972 Canada-Russia series. We were surprised by the strength of the Russian team, especially in the first game, which we lost 7–3. In hindsight, I think that game two was a very important victory for us. Before the match, I told Brad Park, "Look for me, because I'm ready tonight." When I was feeling good, I felt the wind was at my back. Brad gave me a perfect pass, and I went around the defense and scored. We showed the Russians that they'd have to respect us, that we, too, had some speed. Once we knew what we were up against, we adjusted. I'd won too many Stanley Cups to be demoralized by a loss in the first game of a series.

Our Cup win against the very tough Philadelphia Flyers in 1976 was particularly rewarding. They tried to bully us, and we defeated them in four straight games. The victory showed other teams that Philly could be beaten, and I don't think the Flyers were ever the same force again.

The Montreal Canadiens gave me a further challenge when I spent two years as an assistant coach from 1995 to 1997. My primary responsibility was with the power-play and penalty-killing units. We tried to make a team, get the guys working together. Years ago, almost all NHL players were Canadian. Now we have Russians, Americans, Swedes, Czechs—a mixed culture. I do think, though, that after someone plays a few games for Montreal, they feel the Canadiens pride. It's not the same as it was, and hockey is changing, but a good hockey game is still a good hockey game.

Yvan Cournoyer captained Montreal in his last four NHL seasons, winning the Stanley Cup in each of those years and bringing his remarkable career Cup total to 10.
(**Opposite**) *"The Roadrunner" wheels behind the Toronto net with Wally Boyer in hot pursuit.*

Vincent Damphousse

ALTHOUGH I ALWAYS HAD GOOD SKILLS FOR MY AGE, MY parents were crucial to my success. My dad made a rink in the backyard every winter and spent hours playing with me there, but he also took me to a lot of early-morning practices and games. I just loved to play and never even thought about the NHL until I moved up to the Quebec Midget AAA hockey league. When I was successful playing with the best boys in Quebec, I realized I might be able to play with the best in the world.

I started to work out and make any sacrifice necessary to improve my chances of playing in the NHL.

By age 15 and 16, there is peer pressure to do all sorts of other things besides hockey, and I saw many great hockey players choose different paths. They may or may not regret that now, because I missed most of the parties and trips and never went skiing due to my focus on the hockey career I wanted.

I was born in Montreal and grew up near the Forum. Guy Lafleur was my idol, and I tried to imitate him when I played with my friends. He made his NHL comeback when I was playing for the Toronto Maple Leafs, so I later had the thrill of playing against him. Now

that we're both back in Montreal, I've even had the opportunity to get to know him.

Our team was having a tough time just before Christmas 1996, and I asked Guy, as someone from the outside looking in, what I might do as team captain to help turn things around. Guy didn't think we were playing like a team and reminded me that I shouldn't hesitate to share my opinions with my teammates. He cautioned me not to talk as if I knew everything—which wasn't hard because, in truth, I myself wasn't playing very well—but he gave me the confidence to speak up. I took his advice, and I called again to thank him after we returned from a successful road trip right after our conversation.

The Canadiens keep their alumni close to the team, and I'm always open to the insights they have to offer. Even over different generations, I don't think things change in the dressing room. It's easy to believe the alumni when they tell me the team camaraderie is what they miss most. I still keep in touch with a number of guys I met when I started my career in Toronto. They'll be friends for life.

There are a lot of things to take care of as team captain in Montreal. It's good pressure if you can handle it, because it makes you play better. You can't get away with less than your best, or you'll hear about it from the fans and the media. Tradition is so important in Montreal, and there has always been tremendous pride in playing for the jersey. Part of my job is to make sure that everyone on the team knows the team's history and is proud to be part of the club's heritage. The dynasties of the 1950s, 1960s and 1970s are going to be hard to duplicate because of the parity in the league now, but Montreal will always be committed to having a competitive team.

Winning the Stanley Cup in 1993 capped a terrific year for me. I went through a divorce while playing in Edmonton, and it became important to be close to my family back in Montreal. I was ecstatic when the Oilers traded me to the Canadiens in the fall of 1992, but it was an unbelievable thrill to win the Cup in my first year with them. Everything went well for me. I had my best point totals ever, got some big goals and was a factor in every playoff series despite being on my third team in three years. My trades always happened in the off-season. I'm proud of leading the Leafs, the Oilers and then the Canadiens in scoring in each of those seasons, but it's so helpful for a player to make the adjustment to being with a new club and a new city *before* having to concentrate on hockey.

Early in that Stanley Cup drive, we were down 2–0 in games against the Quebec Nordiques, and we went into overtime in game three. I picked the puck up off a dump-in and spun off a defenseman. I threw a quick backhand at Ron Hextall, and he made the save, but the puck bounced off his defenseman's skate into the net. It was a lucky goal but a big goal and saved us from facing an almost-impossible-to-overcome 3–0 deficit. We went on to set an amazing record of 10 overtime victories in a row.

It was a bitter disappointment to lose the final game of the 1996 World Cup to the Americans, but I had some proud moments playing for my country for the first time. Playing with and against the best players in the world was such a great experience. I love to compete when there's a lot on the line, and I always work hard for those opportunities.

Vincent Damphousse led Montreal scorers for the 1996-97 season, his first as team captain. The Habs traded him to San Jose in March 1999. (**Opposite**) *Damphousse speedily weaves up-ice against the New York Islanders.*

Alex Delvecchio

In my day, winning the Lady Byng Trophy didn't really command a lot of respect. I think it has more meaning for players today. I was honored to receive the award three times during my career, but I occasionally was called "Miss Byng" by opponents on the ice. One year, there were rumors that I was going to be traded to the Leafs, and Punch Imlach said, "We don't want any Lady Byng winners in Toronto, so he's not coming here." But that was fine by me. I'm thankful I was able to play my entire career in Detroit.

I started playing for the Fort William Hurricanes, a Red Wings-sponsored team, when I was 15. Three years later, I moved up to the Oshawa Generals in the OHA, where I was coached by Larry Aurie. Larry, a former star with the Red Wings, was able to teach the skills demanded by the NHL clubs at that time. Detroit wanted players who could pass well and play strong positional hockey. If you were on the second or third line, you weren't expected to score. The Red Wings had Sid Abel centering their "goal-scoring" line between Gordie Howe and Ted Lindsay. Everyone else was expected to concentrate on defense.

I was called up to the NHL with Lou Jankowski for the last regular-season game of the 1950-51 season. We were the leading OHA scorers and had just been knocked out of the playoffs. Detroit general manager Jack Adams rested some of his older players for the up-coming NHL playoffs, and Lou and I got a little ice time. I even got an assist. I was back again to stay the next season after a couple of weeks in the minors and played in Detroit for the next 23 years.

We won the Stanley Cup in eight straight playoff games in my rookie year. That was like going to heaven for me. I had never been on a winning team before, even in minor hockey. We had so many stars, but they were a terrific bunch of guys who welcomed me warmly. They offered little tips, and I felt part of a big family. There was tremendous harmony in the club, and we won two more Cups in the next three years.

It was always heartbreaking to lose the Stanley Cup once I knew what it was like to win. I never understood Jack Adams's thinking when he traded about six players from our last Cup-winner. It was as if things were going too well for him. Over the years, we had a few more good opportunities in the Cup finals, but we needed just a little more than we had.

I was very excited when I got the chance to play with Gordie Howe. I remember Metro Prystai and Marty Pavelich telling me, "Make sure you get the puck to 'The Power,' because he'll deliver the mail." I always looked for Gordie first when I had the puck. He was the greatest and had more moves than anyone I've seen. Gordie was the first I saw who could switch hands and change from a right-hand shot to a left. When you play with someone like him, you become a better hockey player. It inspires you to work harder and try different things yourself.

I always communicated on the ice with everyone I played with, but especially with Gordie. I had little arm or glove signals to let him know what I was trying to do on a face-off so that he could anticipate the play. I'll always remember one game against the Montreal Canadiens. There was a face-off in Montreal's end. I told Gordie and the others that I was going to *try* to fire the puck at the net right from the face-off, but everyone was surprised when it went right over the goalie's shoulder for a goal.

Hockey is a rough game, and you have to have luck on your side not to get too many injuries. I did get corked a few times with my head down, but I didn't miss very many games. The Red Wings kept us in tip-top condition, but early in my career, I saw Terry Sawchuk play with an injury and say, "There's no damn way I'm not playing. No one's taking my job." That worry was hanging over our heads all the time. Someone might take your place and look good one night, and you were gone. So you played taped up or with a pulled groin, and your teammates did what they could to help. I'd tell an injured linemate just to go up and down his wing and I'd cover for him. The last thing you wanted to do was let management—or the opposition—know you were hurt.

Once I got my opportunity to be in the NHL, I knew I'd play as long as I could. It got a little more like work when I was in my forties, but I always had fun. Phil Esposito and I would say things at the face-off circle, such as, "Bet you a quarter I win this one" or "You owe me a buck," and that didn't hurt the game or my performance. You have to have a few laughs on the ice. I think it only made me want to win more.

Alex Delvecchio

Alex Delvecchio's 24-season NHL career is the second longest in league history. Captain of the Detroit Red Wings for more than 10 years, he saw his number 10 sweater retired in 1991. (Opposite) Delvecchio cuts sharply to the edge of Johnny Bower's crease while a concerned Bob Baun looks on.

Marcel Dionne

MY HIGHLIGHT—THE GREATEST HOCKEY I EVER SAW—WAS the 1972 Canada-Russia series. I never played, but I look back proudly at being 21 years old on a team with 35 of my heroes. It influenced the rest of my career. I watched how my teammates handled pressure and learned that if you want to win, you've got to find a way. We won on our emotion.

Some guys who weren't playing left when we were in Russia, and I would never accuse them of not doing the right thing. I wanted to leave too. It was very, very tough.

We were aching to play but were pretty much ignored. We even practiced separately. Those who left should have been told, "We love you guys, and thank you very much," but management let them go looking like quitters. Those guys are still my heroes, and I respect them all.

My rookie year with the Detroit Red Wings was the first time I was exposed to problems in hockey. It was something I was not prepared for. The teams I had played for previously didn't always win, but we were competitive and had a winning attitude. My numbers in Detroit were good right from the start, but I was a kid who needed direction, and it wasn't forthcoming.

I had to rely on individual effort, which many people associate with selfishness. They don't understand that you have to protect yourself, you have to survive. My heart was with the team, but there were too many guys pulling in different directions. I liked the city of Detroit and Alex Delvecchio as a coach, but I saw how Gordie Howe—Mr. Hockey, who played 26 years for the Red Wings—got nothing but grief from the team after he retired. I realized I had to look after my own interests. After four seasons, I thought I could get 100 to 125 points a year, but what would be the use? I wouldn't be any closer to what I really wanted: to win. That led to my decision to move to Los Angeles.

I found out the grass isn't always greener on the other side, even though the climate may be! I was determined to perform well in Los Angeles, and I made a commitment to that effect. I had a good coach in Bob Pulford and scored a lot of goals right away, but Bob held me back, the way a jockey restrains a horse coming out of the starting gate. He wasn't happy to have lost Dan Maloney, the heart and soul of the team, as part of the compensation for signing me as a free agent. He was

focusing on defense, and the team was coming off a good season. Once I started putting up big numbers, the guys who had been happy scoring 15 goals wanted to get 25. It worked out in the long run, but initially, there was some turmoil.

Playing in All-Star games and international tournaments really charged my batteries. If we were down a goal, I'd hear, "Don't worry! We'll get one soon." I loved that! The atmosphere was always positive. When your team is accustomed to losing, you hear panic in the same situation. Defensemen are saying, "You're not doing this. You're not doing that." Guys are arguing and swearing at each other. On a great team, guys may not always like each other, but they perform together. They might not like the coach, but they respect him. There's always some turmoil, but you work through it. That's what winning is all about.

Receiving the Lester Pearson Award in 1979 and 1980 was very special. Your peers know where you stand. In 1976, I played right wing in the Canada Cup. I went back to Los Angeles, played the whole year on wing, and the press voted for me as the All-Star *center*. I didn't have to skate as much on the wing, and I had a lot more energy, but playing against really tough guys who didn't give me much room eventually had me back at center where I could freewheel more.

After a couple of seasons in Los Angeles, I started to play with Dave Taylor, and then Charlie Simmer jumped in. Dave played with speed and drove everybody nuts with his aggressiveness. Charlie had good range, and I liked his style. He was a left-winger with a right-hand shot who went to the net. We clicked immediately. It's easy to find a pair, but finding the third guy is very difficult.

Our years together as the Triple Crown Line were probably the easiest of my life. It was as if one guy had a thought and the other two could read his mind. That was an unbelievable feeling we wished would never stop. History looks at playoff accomplishments, but we never had a Paul Coffey or Denis Potvin on defense. Our numbers are astonishing; I think we were as good a line as any that ever played the game.

Marcel Dionne broke into the NHL with the Detroit Red Wings in 1971 and immediately started putting pucks in the net. He retired in 1989 with 731 goals, third highest in league history. (OPPOSITE) Dionne, here working himself free behind the net while playing for Los Angeles, showed that a small man could excel in the NHL.

Bernie Federko

I THOUGHT I HAD COME TO TERMS VERBALLY WITH THE St. Louis Blues for a two-year contract that would take me to my planned retirement. It was the summer of 1989, and general manager Ron Caron told me to come in later in the week to sign the papers. He assured me we'd have everything wrapped up by 10 o'clock. When I went in, he announced that I was no longer in the Blues' plans. I was devastated.

Jacques Demers, who had coached me for three years in St. Louis and was now with Detroit, had just asked if I was available. When Ron found out the Red Wings would part with Adam Oates in return, I guess it was such a good deal, he couldn't turn it down. You can

never get comfortable in professional sports. Very few players get to spend their entire careers with one team, but I thought I had done it. Jacques told me that he had big plans for me as a player and in the Detroit organization after I retired, so I signed my contract to conclude the trade, and my family pulled up roots.

Playing for Detroit was certainly not what I thought it was going to be. I left St. Louis as the Blues' all-time leading scorer—a record I still hold to this date—but eventually was relegated to fourth-line duties. I was even dropped from the lineup for a few games—the first time that had happened to me. Career game 1,000 was my last in the league. I still had a year left in my contract, but I elected to retire after one season in Detroit.

I had had a great career until then, and I wanted to be remembered for the hard work I'd put in to establish myself as a higher-echelon player. I set a number of franchise records in St. Louis, and the Blues retired my number 24 the next year; yet the honor felt something like a consolation prize. It was flattering, but I still had mixed feelings. I felt I'd been deprived of something very special—playing my whole career in one city.

In my final junior year in the Western Hockey League, I was MVP and scoring champion and came to the Blues' training camp highly motivated to prove myself in the NHL. Unfortunately, I found a team rich in centers, with Garry Unger, Red Berenson, Derek Sanderson and Larry Patey. I had made matters worse by breaking my foot playing basketball. I took the cast off the day before training camp, but it still hurt to put my foot down. I fell down a lot and made a bit of a fool of myself. I went to the minors for 42 games and was named

Rookie of the Year before being called up by the Blues.

Brian Sutter and I played together for 10 or 11 years. We had a natural chemistry. Once I was over the blue line, I wanted to dish the puck. I still got my share of goals, because I always stayed involved in the play. Brian and I played with some really good right-wingers, but I also liked to help guys who were struggling. That might have affected my point totals, but hockey is a team game.

We had a great team in 1980-81, but management just wasn't patient enough. Emile Francis had done a masterful job of drafting and trading. We had about 10 guys who had been first-round draft choices, all 25 years old or younger, but we weren't together long enough to fully jell. In talking to Bob Bourne in later years, I found out that the New York Islanders had felt we were about the only team capable of challenging them then. I wasn't surprised to hear it, but it would have been good if that news had filtered out at the time! That way the team might have stayed intact for a couple more years.

The 1986 playoffs were probably my career highlight. Brian Sutter, our team captain, had been injured most of the year, so much of the leadership fell on my shoulders. I centered one line and played wing on another. We were on the verge of elimination in game six of the conference finals on the night they call the "Monday Night Miracle" in St. Louis. It was May 12, 1986—my thirtieth birthday—and we were down three goals halfway through the third period. Amazingly, we took the Flames to overtime and won. I've never seen such electricity in St. Louis since. The people cheered and wouldn't leave the building for half an hour after the game. Unfortunately, we lost game seven 2–1 to the Flames in Calgary.

The day I announced my retirement from the Red Wings, I got an offer to work as a broadcaster in St. Louis. Now I am back with the Blues organization doing color commentary on the radio. The "Blue Note" means so much to me, and broadcasting has given me a connection to the game that's made hockey a lot of fun again. I travel with the Blues, which I enjoy, but now I can really see how much wear and tear the NHL schedule causes. I'm tired a lot, and I don't even play!

Bernie Federko holds a number of St. Louis Blues records, including most games (927), most assists (721) and most career points (1,073). (OPPOSITE) Federko gets ready to tip a shot in front of the Chicago Blackhawks goal.

Sergei Fedorov

My childhood was a fabulous time in my life because I could skate all day. We had natural ice for six to seven months of the year. As long as I was outside, I was happy. I started to skate when I was 3½ years old. When I was a little older, I would stay out on the frozen river for six or seven hours a day. Sometimes it was so cold that school was canceled, but we'd still go out to skate. Ten minutes at a time was all we could take. We'd come in for 20 minutes, drink some hot tea to warm ourselves and go back out for another 10 minutes. I miss those times and think about them a lot.

Because my father was a player/coach, I had the opportunity to play hockey with adults when I was still a young boy. I practiced with my dad's team many evenings, improving my skating and passing. I was amazed that the men would pass the puck back to me. That gave me so much confidence. Most important, I learned that hockey is a team sport.

Sergei Makarov was my hero when I was growing up, so I couldn't believe it when I joined him on the Central Red Army team in 1986. It was a big honor to make that team. I played four seasons, but I'll never forget my first time watching the unit of Vladimir Krutov, Igor Larionov, Makarov, Alexei Kasatonov and Slava Fetisov. They were, are, truly amazing hockey players and great guys off the ice as well. I saw the direction I needed to go in, but I was 16 and the thought of playing in the NHL had not yet crossed my mind.

I played in my first World Championship in 1989 in Stockholm, with Alexander Mogilny and Sergei Yashin as linemates. I was 18 and scored two goals in my first game. I was so happy, because that was the best team I could imagine playing with. We won the gold medal, and I have good memories of the players from that national team. To be honest, no matter how tough life was in Russia back then, I was still having a great time.

In Russia, I played a high level of hockey, and the system was working well for the players then. That system has changed a great deal now. The young players in Russia don't get to see the older players and the best anymore. The Russian system gave me the physical base that I rely upon today. Our conditioning was always excellent. Development in my body language— shifting, faking, deking—for the one-on-one game, improvement in skating backwards and handling the puck and gaining better vision of the play came from practicing on the ice for up to four hours a day. Defense was a big part of our strategy, and our coach, Viktor Tikhonov, made sure that I was always very supportive in our own end.

As life goes on, I wonder how I have been so fortunate in my career. Knowing that I can play 25 minutes in a game and still be fresh the next night leaves me with a great feeling. I'm happiest when I spend a lot of time on the ice. I get chances to try so many things and experience all aspects of the game.

When I first came to Detroit in 1990, I hooked up with Shawn Burr. He's in Tampa Bay now, but he was my good buddy for four years here. He really took care of me, especially in my first year, showing me around and teaching me some of the language. We shared a room when we were on the road, and he likes to talk, so that was really helpful to me. Shawn was an experienced NHL player who cared enough to sit me down a couple of times and tell me to work harder. I appreciate how good he was to me.

The most valuable award I have ever received is the Lester Pearson Award in 1994. To be recognized by my teammates and my opponents as the best player on the ice marked an amazing moment in my career. It got me excited and wanting to work harder and harder. I aim to stay consistent through my entire career and never play at a lower level again. I hope, of course, to win the Stanley Cup, but I want to win some individual trophies again too. Those awards, including the Frank Selke Trophy, have meant a lot to me.

I never thought I'd be reunited with my teammates from the Red Army after playing professional hockey for so many years. I learned some of my first steps from Igor Larionov, Vladimir Konstantinov and Slava Fetisov. We're thousands of miles away from home, and here we are having a very decent time together again. The world is full of surprises.

Sergei Fedorov, two-time winner of the Frank Selke Trophy as the NHL's premier defensive forward, helped Detroit win two consecutive Stanley Cups in 1998 and 1999. (Opposite) Fedorov controls the puck in full flight as he crosses the Toronto Maple Leaf blue line.

Slava Fetisov

From the time I was age 6 to 18, my team never lost a single game, including even regional and national competition. I joined the Red Army club when I was 8 years old. Everyone felt honored to be part of the organization, because it was very difficult to get in. Some years, there were 10,000 kids trying to join. I went through all the stages with them, until I joined the big team (and the USSR national team) at age 18.

Red Army was the most popular club in the Soviet Union, with a great tradition of winning. Three-quarters of the national team came from our club. In every game, every tournament, the pressure was on, especially for our line. I played on the first line for almost a decade with Igor Larionov, Sergei Makarov, Vladimir Krutov and Alexei Kasatonov. Losing was considered a tragedy. It affected our lives politically, economically, in every aspect. The system also couldn't tolerate independent thinking. Anyone who thought differently was shut up or thrown out. Most players' careers were over by the time they reached age 30.

I decided I wanted to try the NHL, but the government wouldn't let me go. I had opportunities to defect, but, I thought, that's not me: I would fight the system for my right, for everybody's right, to leave. It was a six-month struggle that showed me just how powerful the system still was. I had been unaware up to that point just how antihuman and antifreedom the Soviet system could be. It was in the constitution that anyone could sign a direct contract with an NHL club without government involvement. Despite that, the government would intervene, take the player's salary and give him only 10 percent. I knew that wasn't right. It would be *my* contract.

Gary Kasparov, the world-champion chess player and a very intelligent young man, told me that we could break the system. But we would need to stick together and never back up. I was captain of the national hockey team for many years and had made numerous friends. In many ways, my teammates were like brothers. But I had also spent those years in the army. The Soviet minister of defense tried to scare me, demanding that I apologize for asking to leave. He gave me an ultimatum: Apologize or be sent to Siberia, where we will make life very difficult for you. I knew that if I took even a small step back, I would be in deep trouble. I faced a lot of intimidation; most of my friends were afraid to talk to me. It was the toughest time in my life, but I finally won the war. I was the first Soviet to sign a direct contract, and I'm proud to say that not only hockey players followed me. The door opened for people in every profession.

It is still a big surprise to be recognized when I go back to Russia. I've played eight years in the NHL, but people on the street still remember me from the national team. Once we left for the NHL, people thought we were gone forever. The NHL lockout of 1994 allowed me my dream—to bring back the Russian NHL players for a tour. I spent so many years on the national team that I knew how important hockey is to the Russian people. I called Moscow, and the government said we could return. Even Alexander Mogilny, who had defected and been considered an army deserter, got his passport back. Most of the guys had run from the Soviet system; it was so gratifying to see them surrounded by their families and old friends. We all got a hero's welcome in every town we visited, including in Siberia. Now everyone can go back whenever they wish.

I grew up dreaming of playing for the Soviet national team and competing in the World Championships and the Olympics. I was eventually selected to several All-Star teams and named Soviet Player of the Year three times. Two Olympic gold medals and eight World Championships topped my accomplishments during my prime years. I went from hero to enemy of the country in six months. I won the big fight against the army but only had two weeks to prepare myself for my first NHL season. I was 31 years old and hadn't trained for months, far from my usual routine. The language barrier, a different lifestyle, different tactics and different teams made for a difficult first season. It really took two or three seasons to adjust.

I've especially enjoyed my past few seasons in Detroit. It's a great organization, with good people and a strong tradition. By chance, I saw Ted Lindsay's story told in a television movie. I was flipping channels but was completely gripped by the show, seeing some strong similarities to my own experience. I have a lot of respect for that man. I sit in Gordie Howe's old stall in the Red Wings dressing room, feeling better every year that I play in the NHL. Many of the younger Russians in the NHL now call me "Godfather." I'm 39 and my pride feels restored.

Slava Fetisov, a member of eight World Championship teams and a two-time Olympic gold medalist, helped Detroit win two Stanley Cups. (Opposite) The New Jersey Devils signed Fetisov to his first NHL contract in 1989. After retiring as a player, Fetisov returned to the Devils and won a third Cup ring in 2000 as assistant coach.

Theoren Fleury

My size was always a motivating force for me. I made it with speed and skill combined with fearlessness and all-out determination. I wanted to prove wrong every person who ever said that I was too small. The scouts have a "big man" mentality. A big guy has to prove that he *can't* play, and a little guy has to prove that he can. Most times, the bigger guy gets the nod because of the belief that through good coaching, he'll eventually be the better player.

There's always room for small players in this game. Henri Richard was no bigger than I am, and he won 11 Stanley Cups. Marcel Dionne also comes to mind right away, but there's a long list of small men who have had amazing careers. Whenever a small guy made it, I took hope. I want to be remembered as a hockey player first and foremost, but I'm thankful that I might be providing the same kind of hope to some kids today. Because they can do it.

It was great to have my mom and dad with me during the 1996 World Cup. My mother isn't the biggest hockey fan, but she has been supportive of me, often making the 10-hour drive from Russell, Manitoba, to see me play in Calgary. My parents loved meeting the great players we had on the Canadian team. I know that my dad would have loved to be an NHL hockey player himself. I'm really glad that he can experience some of his dreams through me.

A tournament like the World Cup is the most fun in hockey. The whole country is going to live and die with the team for a month. There is such a big emphasis on performance and winning. That brings out the best in elite players. Any athlete will tell you that competing at the highest level is the most enjoyable. That's why we strive to win the Stanley Cup in the NHL. It's all about working under the highest pressure, pressure that we ourselves create.

I remember my first NHL goal as if it were yesterday. It was my third game, and we were playing the Edmonton Oilers on *Hockey Night in Canada*. It was an incredible feeling to know that my family and friends were back home watching. I could picture them jumping all around the house when I put the puck in the net. I even scored a second goal that night. My aunt, uncle and some cousins had driven in for the game, so we went out for a big celebration afterward.

It's always great to share the good times with your family. They're my support system, the people who are there when things aren't going well, when I need someone to talk to. I think of my dad as a good-luck charm. Whenever we're struggling, I ask him to get in the car and come to Calgary. If he's there, I think our chances are pretty good.

I like to reminisce about the days back home when hockey was just for fun and there was no pressure. It gives me a good feeling and gets me focused on what the game is all about. But I also look back at all the years of practicing, the outdoor ice surfaces, the cold rinks and the long bus rides. There were days I didn't want to be there. When I really think about it, being in the NHL is the most fun. But sometimes—because there are a lot of demands and we get paid an unbelievable amount of money—it's hard to think of hockey as just a game. That's when it's important to remember the way you played as a child.

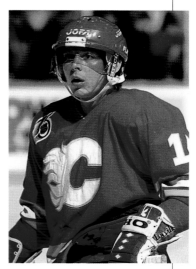

We had a big, tough, established team with great balance when we won the Stanley Cup in 1989. I got called up on New Year's Day to provide a bit of spark. I wasn't expected to make the team, let alone be part of winning the Cup. I've always been a cocky guy, which I think is one of my strongest qualities, but it didn't make it easier to mesh with the team. I came with the intention of staying, and I played well enough that the coaches had to keep me in the lineup. Unfortunately, that meant someone else had to sit out. I wasn't welcomed with open arms, but over time, I earned respect.

The Calgary team was so good that even after playing well, I never felt I'd earned a spot. That insecurity was probably good for me, making me the team's hardest worker. Once you get a taste of the NHL, you're loath to go back. I thought we had a good enough team to win for a couple of years, but we haven't been too close since. I want to win another Cup with Calgary because they gave me a chance to play when no one else thought I could.

In 1989, the speedy and determined Theo Fleury worked his way onto a powerhouse Calgary team which won the Stanley Cup that spring. (Opposite) The Flames traded Fleury to Colorado in March 1999, but four months later, the New York Rangers signed him to a lucrative free-agent contract.

Ron Francis

It was really tough to be traded to Pittsburgh in 1991, because I had virtually grown up in Hartford. I had spent my entire 10-year NHL career there, starting at age 18. My wife and I had a lot of good friends in Hartford away from the game too, but I knew that professionally, it was probably the best thing for me. It certainly worked out well. Three months later, we were carrying the Stanley Cup. We won again the following season. It's a privilege to have been on two Cup winners. We worked hard, but I know that everyone who reaches that goal has to get some breaks the way we did.

The Pittsburgh players had a party about three or four days after the trade. John Cullen had been a good friend to most of the guys and had been having a great season. There was certainly sadness and regret seeing him leave for Hartford. Despite that, the players made it clear to me that as much as they were going to miss John, I was going to be a big part of the team. They were ready and willing to rely on me. I felt welcomed and at ease right away.

I remember playing as a boy under the stars in Sault Ste. Marie and how much fun I had, no matter how cold it got! I still feel that genuine love of the game and am thankful to be a professional hockey player. I must say, though, it's easier to give your best when the team is winning. We had some lean years in Hartford, but I'm proud of the consistency I had there. People pay to see us play, so I have an obligation to maintain my mental state—not get too high or too low—so that even if the team isn't doing well, I can still play a strong game.

When Mario Lemieux took a year off, for the entire 1994-95 season, I got a great opportunity to play more. Jaromir Jagr stepped up his game to the next level at the same time. I benefited from that as Jaromir's center and won my first NHL individual awards. I'm grateful that the Frank Selke and Lady Byng trophies now have my name on them, but if all my teammates hadn't played well, I would not have won them.

It's a lot easier to play *with* Mario and Jaromir than it is to play *against* them! They are both tremendous talents. Mario is a great individual, and Jaromir is a hard worker and fierce competitor. It's obvious that when I'm on the ice with those two, my job is to concentrate on the defensive aspect of the game and allow them to be as creative as possible. Of course, I still get my share of points. Recently, we three have been playing on a line together. I'm one of the luckiest centers in the league, with the tough decision of whether to pass left to Mario or right to Jaromir.

Ulf Samuelsson is one of my best friends. Everyone hates to play against Ulf, but everyone in the league would love to have him on his club. We played together for almost 12 years in Hartford and Pittsburgh and were roommates most of that time. I got to know Ulf off the ice. He's a great guy. Our wives are good friends, and we have three kids each who are roughly the same age.

Away from the rink, Ulf is a quality individual and a guy I'm proud to call my friend. It's only tough to be friends with him when we run into each other on the ice now that he's a New York Ranger. Ulf is a competitor who plays to win. I don't expect any favors from him, and he doesn't give any. Of course, that works both ways!

I had a big disappointment at a critical point in the 1996 playoffs, getting injured just before we started the Eastern Conference Finals against Florida. I had had a good year, and we were making another promising run at the Stanley Cup. Despite not being able to play, I thought I could still contribute. I took a spot behind the bench to help my teammates stay calm, relaxed and focused, particularly in times of frustration. I shared what I saw from my position, especially with Jaromir and Petr Nedved. I've played with Jaromir for so long that I understand a lot of the defenses that are used against him and what can be done to break them down. We worked hard but unfortunately lost to Florida in seven games.

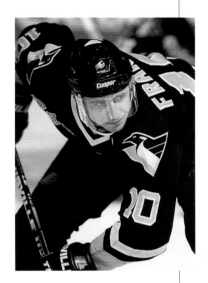

I was glad to help behind the bench, but I have no aspirations ever to be a coach. To do the job properly requires a tremendous time commitment. My family has suffered enough with my playing schedule for the past 16 years. Professional hockey is not as glamorous as many people might like to believe. There is a lot of travel involved and large amounts of time spent away from your family. All things considered, I have no beefs. But I missed my daughter's first steps and first words. Those are things you can't make up for.

Ron Francis won two Stanley Cup rings playing for Pittsburgh after 10 exceptional seasons with the Hartford Whalers. The Whalers moved to Carolina for 1997-98 and reacquired Francis the following season. (Opposite) Francis muscles his way around Doug Gilmour and the Maple Leaf net while his Penguins linemate Jaromir Jagr looks on.

Grant Fuhr

It's going back a while, but I remember advice I received from Glenn Hall. I was a teenager at hockey school, eager to learn as much as I could from one of the greatest goalies ever to play. "Don't be a goalie," he said. "Goalies are insane." More important, Glenn explained, you have to have fun when you're playing. If it turns into a job, you should get out. I've carried that philosophy through my career. I really enjoy what I do. But as soon as playing hockey becomes a job, I'm done.

I'm primarily self-taught. I wouldn't say that I have an acrobatic style. I'd describe it more as "mad panic." I do whatever I can to get in the way of the puck. If it means diving, somersaulting or whatever, I do it. It doesn't matter to me which part of the body I use; I just throw whatever is closest at the puck. I never had a full-fledged goalie coach. I've just picked up little bits from different guys, trying to add something every year.

My aim was to make the NHL. I was surprised to be drafted in the first round, but going to Edmonton in my home province made the transition to the NHL much easier. It was always a lot of fun to play for the Oilers. I knew our team would score four or five goals every game right through the 1980s; my job was to keep the other teams under that. I might not have had the best numbers in the world, but we won. That's all that matters.

The best game I ever played was against the Islanders in the opening game of the 1984 Stanley Cup finals. It was one of those games when everything went well. The Islanders had swept us four straight in the finals the year before for their fourth consecutive Stanley Cup win, but we beat them that night 1–0. You hope for more games like that, but I haven't had one lately. There's a zone that an athlete gets into. The closest thing I've found to that sensation, perhaps the only better feeling, is having kids. You go through spans when you get in the zone, but just as fast as it comes, it goes. You really don't know what gets you there or what keeps you there, but if you're lucky, good things happen. We went on to win our first Stanley Cup.

That first Cup was special, but it was even better to win back-to-back. Everyone had told us that repeating was even harder than winning. I can't say that I had a bad year in Edmonton. Life was easy for a goaltender then. I didn't face tight 2–1 games. You can win different ways, but I enjoyed the wide-open hockey. I was never surprised by breakaways, because I was prepared for that kind of game. I'm still making an adjustment to being a St. Louis Blue because of the style of hockey we play. The defensive game is a little boring to me, but if it wins, I'm all for it.

There was no way that I wanted to retire after a somewhat disappointing stint in Los Angeles. My career was dragging, St. Louis was looking for a goalie, and they gave me an opportunity. I had no warning that I'd start so many games when I joined the Blues in the fall of 1995. I got off to a good start, and day by day, the chance to set the record for most games in a season by a goalie appeared. I like a heavy workload; playing a lot agrees with me. My playoffs got off to a good start too, but in only my second game, I was injured in a goalmouth collision. That's playoff hockey—there's nothing to be done about it—but it made me eager to get back to the playoffs and pick up where I left off.

Competition between goaltending partners helps keep things fun and makes each goalie better. I've been lucky to share duties with a super mix of veterans and kids over the years. Ronnie Low really welcomed me and helped me get comfortable in my first couple of years with the Oilers. I coached Felix Potvin in Toronto when he first came up. He's a great guy and was fun to play with. I've enjoyed seeing him do so well. I think that most goalies get along. We respect each other.

I got into trouble with substance abuse through some of the people I hung around with outside hockey a few years ago. But hockey made a big difference by giving me a place to go to sort things out again and get through a rough time. It has always been good to come to the rink. I had to learn the hard way, but every time I hear rumors that I'm near the end, I try to find a way to resurrect my career. When I leave, I want to go on my own terms.

Grant Fuhr stands with his protégé Felix Potvin during the time of their Toronto Maple Leaf goaltending partnership in 1992. (Opposite) Fuhr set an NHL record with 79 starts for the St. Louis Blues in 1995-96. He completed his outstanding career with the 1999-2000 Calgary Flames.

Mike Gartner

Playing in the WHA was a great stepping-stone. I was lucky to play a year for Cincinnati when I was 18. The NHL draft didn't occur until players had reached the age of 20. There were a few of us, including Mark Messier and Wayne Gretzky, who got the same chance. The WHA had become a major threat to the NHL, not only by signing underage players but by the caliber of its teams. The weak clubs had been weeded out, and the league was solid, made up primarily of players capable of playing in the NHL. The NHL absorbed the WHA the following season.

The Washington Capitals made me the fourth pick in the 1979 NHL entry draft. They had a poor team, so I got

a lot of ice time, even as a rookie. I was actually surprised to develop into a goal scorer. I had come into the league as a two-way hockey player, not a scorer. Of course, I could always skate and shoot, but I scored more goals (48) in my second year in the NHL than I ever did in junior. I then had a streak of sixteen 30-goal seasons, broken only by the owners' lockout in 1994.

In Washington, I had 10 great years. I grew up with that organization and put a lot of myself into the club and the community. We went from a struggling team to respectability in the league. It was a low point in my career to be traded from the Capitals, a pill that I had a hard time swallowing. Phoenix is the fifth team that I've played for in 18 seasons.

Trades have become more familiar to me, and I know what to do now, but they have become increasingly difficult. I've never grown used to being traded. It's hardest on my children, who have to leave their friends, go to new schools and establish new friendships. The hockey is the easiest part of the transition, because it's what I do best. No matter what team I'm on, whether it's in the NHL, playing for my country or in an All-Star game, I can adapt to my teammates.

I've seen a lot of changes in the league since I started. Overall, the game is better. There are more quality players who are bigger and stronger and better skaters. I've also seen shifts from a game of intimidation, personified by the Philadelphia Flyers of the 1970s that carried over into the 1980s, to more of a New York Islanders checking and positional game in the early 1980s to a skating game best played by the Edmonton Oilers of the later 1980s (when I had the most fun). The game

today is much like that old Islanders style but faster. I've had to continually adapt and develop goal-scoring strategies to cope with those shifts in the league as well as with new coaching systems. When I started, I counted almost exclusively on my speed. In the past few years, I've had to get in front of the net, get pounded and bang away at rebounds.

Today's hockey has made me into a pioneer of sorts in Phoenix. We have to introduce and sell the game in the desert—which naturally has no history of NHL hockey. But bringing the game to such locales has shown that expansion is feasible in a number of other areas. This is really as good for the players as it is for the owners, because it creates more jobs. And even with the higher number of teams in the league now, any lower-echelon team is capable of beating the best teams on any given night. That wasn't the case when I first joined the league. In the late 1970s and through the 1980s, there were usually only two or three teams that had a shot at winning the Stanley Cup. It would be a real feat for anyone else to win. There are still a few favorites, but there are probably a dozen teams that have a reasonable chance of winning the Cup now.

I have some God-given skating talent, but going to power-skating school as a boy helped me develop a strong skating technique. It was a lot less fun than hockey school and I didn't appreciate it at the time, but going on the ice without pucks really paid off for me. I always felt that I was one of the faster skaters in the NHL, so I enjoyed it when the league instituted some competition at the All-Star game. I especially got a kick out of winning the skating race (for the third time) at age 37. It's a pretty short race and not all that important, but the competitive juices start to flow. The atmosphere is very loose, but as in most things, once we get to the starting line, we all want to win. That attitude is what got us to the NHL.

Mike Gartner

Mike Gartner tallied his 17th 30-goal season (an NHL record) in 1996-97 as a Phoenix Coyote. (Opposite) Shortly before his retirement in 1998, Gartner, a Maple Leaf from 1994 to 1996, became the fifth player to tally 700 NHL goals.

Bernie Geoffrion

I WAS PLAYING JUNIOR HOCKEY AT THE MONTREAL FORUM when Charlie Boyer, a newspaperman with the Montreal *Gazette*, first called me "Boom-Boom" after seeing me shoot the puck and hearing it echo off the boards. I thought, "If Mickey Mantle can handle being called 'Mickey,' I can live with 'Boom-Boom.'" The name stuck.

I slapped the puck for the first time behind Immaculate Conception church when I was about 10 years old. I was practicing my shot—wrist shots and backhands were all we knew then—and not doing too well. In frustration, I took a whack at the puck, and it took off. I was impressed and started to practice what became known as the slap shot.

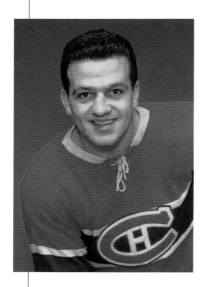

I worked on my shot constantly. In junior, I would shoot 50 to 70 pucks after practice, and when I was a pro, I was up near 150. The slap shot didn't catch on with other players right away. The Rocket only used it once in a while, but eventually, even Jean Beliveau and Gordie Howe added it to their game. I was glad of that, because it's a shot that players enjoy. The coaches hated it at first, because accuracy only came with practice. But it's part of the game now.

In the 1950-51 season, I got called up to the Canadiens for a three-game tryout and had three goals. When I used my slap shot, the goaltenders were pretty surprised. They didn't like it and complained that they didn't know where the puck was going. I just replied that it was going in the net! I got several more call-ups before the season was over, but Montreal was careful to keep my rookie eligibility for the coming season by playing me fewer than 20 games.

The next year, I won the Calder Trophy with 30 goals. That was a thrill, but my first priority was to get my name on the Stanley Cup. I won six in all. The first, in 1953, was so exciting. I don't think anyone will ever beat our record of five in a row. Even if they do—records are made to be broken—your name stays on the Stanley Cup forever. Rookie of the Year was great, as was the scoring title and being named MVP, but winning the Cup was best.

What I loved about hockey was the speed of the game, the intelligence needed to play well and the togetherness of the team. I enjoyed every minute I played and wanted to win as many awards as possible. The fans got on me when I won my first scoring championship in the 1954-55 season because I passed Rocket Richard by a single point in the last game while he was serving a suspension. But what could I do? I got paid to help the Canadiens win the Stanley Cup. The fans later realized they made a mistake, but it was hard at the time.

It was a big thrill to score 50 goals. I was only the second player to do that, after the Rocket. I was playing on a line with Jean Beliveau, as I did for much of my career, and in 1960-61, Gilles Tremblay was on the other wing. Everything went well. I shot the puck a lot, and it just seemed that most went in.

There was nothing I wanted more than to play for the Montreal Canadiens. I would have loved to have finished my career with them, but it was not to be. I retired in 1964 and went into coaching when a young Yvan Cournoyer looked to inherit my spot on the wing. I had success coaching but decided to play again after two seasons behind the bench. It was a difficult comeback, and I felt as if I were sacrificing my body to the goal of proving I could still play. Montreal couldn't protect all their players, and the New York Rangers made me their first choice in the internal draft. That turned out to be one of the greatest things that ever happened to me.

When I first played with New York against the Canadiens, I saw that the Montreal jersey was only a sweater. Wearing the blue sweater instead of the red didn't make any difference, and I scored two goals. You can't live in the past. Being with New York opened so many doors for me. I did a lot of commercials and endorsement work, and I've been very happy in the U.S. I was pleased for Guy Lafleur when I saw him make a similar

comeback in 1988. I could really relate to what he was going through.

I'm proud of what we did when we first brought hockey to Atlanta in 1972. I had my first crack at coaching in the NHL with the Rangers in the 1968-69 season, but by the time I was coach in Atlanta, I hadn't played with or against 9 out of 10 of our players. I had a hard time motivating the team at first. It took them some time to realize that it's more fun to win than to lose and

to look at my record with respect. Although I stopped coaching in 1975, I did radio and television commentary for years and really enjoyed that side of hockey too. I stayed when the team moved to Calgary, and I've lived in Atlanta ever since.

Bernard Geoffrion

Bernie Geoffrion counts six Stanley Cup victories as highlights in an NHL career that also included winning the Calder, Hart and two Art Ross trophies. (Above) "Boom Boom" battles in deep against a swarm of Maple Leafs.

Rod Gilbert

I remember being at Rendez-Vous '87, the NHL-Russia series. I was talking with Henri Richard and Yvan Cournoyer. A photographer wanted a picture of us, so I remarked, "Look at this. Among the three of us, we have *twenty-one* Stanley Cups." The photographer was amazed. "That's incredible," he said and asked Henri how many he had. "Eleven." Then he asked Yvan. "Ten."

We all laughed, but the desire to win a Cup made my career exciting. My pursuit was intense and made me a better player. I pride myself on that. Playing for Team

Canada in 1972 was my Stanley Cup. The Rangers had enough talent but not a complete enough team to win. Our coach and general manager, Emile Francis, just didn't believe in the style of play that Boston and Philadelphia practiced. We were outsmarted. Peripheral opposition players would take key players from our club off the ice by luring them into fights. I was not a fighter, but if someone attacked me, I had no choice. Of course, we also ran into Bobby Orr and some hot goaltending by Bernie Parent in Philadelphia. But for them, we would have won. Bobby Orr was in his prime then. I remember chasing him while he was killing a penalty. I yelled, "Bobby, give us the puck. It's our power play. Throw it down the ice." He just answered, "Come and get it."

We won the championship in my last year of junior with the Guelph Biltmores, and I was nominated as best player in the league. Unbelievably, I suffered a major injury with one game left in my junior career. I was paralyzed for two months and sent to the Mayo Clinic for a spinal fusion. My career was in great jeopardy already, but more complications arose. My tibia became infected, and there was talk of having to amputate my leg. Then I got a staph infection in my back. I was thankful that the Rangers stuck with me and gave me the eight months I needed to recover.

I played pro in the minors late in the 1961-62 season but finished the year in the NHL when the Rangers made an emergency call-up for the playoffs. I scored two goals in the first period I played. It felt like a dream after all the anxiety I'd suffered. Unfortunately, I had to play with a back brace, which hindered my breathing considerably. But things got worse. After four years, I got hit into the boards and the spinal fusion broke.

The doctors decided to take a bone from my pelvis instead of the tibia and fuse it to the three vertebrae. As a preventive measure against the infection I got after the first operation, they fed me antibiotics for seven days and no food. I suffered acute indigestion, and during a visit by Emile Francis and Bill Jennings, the Rangers team president, I actually choked to death. I was clinically dead for four minutes. I had an out-of-body experience, watching the nurse working on me, Bill Jennings running around the room and Emile Francis yelling, "Bring him back, damn it! He's my best player!"

The nurse finally cleared my breathing passage, gave me CPR and oxygen, and I woke up as if nothing had happened. They gave me a blood transfusion to get my strength back, and I felt perfectly well. I believe that I had been given a choice to exit this life and I had declined. I was dreading another eight-month recovery, but I think that my soul *needed* to come back to live out my dreams. I've felt connected to a superior force since I was a kid, and I made a lot of promises to "the big guy."

I didn't want to be a blacksmith like my dad. He worked like a dog. You should have seen *his* back! I'm still thankful every day. My back became strong enough to allow me even to take my brace off.

I first met Jean Ratelle when we were both 8 years old. I wanted to play with him immediately, and because he followed a similar path, I got my wish—I played with him almost my entire life. We're still close, so it was quite depressing when Jean and our tremendous defenseman Brad Park were traded to the Boston Bruins in 1975. I never understood that trade. I played only a few years after that. I tried to be very professional, but I really lost some of my feelings for the game.

I've always believed that if a player has a team tattooed on his heart and he's still able to produce, why trade him? I was lucky to be chosen to sell the Rangers to the fans early in my career, probably preventing any possible trade. For years, I was the biggest hockey evangelist in New York City. I went on all the TV shows, including *What's My Line?* I was the "Mystery Guest" and stumped the panel when they had their masks on *and* when they took them off. I once tried to impress a woman by telling her I was a Ranger. She asked if I put out forest fires. The New York Rangers were completely unknown to all but about 25,000 fans in a city of 8 million, but I saw that change over the course of my career.

Rod Gilbert

Rod Gilbert holds the New York Ranger records for most career goals, assists and total points. Gilbert's number seven now hangs from the rafters of Madison Square Garden. (Opposite) Here, we see him in the late 1960s, carrying a "banana blade" and looking for a rebound off Toronto Maple Leaf Bruce Gamble.

Doug Gilmour

BEING A HOCKEY "CELEBRITY" HAS GIVEN ME THE SPECIAL opportunity to get close to some children afflicted with cancer, and I have witnessed how fragile life can be. My wife Amy and I have a little boy now, and my daughter Maddison is 12. I treasure my time with them. I'm as fiery on the ice as I ever was, but I don't take a loss in hockey as hard as I once did. Am I going to cry over a hockey game when I know there's a child fighting for his life in the hospital down the road? I don't think so. Hockey is a game I love, but it's people who are most important to me.

Bobby Orr was my hero when I was growing up. Like him, I played defense and loved to rush the puck up the ice. I was small for my age (I never did get too big!), but I was a good skater and stickhandler. Still, like most small kids, I repeatedly heard that I'd never be able to make it in hockey. I got so discouraged by this that I actually quit the game for a while. I was always a fierce competitor, but it's hard to be told that, through no fault of your own, you can't do what you love.

Fortunately for me, Gord Wood, a hockey scout, saw some potential in me and encouraged me to get back in the game. He got me on a Tier II junior team in Belleville, Ontario, not far from my hometown of Kingston. Larry Mavety was the coach there, and he switched me from defense to forward. My size became less of an issue, and since I had been an offensive-minded defenseman, the transition wasn't all that difficult. Gord drafted me to the Junior A Cornwall Royals a couple of years later, and I was on my way to a professional career.

I really enjoyed playing OHL hockey in Cornwall, but even to get on that team was a struggle. I felt I needed to prove that I belonged and got 119 points in my first season. It was a satisfying year capped by winning the Memorial Cup, the greatest achievement in Canadian junior hockey. It was my draft year, and I was really proud of my accomplishments. It felt like a slap in the face to be drafted by St. Louis in the seventh round, 134th pick overall, in the 1982 NHL draft. I thought I deserved to go higher and grew more determined to show the hockey world that they were wrong about me.

The next year was even better for me personally. I went back to Cornwall for another year and won the OHL MVP award. I also led the league in assists and total points, with 70 goals and 107 assists. But if I thought my junior success would make it easier to establish myself in the NHL, I was wrong. I continually have had to prove myself, again and again. I've been traded twice when I felt my club undervalued my contributions. The fan reaction to the trades in St. Louis and Calgary seems to show that wasn't only my opinion.

I had tremendous highs and lows in Calgary. We won the Stanley Cup, which is as good as it gets. My only regret is that I didn't skate around the ice with the Cup.

We had such a good team that I thought I'd have lots of opportunities. I get a little extra motivation thinking about that now. It's a little thing, but I'd love to get the chance to do that.

I really locked horns with Calgary GM Doug Risebrough in contract negotiations. He took me to arbitration, which is a terrible process to go through. To prove the team's case for a lower salary, Doug exaggerated every possible flaw in my play and demeaned my value to the team. Every good thing that I did was made to seem worthless. I like Doug, we're very similar people, but he was new to his role and this was the first time he'd been through the arbitration process. After hearing that Calgary didn't even think I'd be on the team in a year, I realized I had no desire left to be a Flame. I demanded a trade, which was sad for me then, but being a Toronto Maple Leaf was great.

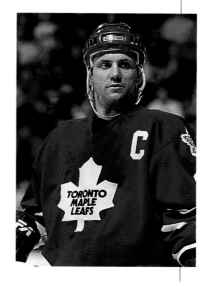

My parents and family got to see me more often after the trade to Toronto, and that was worth a lot. My parents can be very funny in their critiques of the game and my play. My style has always been a bit on the scrappy side, but my mom thinks that any trouble I get into is always someone else's fault. If the team doesn't do well, it's because of what others didn't do. My dad, while supportive of me personally, is the opposite. If the team doesn't win, it's because of what I didn't do; I shoulder the blame because of the goal or pass I missed. Both my parents have strong personalities, and I've been lucky to inherit some of their character.

Doug Gilmour was a popular team captain of the Toronto Maple Leafs until his trade to New Jersey in February 1997. He signed with Chicago in the summer of 1998 and joined the Buffalo Sabres in a March 2000 swap. (OPPOSITE) Gilmour squeezes past Brett Hull behind the net of the St. Louis Blues.

Michel Goulet

I PLAYED IN THE WHA AS ONE OF BIRMINGHAM'S "BABY" Bulls. Too young to play in the NHL, Mark Messier and Mike Gartner were in Cincinnati, Wayne Gretzky was in Edmonton, and Rick Vaive, Craig Hartsburg, Rob Ramage, Pat Riggin, Gaston Gingras and I played in Birmingham. That was a lot of fun. We were the youngest team in the league. At the end of that year, every one of us were first-round picks in the NHL. I was excited to be selected by the Quebec Nordiques, because I played my junior hockey there and really love the city. It was, and always will be, a great place to play hockey.

We had a strong first half in the team's inaugural NHL season and my rookie year, but then it was tough. We really appreciated what we accomplished in later years, because we grew as a team together. Peter and Anton Stastny and Dale Hunter were important additions in our second season. I had Dale as my center for seven years. I loved playing with him because of what he brought to the team offensively and defensively. When you look at *all* his numbers—more than 300 goals, about 1,000 points and well over 3,000 penalty minutes—you see he's more than just a tough little distraction to the other team. He's also one of the league's best players.

I had talent, but I also practiced a lot. I always arrived early and worked on my shot every day. It was important to me to be one of the best left-wingers in the league. That drove me. I knew I had to go to the net to score goals, and I was never intimidated, never afraid. Seeing my goal-scoring totals go up was rewarding, but above all, I tried to be a complete hockey player, a guy who goes just as hard both ways.

Winning the 1984 Canada Cup was a big thrill for me. I played on a line with Wayne Gretzky and Rick Middleton and was the top scorer in the tournament. I knew Rick's game a little better than Wayne's, because the Nordiques generally played his Boston Bruins about eight times a year. He was one of the most underrated players in the league. He did everything—at both ends of the rink—with a lot of skill. What can I say about Wayne Gretzky but that there was good chemistry among the three of us as soon as Glen Sather put our line together at training camp. Playing with Canada's best was always great. In 1987, I had the chance to play with Mario Lemieux a little bit, and we won the Canada Cup again.

Probably the best game I ever played was against Quebec's archrival, the Montreal Canadiens. We were losing 3–0 after 10 minutes of play, and the Montreal fans turned the Forum into a big party with their singing. We called a time-out and quieted the crowd when we started to turn things around. We were only behind 4–3 at the end of the first period, and I eventually had four goals and two assists in an unbelievably dramatic contest. We won 8–6.

I had knee surgery in 1989 and got more bad news when the team decided to make changes and traded me to Chicago. My best times with the Blackhawks were the three years of my five there when I played on a line with Jeremy Roenick and Steve Larmer. We came close to winning the Stanley Cup in 1992. It was a discouraging loss, because we went to the finals with 12 straight playoff victories and were winning by three goals in the first game against the Pittsburgh Penguins. We tried to tie up Mario Lemieux, but then Jaromir Jagr responded with three goals. We stayed tough, but Mario broke our hearts with a beautiful goal. We ended up losing 5–4 and never really recovered.

I don't know anyone who was *really* ready to retire, but my last game came as a shock. I was skating toward the corner when I lost an edge and slid about 10 feet headfirst into the boards. I was in a coma for eight days with injury to various parts of my brain. I lost my memory and coordination and spent the next three years learning to do things all over again.

No one can say for sure that another helmet would have helped me, but I would feel better if the league acknowledged that players need better protection. I was wearing the same kind of helmet that is still worn by some players, and it did not provide even standard protection. The National Football League wouldn't allow one of its players to wear less than standard equipment, and neither should the NHL. What happened to me could happen to anyone.

I'm pleased to be where I am now. I joined the Colorado Avalanche as director of player personnel in 1996. I know what a good job is, because I had the best one in the world for 16 years. I appreciated every minute I had as a player. But there comes a time to try other things. I feel good that I was able to realize my dream of playing in the NHL. Many share the dream, but it takes a little extra to bring it to reality. I'm thankful I found what it takes.

Michel Goulet scored his 500th career goal on February 16, 1992, while playing for the Chicago Blackhawks.
(**OPPOSITE**) *Goulet was an NHL All-Star five times during the 11 seasons he skated for the Quebec Nordiques.*

Wayne Gretzky

I REMEMBER MY FIRST HOCKEY TRYOUT. I WAS 5 YEARS OLD. There was no organized hockey for kids my age, so I tried out for a team of 10-year-olds. I made the team but was really disheartened when I wasn't allowed to play because I was too young. They said I had to be at least 6. We drove from Brantford to a little town called Paris, where we thought I could play, but they, too, said I was too young. I wasn't able to play that year.

When I was 6, I tried out for the Brantford team again and made it. I played on that same team for five years and then played with the same boys from about age 9

until 13. We spent a lot of time together, and good friendships were made. Whether we were playing baseball in the summer or pickup hockey in the backyard, on frozen ponds in the winter or in organized hockey tournaments, it was all fun. There was never any pressure until I was about 12.

I looked forward to winter so that my dad could make a rink in the backyard and I could skate and play with my friends. There was usually a crowd to scrimmage with, but there were times when I'd skate by myself. In the early mornings before school or after everyone went

home at night, I'd have an extra half-hour or so. My dad, a gifted teacher of the game, would come out and give me some little drills for shooting or stickhandling. He made it interesting while he helped me develop my skills.

Parents come up to me now saying, "We'd like you to tell our son that he has to practice hockey the way you did, for six, seven or eight hours a day." I tell them that's not my philosophy. It really wasn't practice, it was fun. I enjoyed myself. My life revolved around playing games. If I had considered it practice, I would not have done it. It's human nature to be a little rebellious when someone tells us we have to do something.

A lot of what I do comes from within. It's instinct. I'm not a good teacher like my dad, but I'll always enjoy skating and having fun with my kids on the ice. What I can pass on from my dad is a motto that my wife and I believe in: Whatever you start, you have to finish. We'll encourage our kids to do everything they want and make their own choices, but our job is to help them stick with their decisions.

With all of the good things that were said about me when I was growing up, there was always some skepticism. The doubters motivated me, and I kept working hard. I focused on doing well in school too. Until I actually signed a pro contract, I really didn't know whether I was going to make it in hockey. I was never the biggest or overly fast, and there were always question marks.

The hockey in Brantford was as good as anywhere, but the day came when it seemed to be in my best interest to leave home and move. For my everyday life, going to school and fitting in with kids, it was probably the best thing I could have done. Still, if I had to do it all over again, I'd probably choose differently. I missed a lot of time at home, and some days were very difficult. I remember some sadness playing for Team Canada in the World Junior Championship when I was 16. As exciting as it was, that was my first Christmas away from home. I was no different than any other 16-year-old; I dreamed of playing in the NHL and winning the Stanley Cup. Dreams are great, and we should all have them. But then there is the reality that no one just hands you your dreams.

A dominant hockey memory from when I was a boy is of Jean Beliveau lifting the Stanley Cup. For some reason, he sticks out in my mind. Before we won our first Cup in Edmonton, we had pictures in the dressing room of a few players, including Jean, raising the Cup in triumph. I can't even describe how wonderful it was when I first got that opportunity. There is no feeling like it. I'd dreamed of that moment in my backyard, in the street and on the ice for so long.

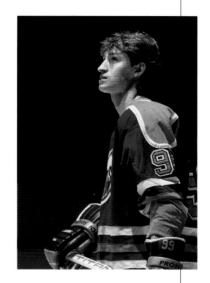

I was fortunate to play for Glen Sather. Glen had played in Boston with Bobby Orr and Phil Esposito and in Montreal with Guy Lafleur and other great players. He was a big believer in the team concept, but he also encouraged individualism. I don't know what might have happened in my career if I had been on another team. I've won a lot of individual awards, and I know I owe a great deal of that success to Glen and my teammates. I'm proud of the awards, each and every one of them. There are moments when I look back on winning 10 scoring titles. It's fun! I can hardly believe it myself sometimes. But I know that I've had the right group around me, from the coach to the players.

Wayne Gretzky

Wayne Gretzky, rightfully known as "The Great One," played nine spectacular seasons for the Edmonton Oilers, winning four Stanley Cup rings and establishing himself as a hockey legend. (OPPOSITE) Gretzky, here moving toward open ice in front of Pittsburgh's J.J. Daigneault, continued to be a dominant player right up to his retirement as a New York Ranger in 1999.

Glenn Hall

I ALWAYS FELT I PLAYED BETTER IF I WAS PHYSICALLY SICK before the game. If I wasn't sick, I felt I hadn't done everything I could to try to win. I had no trouble getting "up" for a game; I was always completely ready.

I liked the deep crouch that I saw Terry Sawchuk use. Most goalies would try to look over the players screening them, but Terry would often look underneath the screen. That worked well for me too, but in those days, goalies never talked about goaltending. I was called up a few times to fill in for Terry when he was injured, but he never told me a thing. No goalie ever did.

I developed my "butterfly" stance somewhat by accident. By swinging my legs, I could pick up shots near the post, but to do that, I needed to keep my legs apart. To protect the "five-hole," I brought my knees together. I also wasn't strong enough to stop the puck from going in with just my stick; going down in the butterfly supports the stick.

I think, as well, that I started the butterfly partly through favoring groin injuries. "Doing the splits" would really aggravate that injury. In those days, the splits was considered a beautiful play. It *was* picturesque if you made the save, but as soon as you made the move, there were holes all over the net. The butterfly closed up most of those holes.

My style was not the accepted way to play net. They called it "flopping." I didn't realize at the time how much criticism was being directed at me through the media, because I didn't read the hockey section of the newspaper until I retired. I'm thankful for that. I knew the style was good for me. The critics didn't understand what I was doing. The butterfly keeps the body erect. When the body is erect, you can recover easily. It's actually the *opposite* of flopping.

Our biggest injuries came from pucks in the face. We were very eye-conscious, because permanent eye injuries were not uncommon. I had little confidence in the masks we wore, but I put one on for my last 2½ seasons. The game was changing. Instead of beating the defenseman wide, the forwards often put the puck back to the point and went for the screen and the deflection. As a result, there were more injuries to the goalies.

I believed that exhibition games during the regular season were a no-win situation. I remember Jack Adams trying to tell us how good the Red Wings were to take us to play an exhibition game in Cleveland rather than stay home and practice. I failed to see the logic. I also disagreed when I was told by management not to talk to Ted Lindsay when he was trying to form the first Players' Association. I told them that if they had an argument with Ted, it shouldn't and wouldn't affect anything I did.

Management had total control of the players. Claims that the players then had no guts and should have stood up to the owners are totally untrue. There's a long trail of the ones who did stand up, and it leads to the minors and Timbuktu. They simply got rid of you. The team representatives who were supportive of the Players' Association were traded to Chicago. Doug Harvey, who was still at the top of his game in Montreal, was about the only exception. Ted was the only really big star to go. I wasn't even entirely sure I could play in the NHL yet.

Ted made a huge contribution to the Blackhawks. He brought attitude and a belief that *collectively* we could do well. It was Teddy more than anyone who suggested that *we* could stop the puck, not just the goalie, not just the defensemen. He brought the message that hard work can overcome many weaknesses and that we really weren't as bad as many people thought. It was obvious to everyone that Ted was not only a great hockey player, he had the makings of a good coach or general manager.

Playing 502 consecutive games meant two things: I wasn't injured, and I was doing a good job. That breeds confidence. It also meant that the team was careful not to burn me out. So much of the game is left on the practice rink today. I remember telling Chicago coach Billy

Reay, "I can play in the games, or I can play in practice. I can't do both, so take your pick."

Winning my only Stanley Cup with Chicago in 1961 was certainly an excellent event to be part of, but I always thought results were secondary. Playing in three consecutive Stanley Cup finals for the St. Louis Blues was great. The original six teams gave nothing to the expansion clubs but old guys they thought couldn't play anymore or young kids they didn't think would ever amount to much. We had a team of 20- and 40-year-olds, but I feel good about how well the Blues represented the expansion teams. I don't think the NHL would be enjoying the success it is today if we hadn't done so well.

Glenn Hall

"Mr. Goalie" Glenn Hall backstopped the Chicago Blackhawks to their last Stanley Cup victory in 1961. (ABOVE) Dave Keon of the Maple Leafs is thwarted as Hall covers the net with the butterfly style he pioneered.

Dominik Hasek

I GREW UP IN A CITY OF 100,000 PEOPLE IN CZECHOSLOVAKIA. Of the 200 or 300 six-year-olds who wanted to play hockey, only 40 were allowed to start. We had tryouts, and I made it. I was the goalie right from the first practice. I had always chosen to play net, whether on the pond with my friends or in the kitchen with my dad or grandfather. I actually started to play with kids who were two years older, because they had no goalie. I moved back a year, but all the way up, I was good enough to continue playing with kids one year older.

We had the best team in Czechoslovakia and won all the tournaments. One season, we lost only one game. The coaches taught me how to skate, but no one taught me how to play net. The only advice I got was to keep my stick on the ice, watch the puck and make the save. I learned by watching every goalie I could find. My hometown, Pardubice, had a First Division team, and I tried to see every game. I didn't have an idol or try to copy one particular goalie; I studied them all.

I never felt like a star as a youngster. I got some awards, but I just felt part of a great team. My dream was to make the First Division. I don't want to say

that I didn't think of making the national team, but I doubted I was good enough.

Some saves I've remembered for years. Unfortunately, I also remember some goals! When I was 16, I played my first game in the Czechoslovakian First Division. We won 5–1, but I still remember the goal I let in. It wasn't even a bad goal! I got established in the First Division, and my numbers were quite good. I got my first invitation to play for my country at age 18. I played in the 1984 Canada Cup tournament at age 19, but there was still a fight for the starting position on the national team. By age 21, the job was mine.

I was drafted by the Chicago Blackhawks in 1983 but didn't even hear about it for a couple of months. I didn't know what it meant, or care. Later, the Chicago scouts came to see me, and even the general manager, Bob Pulford, paid a visit. He offered me a five-year deal when he caught up to me in Vienna in 1987. We talked for an hour or so in his hotel room, and he told me I'd be the third-best-paid player on the team. I turned him down because I was very happy where I was. I was single and had enough money—I could eat in restaurants, I could buy what I wanted, I had a car. I didn't need anything else, and I was having a great time. I was also attending university and wanted to graduate.

By 1989, I had my degree and was married. I thought more about the NHL and decided to try it. It was a tough transition, because in Czechoslovakia, I was a pretty big star. When I finally got to Chicago in 1990, the coaches sent me to the minors. I had to learn to play with my stick. In Czechoslovakia, the goalie never went behind the net or into the corner. That was considered the job of the defense.

Because my style was unorthodox, I constantly heard and read that I didn't have NHL skills. Vladislav Tretiak was the goaltending coach for the Blackhawks, but he came only twice a year for a couple of days. Regardless, he spent most of his time with Eddie Belfour, Chicago's starting netminder. I had a tough time proving that I was good enough. Being traded to Buffalo was a big break. I didn't get an opportunity right away, but I saw that my chances were better. I even liked the city more.

Each goalie has his own particular style. I'm flexible and do a pretty good butterfly. What I do is what is best for me. The game is so fast that you have to be constantly prepared. Everything has to be automatic. There's no one in the NHL that I'm particularly afraid of, but it's wise to be most aware of the proven goal scorers. Once they're over the boards, I know where they are on the ice.

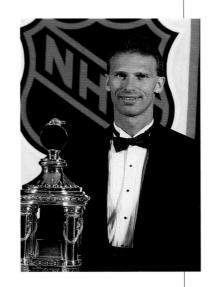

There's a good feeling whenever you receive an award, but winning the Vezina two years in a row felt like a great accomplishment. I'm proud of that, as well as coming runner-up for the Hart Trophy in 1994. I don't think I did anything differently that year. With a little luck and the Buffalo Sabres keeping to the very disciplined hockey they played that year, I can repeat that kind of season.

I love to have a low goals-against-average, but there's no better feeling in hockey than winning a game. Individual awards are nice, but winning with a team is even better. I don't really care if the score is 5–4 or 1–0. I mean, I'd love a shutout every game, and reporters crowd the goalie after a shutout, but otherwise, the feeling of victory is just the same. I like playing so much because I like to win.

Dominik Hasek, shown above with the Vezina Trophy, won the award for the sixth time in 2001. He is the only goaltender to have earned the Hart Trophy twice, in 1997 and 1998. (**Opposite**) *"The Dominator" played nine seasons for the Buffalo Sabres before being traded to Detroit in June 2001.*

Dale Hawerchuk

I WAS ONE OF THOSE KIDS WHO LOVED HOCKEY AT FIRST SIGHT. Whenever a teacher asked me what I wanted to be, I always answered, "A hockey player." I'd be encouraged to choose something else, but I never would. When I got home from school, it was road hockey, shooting pucks on the net and playing organized hockey.

I worked my way up the ranks and had quite a bit of success in minor hockey. Our Oshawa team won the Ontario championship when I played bantam and the Metropolitan Toronto championship in Junior B. I then

made Junior A and won two Memorial Cups in Cornwall. Winning the Memorial Cup really means a lot to a town like Cornwall. Playoffs were sold out every night, and tickets were scalped for huge prices. The town really got behind the club, and the club helped put the town on the map for a while.

There's nothing better than winning with a team after you've been grinding it out all year. It's difficult to explain to people how great it is. Being in a hockey dressing room is almost like having 20 brothers. When you share a moment like that, it's unforgettable. I was happy to come to Philadelphia, because we really have a good shot at winning. I'm not concerned about being one of the guys who had a great NHL career but never won a Stanley Cup. I want to win the Cup because I know what it's like to win a championship. There's no greater feeling.

I was drafted by Winnipeg as the first choice in the 1981 NHL entry draft. I was never a cocky kid, but I was very confident in what I could do. I had desire, but you never know if you're good enough. When I went to my first pro training camp in Winnipeg, the first week was very tough. It dawned on me right away that I was only average. I really had to push and try to keep up, and though I ended up winning Rookie of the Year, I was really worried that first week. I wasn't sure I was ready. I was only 18, so I knew that I had time, but I really wanted to do it then. I had accomplished a lot in junior, and I really didn't want to go back.

That was my dream, to play in the NHL, and I think it was my grandfather's dream too. He was having a serious fight with cancer, but he drove all the way from Ontario to watch my first couple of games in Winnipeg. I look back and appreciate that more now than I did then. He cheered me on for my first season but died within a year.

I hit two or three posts, and we got hammered about 5–1 by Toronto in my first game. We played the Rangers two nights later. I got two goals and two assists, and we won 6–4. I was on my way. I finished with 103 points, and the team finished with a .500 season and made the playoffs for the first time. Winnipeg was a good place to start, because the team had finished dead last by a large margin the previous season. They were looking for *anything* to help. General manager John Ferguson brought in about seven or eight new players besides me. They were good guys and we were hungry. It never dawned on us to feel connected to a losing past; we came to win.

I had a heck of a year in 1984-85 and made the Second All-Star team, finished third in scoring and second to Wayne Gretzky in the voting for the Hart Trophy. Everyone was in Edmonton's shadow then. And who was going to unseat Gretzky as the best centerman in the league? A lot of individual accolades came my way, but going to the rink every day when you're winning is so much more fun. I don't know that hockey will ever become work, but it's harder when you're struggling or you lose.

One of the problems we had during my time in Winnipeg was that we invariably met Edmonton or Calgary in the first round of the playoffs. Both were powerhouse teams then. We beat Calgary that year, but I broke my ribs and couldn't play the next round. We lost four straight to Edmonton, so while we made a move as a club, in the end, it was a disappointing year that left a sour taste in my mouth.

I enjoyed my time in Buffalo, but we had the same problem every year. We had a better team than showed in the playoffs, because we always ran into major injuries. That's spilt milk now.

Five hundred career goals was a nice milestone to reach, but I'm most proud of hitting the 1,000-point mark. I get as big a thrill setting up a play as the guy who puts it in. When you're young, you think goals are great, but I've always realized that the goal scorer is not always the most important man in a play. More often than not, the guy who sees the ice, makes the plays and creates the chances for the goal scorer—he's the key guy.

At only age 18, Dale Hawerchuk broke into the NHL with the Winnipeg Jets in 1981 and won rookie-of-the-year honors with 45 goals and 58 assists. (OPPOSITE) Hawerchuk enjoyed five successful seasons with the Buffalo Sabres in the early 1990s. He retired as a Philadelphia Flyer in 1997, then the 10th-highest scorer in NHL history.

Paul Henderson

WHEN I WAS A YOUNG BOY, MY FAVORITE PLAYER WAS GORDIE Howe, and it was a dream come true to play with him on the Red Wings. Being traded to Toronto was traumatic for me at the time. I cried like a baby, I was so devastated. It was my first experience of rejection. I didn't see that Toronto wanted me, only that Detroit didn't. A lot of players were involved in the trade, but I took it personally. I grew to love Toronto in a short time, but it was a tremendous shock to leave the Detroit organization I'd been in from boyhood.

When Team Canada was being chosen in 1972, I looked down the list of prospective left-wingers and felt I deserved to be among those invited to the large squad of 35 players. I had scored 38 goals the previous season and was a fast two-way hockey player. But if the team had been only 25 guys, I probably wouldn't have been there.

I decided that I was really going to enjoy myself in the series but was committed to do whatever was asked of me, no matter what. Bobby Clarke, Ron Ellis and I went to training camp as underdogs. We wanted to prove that we belonged there, and we got serious pretty quickly, working our buns off. The chemistry on that line was just right. Clarke was like a younger Norm Ullman (Ron's and my center in Toronto, an aggressive forechecker). We started beating up on the other lines in camp and got some real confidence up. There's an old saying, "You never know when opportunity is going to knock. The secret is to be ready." Well, we were ready. Even in the first-game loss, 7–3, our line was plus one. We scored two goals and only had one scored against us.

Finally having Canada's professionals play the Russians was supposed to be a wonderful experience, and all of a sudden, it was bloody war. The series went far beyond hockey. I'm really glad that I've since got to know a lot of the Russian players, because they're classy, down-to-earth people. I give them credit for managing to be good husbands, fathers and athletes under that system. They're great guys, but I hated their guts in 1972. I hated everything about them. They couldn't understand our intensity, our ferocity. I believe that's why we won, though. We dug down and went beyond our normal capacities. Hockey was our game, and we couldn't let those guys beat us.

The series became the pinnacle of my hockey career.

I was fortunate to score seven goals, including the winners in the last three games. In the seventh game, I went through the whole team to score with about 2½ minutes left. I thought, "This is the highlight of my hockey career," and I couldn't imagine a better goal. I just wasn't the kind of player to do things on my own like that. Now, that goal seems insignificant, but I relive that moment as much as I do the final goal. I was actually off my feet with a guy on my back as I lifted the puck just under the crossbar.

I was sitting on the bench at the end of the final game, and I had a sense that I could get a goal. I'm not saying that that's unusual for a hockey player, because we were all confident players who had had that experience before. But I stood up and started yelling at Peter Mahovlich to come off the ice, something I'd never done before and I never did again. I *needed* to get out there to score a goal. Even when I was tripped and flat on the ice behind the net, I looked at the clock ticking off the last 40 seconds and thought, "Good, there's still time. They'll take it down ice, but we'll be able to bring it back." And then events happened so quickly that I panicked. The puck came to me, and I fired it along the ice. Tretiak got his pad on it, but the rebound came back to me and I had a fair piece of open net to shovel it in.

Destiny is a word people often use. I don't know. When the series ended, I was the toast of Canada. I was 29, had some fame, a great wife and family, a beautiful home, but I was still far from content. I started to develop a spiritual dimension to my life, and in 1975, I became a Christian. Hockey gives a lot of highs, but they're so transitory. As an athlete, I lived and died with the wins and losses, which didn't deal with who I am.

Christianity has helped me to even out those experiences, put them in the context of my life, and today I work in ministry. As a young hockey player, I could have really benefited from a mentor. We had so many great players on the Red Wings, but all were so afraid for their jobs then that they never talked. I try to be a mentor for others myself now, for life rather than for hockey, though I still love to play and watch the game.

Paul Henderson

Paul Henderson became a national hero in 1972 after he scored dramatic game-winners in the final three games of Team Canada's epic series against the Soviet Union, the last coming with only 34 seconds left. (OPPOSITE) Henderson, who broke into the league with the Red Wings, shows his speed and tenacity as he tries to strip the puck from the Rangers' Rod Seiling.

Gordie Howe

MY MOM GAVE A COUPLE OF DOLLARS TO A WOMAN WHO WAS in desperate need of milk for her family. In return, the woman gave my mom a gunnysack full of things, including a pair of skates. My sister Edna grabbed one, and I got the other. We went outside and push-glided around an ice pond. When Edna got cold and took her skate off, I put it on my other foot.

From that moment on, I loved skating. I think the two dollars my mom gave that woman was the down payment on my career. My wife Colleen has continually demonstrated to me that when you give something

away, it comes back twofold. It's the law of giving.

As a boy, I even ate meals with my skates on. Hockey meant everything to me. I'd go off the ice straight into the kitchen. My mom put some papers down so that I wouldn't mark up the linoleum. As soon as I finished eating, I'd go right back on the ice, missing only a couple of shifts.

My dad never saw me play hockey as a kid, but he was always supportive. He took an old washing machine and put an attachment on the flywheel so that he could sharpen everyone's skates. He was a tough old

bird. The two of us once picked up a huge rock five other guys couldn't lift. When we leaned over, he quietly said to me, "Don't let me down." We threw the rock into the back of a truck. Although I was a strong young man then, I did have a hernia operation the next year! The first real pro game my parents saw me play was in my thirteenth season with Detroit. They came in for a "Night" in my honor at the Olympia. I was surprised and cried when I saw them.

As a teenager in Saskatchewan, I played against Harry Watson and other NHL players who were serving with the Canadian Forces during World War II. We spoke together briefly, and Harry liked me. Later, in the first NHL game I played against him, he yelled, "Look out, Gordie!" when he had a chance to hit me. I wondered why, because I was turning into the flow of play and he could have checked me really hard. I found out later when I caught him in a similar situation. I said, "Look out, Mr. Watson!" He looked over his shoulder and said, "We're going to get along just fine." You have to hit everyone, but you can warn the player. If someone doesn't like you, the first words you hear *after* a hit are, "Look out!"

I loved playing against Bobby Hull. You knew what he was going to do—you could read him like a book—but he was so strong, he'd do it anyway. We weren't allowed to talk to one another on the ice, but while watching a ridiculous fight between a Chicago player and a Detroit player, Bobby leaned over and said, "If we'd get rid of a few of these brawlers, this could be a great league."

I'm glad to see how things have improved medically for the players today. When I tore my rib cage on an open gate one game, the team trainer undressed me, taped me up and gave me a card with the name of the hospital and a doctor on it. The only question he asked was whether or not I had the cab fare to get there on my own. Longtime Red Wings general manager Jack Adams, often portrayed as a miserable individual, sometimes showed another side. When I was seriously injured, he stayed up all night with me and made certain my family was brought to Detroit to be with me. Hockey, like most things, was rarely black or white.

I retired from the Red Wings after 25 years and achieved my longevity goal. By then, I was really wrought with arthritis pain, which never goes away. Two years later, though, I made a comeback for the chance to play in the WHA with my sons Mark and Marty. I was hurting, and I called Colleen to say that I may have made a big mistake. Mark and Marty had also called her with concern that my color was gone and I was breathing very heavily. She told them to give me a chance to reach my dreams.

Even the coach offered to excuse me for the latter half of a double practice one day, but I said, "No, if I'm going to be one of the guys, I have to do what it takes." Somehow, during that practice, I went through what runners call "the wall." My sons looked at me and said, "Feeling much better, aren't you, Dad?" I asked how they knew. "Well, your color is back, and we weren't running all over the ice for your passes today."

I've always been in love with hockey—I loved it too much to retire early. The years I played with Mark and Marty in Houston and in international play are the most memorable for me. I was very proud of them, that team and my own performance. Every game was special, but I'll never forget the pride I had when the three of us first jumped on the ice together. It's a feeling that will last forever.

Gordon Howe

*Gordie Howe received the Hart Trophy as the NHL's most valuable player six times in an illustrious 32-year professional career. (**Opposite**) Howe powers the puck into the net against fellow Hall of Famers Allan Stanley and Johnny Bower of the Maple Leafs.*

Harry Howell

THERE WAS NO ORGANIZED HOCKEY FOR REALLY YOUNG BOYS in the 1940s, so I was 13 before I played on an actual team. At age 16, it was time to make the move to junior hockey. I planned to play for my hometown Hamilton team, but I got a phone call from the New York Rangers telling me that I would be playing for Guelph. Unknown to me, I had been on the Rangers' "list" since I was 14. If I wanted to play, it would be in Guelph.

Guelph had a heck of a team, and we won the Memorial Cup in 1952. Many of my teammates graduated to the NHL the next year, but I was still eligible to play junior. Five games into the NHL season, the Rangers lost three defensemen to injuries. They called me up

to play a game against the Leafs in Maple Leaf Gardens. I had played in the Gardens as a junior, which had been thrilling, but to play there in an NHL game was another matter entirely. I still love that building. It *is* a hockey shrine.

I scored my first goal in that game. The puck came around the boards to me at the point, and I floated a backhand in the general direction of the net. It made a large arc and came down just over the shoulder of Leaf goalie Harry Lumley. I laughed when I saw the photo of the goal in the newspaper the next morning. It looked as if I'd blasted a slap shot from 50 feet out. We lost the game, but the Rangers decided to take me back to New York. I played for them for the next 17 years.

The Rangers floundered in my first 10 seasons. We always opened the year with a five-game road trip because the rodeo would be using Madison Square Garden. Even in the playoffs, we could get only two home dates before the circus took over. The owners didn't really care whether we won or not.

Our practice facilities were horrendous. We used a figure-skating rink on the fourth floor that was only 150 feet long, had aluminum boards, purple and pink lights and mirrors on all the walls. (They had to put up netting when the guys took aim at the mirrors.) The figure skaters even got the preferred ice times. Everything was handled poorly. We finished a strong second in the league in the 1957-58 season. Most of us were about 25 years old, but the next summer, management traded five guys, including most of our power play, thinking they had five juniors who could step in. We dropped to fifth place and went through a long dry spell of not making the playoffs.

There were so many bad trades, a reflection of our second-class status, until Emile Francis took over as general manager in 1964. We got better and grew in popularity in New York. Then it became important to win, to the players *and* management.

I won the Norris Trophy for the 1966-67 season. My 12 goals and 40 points were high totals at the time. They held a "Night" for me in Madison Square Garden halfway through the season, marking my thousandth game. I was only the third NHL player to reach that milestone. I had a hard time concentrating, remembering how Doug Harvey was on the ice for six of our goals when we hammered Montreal 7–2 on "Doug Harvey Night" in Montreal. We'd also got a rare victory against the Canadiens on "Maurice Richard Night." I was so relieved, and grateful to Eddie Giacomin for having a great game in net, when we beat the Bruins 2–1. I even assisted on the winning goal.

I just found out this year that Brad Park had an agreement with the Rangers that he would play with me as a rookie. It's a great compliment, because I didn't have to teach him very much. I worked with him on positioning and playing the man. I'd remind him about taking people out with two hands on the stick, and we'd talk after games and during practice.

I missed only 17 games in my first 16 years, but then I had to have a back operation, a spinal fusion. Emile Francis tried to talk me into retiring and taking another job with the Rangers, but I thought I could still play. The Rangers had too many good youngsters, so I asked to go to the West Coast. I played for Oakland and Los Angeles before signing four years later with New York in the World Hockey Association.

The New York team went broke 10 games into the

season. We moved to New Jersey and played in a condemned arena in Cherry Hill. I became player/coach, and we had a great season, because opponents hated to come into our rink. We rigged up an adequate dressing room for our club, but the other team—even great players like Gordie Howe and Bobby Hull—had to get dressed for the game in their hotel rooms and walk into the arena with their stick and skates slung over their shoulder. I retired two years later, with 24 professional seasons under my belt. I got a ring as a scout for the 1989-90 Edmonton Oilers and finally did get my name on the Stanley Cup.

Harry Howell

Hall of Famer Harry Howell holds the New York Rangers team records for most games (1,160) and most seasons (17). (Above) Howell, winner of the Norris Trophy in 1967, races to the corner for a loose puck in front of Toronto's Ron Ellis. Goaltender Gilles Villemure and Rangers teammates Walt Tkaczuk and Arnie Brown look on.

Bobby Hull

We won the Stanley Cup in 1961 when I was 22 years old. We had an equally good or better team in later years but came up just short each time we got to the finals. I thought that 1961 victory was only the first of many to come, but I never did drink out of the Stanley Cup. As the festivities began, I started drinking beer out of the owner's son Mike Wirtz's dirty old felt hat. I got sick as a dog and had to go to bed instead of celebrating that night.

Hockey was my life and my love as a kid. I can't remember when I thought of anything *but* being an NHL player. It was just a question of getting old enough or big enough. I couldn't wait for winters to come and would have my equipment on two or three times in the summer. I was an energetic boy on a dogtrot wherever I went.

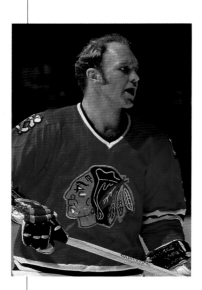

From ages 10 to 12, I worked as a stickboy for the local Belleville Junior B team. I watched a player named Harry Brown set Coke bottles on the boards after practice and try to knock them off with slap shots from the other side of the ice. He inspired me to practice my own shot.

I left home at 14 to play Junior B hockey. My dad, a pretty good former Senior A hockey player, taught me the fundamentals, but I had to grow up quickly when I started playing with players as old as 20. In minor hockey, all I had done was grab the biscuit and go with it. I wasn't taught a lot of teamwork, so I had a tough time at first. Within a couple of years, I understood more of the game and blossomed as a complete player.

I wore three different numbers with the Blackhawks, all chosen by our trainer, Walter "Gunzo" Humeniuk. Some great things happened while I wore number 16, the sweater first given me when I arrived in Chicago, but I got off to a horrendous start to the 1961-62 season. Halfway through the 70-game season, I had only 13 goals. Gunzo gave me number seven, and my luck did change, although I'll admit I also got better rested after putting a sheet of plywood under the swaybacked mattress I had been sleeping on at the time. I went on a 37-goal tear for my first 50-goal season. I wore number seven for almost two years, but when I went to training camp for the 1963-64 season, Gunzo had number nine—associated with some of the best players ever—ready for me. And that's the number that was later retired by the Blackhawks and the Winnipeg Jets.

My brother Dennis was just a little boy when I left home. We really didn't become great friends until after we were retired, but we had some good times together in Chicago. What I liked to do most was score a goal on my first shift, but if I wasn't going to accomplish that, I would fire a puck high off the glass over the goalie's head—just to give him something to think about. Dennis and I used to enjoy getting the goaltenders up on their heels, and then we'd rip one along the ice when they couldn't move.

When I jumped to the WHA in 1972, I was denied the chance to play for Team Canada against the Soviet Union. That was the biggest disappointment in my career. I experienced my biggest high in hockey in the first game of the WHA series against the Soviets in 1974. I couldn't even put my stick on the ice to receive a pass on my first shift—I literally felt elevated—but the series was satisfying only in a personal sense. I loved playing against such great athletes, and I became the highest-scoring North American against the great Russian goalie Vladislav Tretiak.

Although I hated to leave Chicago, I was obligated to go to Winnipeg when they met my request. I had asked for a million dollars just to get Ben Haskin and the WHA to go away. If I'd ever thought they'd actually raise it, I would have said an impossible 20 million. Overall, I have no regrets. It was a joy to play in Winnipeg with so many great players, including my linemates Anders Hedberg and Ulf Nilsson. I don't think there was ever a more entertaining line in hockey. My move also gave *all* players a little more bargaining power and helped pave the way for players to make the big money they get today.

Wayne Cashman is the only guy who ever thanked me personally for that. I was visiting with Dennis and some other Team Canada '72 members when they were playing the Soviets in Vancouver. My good friend Ewen Lazaruk was looking for tickets to the game, and I asked Wayne if he had any. He immediately fished four tickets from his pocket and handed them to me. When I asked what I owed him, he said, "What do you owe me? What do *I* owe you? My salary just tripled because of you!"

Watching my son Brett play ranks as the greatest feeling I've experienced in hockey, along with making my childhood dream of playing in the NHL a reality. Competing against the best and occasionally coming out on top made that accomplishment even more satisfying.

Bobby Hull broke the single-season goal-scoring record twice during his award-filled years with the Chicago Blackhawks. (Opposite) *Always a scoring threat because of his speed, strength and shot, "The Golden Jet" moves in close with several Montreal Canadiens in close pursuit.*

Brett Hull

HOCKEY MEANT EVERYTHING TO ME AS A BOY, BECAUSE THAT was all we did—we played on the ice, in the driveway, in the basement, or I watched my dad or brothers play. My older brothers probably remember my dad's days in Chicago better than I do. My sharpest memories go back to when he signed with the Winnipeg Jets in 1972. I was pretty oblivious to his stardom up to that point, but when I watched the Bobby Hull parade celebrating his arrival in Winnipeg, I realized he was someone special.

Some might think it would be difficult growing up in a Hall of Famer's shadow, but it was always positive for me. My parents didn't get along, so I had to get out on my own before my dad and I were able to see each other more regularly, but there was always a lot of love there.

I was never the best player on my team when I was growing up. I played for fun. Only when a friend of mine

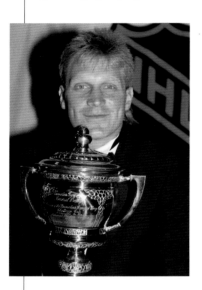

talked me into trying out for a junior team did I take the game seriously. Actually, I wasn't very serious in my first year of junior either. But then I thought, "Hey, this could take me somewhere"—whether it was going to college and getting an education or maybe even having the chance of one day following in my dad's footsteps, never imagining that I might be able to do anything close to the things he did.

I held dual citizenship in Canada and the U.S., and representatives from both countries came to watch me play at the University of Minnesota in Duluth in 1986. The Team Canada coach had no interest in me, but Dave Peterson asked whether I'd like to go to the World Championships with Team USA. I was a college sophomore and jumped at the opportunity to go to Moscow and play against the best in the world.

From day one, Team USA treated me like one of their own. They gave me an opportunity to better myself and my career, and I've played for the U.S. in international competition ever since. I would feel badly if I turned my back on them now. It seems natural that I would stay loyal to the group of people who made that commitment to me.

Winning the World Cup in 1996 is something I'll never forget. Spending a month with a team of talented and great guys was the key to our win. We got along so well, and our coach, Ron Wilson, was number one. He handled every single player perfectly, even in situations where they weren't playing. He was a

big part of our victory.

St. Louis was rebuilding when Calgary traded me late in the 1987-88 season. Calgary had Lanny McDonald, Joe Mullen, Hakan Loob, Joe Nieuwendyk, Colin Patterson, Perry Berezan— all on the right side— along with Tim Hunter, a regular tough guy. There was just no room for me in the lineup. When I came to St. Louis, they gave up a couple of veterans in Rob Ramage and Rick Wamsley, so they gave me a chance to play right away. They wanted to show they hadn't made a mistake. The team started to play well at the same time that things started to roll for me. Attendance went from 10,000 to 15,000 to 18,000 a night. It was great to be part of that.

I couldn't have dreamed what's happened to me. To be able to share a father-son record (500 goals for each of us) and being in the record book with Wayne Gretzky (for 50 goals in 50 games two years in a row) is really special. The 31 games Wayne played for the Blues in 1996 were one of the best times I've had in hockey. He's a friend, but he also made our team so much better. It was devastating to see him leave, the worst thing that's happened in my career.

I still have fun every time I play the game. I was born in 1964, but every time I get on the ice, I feel as if I'm 12 again. Scoring goals in front of a crowd is the greatest feeling I know and what I enjoy doing most. I've always liked the slapper, but I realized I was not going to score a lot of goals until I learned to take a wrist shot. I always had a quick release, but when I really started to work

on it, the goals started to go in more. But I can't even begin to explain my 86-goal 1990-91 season. I was helped by having so many great players on the team, but it was almost magical.

The only award that stands out for me is one I don't have—the Stanley Cup. All I can do is play the best I can and hope the organization can put the group of guys around our core players so that we can accomplish that in St. Louis. The fans and the organization have treated me so well. St. Louis is also a great city to live in and raise a family. I'm not interested in winning the Cup anywhere else.

Brett Hull came into his own once he joined the St. Louis Blues, where he set many club records, but he won his only Stanley Cup ring as a Dallas Star in 1998-99. (Opposite) Hull holds the Lady Byng Trophy he won in 1990. He earned the Hart Trophy and the Pearson Award in 1991.

Dennis Hull

I NEVER WOULD HAVE GONE TO DETROIT AFTER I RETIRED from the Chicago Blackhawks if it weren't for Ted Lindsay, who was then the Red Wings general manager. When I was 12 years old, my mother was in a boating accident and in hospital for 16 weeks. On one of my visits, there was a red 1957 Thunderbird with Michigan license plates in the parking lot. I admired it, and when I went to my mother's room, I found out my brother Bobby's teammate Ted Lindsay had read about the accident and had made a five-hour drive just to visit my mother. So when he called years later and asked me to join Detroit just after Christmas of 1977, I didn't want to say no. We went a couple of rounds into the playoffs, but I didn't enjoy the experience at all.

Once Chicago let Billy Reay go—the most instrumental person in my life and my only NHL coach—I lost all my desire to play. I was 19 when I arrived in Chicago in 1964, and Billy taught me everything an adult needs to know about how to treat people properly, not just how to play hockey. He's still one of my best friends.

Sometimes people said to me, "Wouldn't it have been great if you'd been on another team so that you wouldn't always be referred to as Bobby Hull's brother?" I would respond that they must have grown up as an only child. I came from a family of 11, and we all liked each other. When I did well, the happiest person on the team was Bobby. I wanted him to succeed too. My favorite goal is not one of mine but one that Bobby scored. I made a good move in a game against the Boston Bruins to get the puck to Bobby for his 600th career goal. Bobby Orr made that assist even more special by telling me, "Nice play," as we went to face off again.

I got an extra look as a junior because I was Bobby's brother, and I even got my best linemates from him. The Blackhawks decided to seek out two players who'd complement Bobby best. They traded for Jim Pappin and Pit Martin, but when they were supposed to start playing together, Bobby wasn't at training camp because of a contract dispute. Billy Reay put me on left wing for the interim, and by the time Bobby came back, our line was so successful that they picked two other guys to play with him.

I played with Pit and Jim for eight years. We weren't just linemates, we were best friends. That was when hockey was the most fun for me and when I was most productive. We were the Blackhawks' highest-scoring line and were also good defensively, the team's best penalty killers. I remember one game when Jimmy and Pit had to kill one of *my* penalties. They both scored shorthanded goals. When my penalty was almost over, I signaled to Billy Reay to see whether he wanted me to join the play or come to the bench. He signaled back, "Stay in the penalty box!"

In 1971, the press decided to vote for the Conn Smythe Trophy just prior to the seventh game of the Stanley Cup final. It was secretly decided that if Chicago won, I would get the award because I led the league in playoff points. If Montreal won, Ken Dryden would get it. We lost the game—and I lost the Conn Smythe—in the third period.

The winner of the Conn Smythe also received a new car. During the warm-up of an exhibition game against Montreal early the next season, Yvan Cournoyer called me to center ice. He said, "I have a message from Ken Dryden. He says your car is running real good." Yvan wasn't the only funny guy on that team. In every game I played against Henri Richard, he'd come up behind me at some point and say, "My brother's better than your brother." I loved to play against the Montreal Canadiens most and went to the Stanley Cup finals three times against them. Unfortunately, they always found a way to beat us.

In the fifth game of that 1971 series, Pat Stapleton got cut by a skate and took 80 stitches in the face. We were flying to Montreal for game six and, coincidentally, the Chicago Cubs were also going to Montreal to play the Expos. Leo Durocher was the Cub manager, and he offered some sympathy about losing Pat at such a critical time. We said, "What do you mean? He's playing. He's right over there." Leo couldn't believe it and said, "If Pat Stapleton's playing tomorrow night, I'm going to get kicked out of our game in the first inning and come watch." True to his word, he was at the Montreal Forum 10 minutes after getting himself ejected from the game.

Not winning the Cup was disappointing, but the saving grace for me was playing for Team Canada in 1972. After the final game in Moscow, we came storming into the dressing room on an unbelievable high. I was sitting next to Yvan Cournoyer, and I asked him if this was like winning the Stanley Cup. He replied, "No, this is ten times better!" I still think to myself that I've won only one less Stanley Cup than Henri Richard.

Dennis Hull

Remembered most for a slap shot that rivaled his brother Bobby's, Dennis Hull also excelled in the defensive side of the game. (OPPOSITE) Hull, shown sweeping around the Detroit Red Wings defense, broke into the NHL in 1964 and scored more than 300 goals in a 14-season career.

Dale Hunter

When my dad took my brothers and me to the rink, he was taking time out from farming. He coached us right through minor hockey and made sure that we gave our best effort. He goaded us by saying, "It's a fun game to play, but don't waste my time." If we didn't hustle on the ice, he wouldn't bring us to the rink. We learned the value of hard work at a young age.

I've been playing hockey since I was 5 years old. I feel lucky to still be playing, because it's always been a lot of fun. My older brother Dave and younger brother Mark

also had long NHL careers, and my oldest brother Ron played Junior A. Ron, Mark and I still farm with my dad in the summers. Going back to the farm— baling hay, doing the chores—brings me back to reality. I can't wait for training camp to start! It's easy by comparison! If anyone thinks they work hard playing hockey, well, other people work hard too.

Having older brothers who played Junior A and professional hockey before I did made my progression easier. Dave let Mark and me know what to expect. His most helpful advice was, "Be noticed!" To make a team, you have to do something to draw attention to yourself. You can't just be another body out there, counting on your talent alone.

I'm a smaller guy, so I've always needed to play the same energetic and aggressive style to show that I can compete against bigger players. Unless he's super-talented, a small man doesn't play in the NHL. I'll never forget my first year out of junior. I was 20 years old and had no desire to play in the minors. I remembered Dave's advice, and I guess I racked up a few penalty minutes as a result. I almost went out of my way to knock heads with the toughest guys on the other teams just to prove that I wasn't afraid to play in the league. I got beat up quite a few times, too many to count!

Moose Dupont was captain of the Nordiques when I first broke in. He helped me a lot. He had been one of the main guys from the Cup-winning Philadelphia Flyers and brought his love of the game to the rink every day. He laughed, had fun and played hard. He didn't let it get to him if things didn't go the way he wanted. I loved his attitude.

The Quebec Nordiques were rebuilding when I was traded to Washington in 1987. They traded Peter Stastny and Michel Goulet at the same time and then didn't make the playoffs for five consecutive years, so I was grateful to have gone to a good club. I jelled with the guys on the Capitals right away.

Whatever you accomplish, it's always judged by what you do in the playoffs. Facing elimination adds some pressure, but the more pressure there is, the bigger the win. It's a great time of year. Pressure and fun go hand in hand, so it's the playoffs that I most enjoy. I've had a couple of good runs, but we've met the Pittsburgh Penguins early on in the past few years. They've beaten us out every time. We have a lot of young guys on the team, so now that they have more experience, I think we'll do better.

I still have to play hard every night, but my first few years set a tone that gave me less need to prove myself. I've always taken a lot of penalties, but I have no regrets. There has been trouble a few times, from incidents occurring in the heat of the action. We lost three over-time games before we were eliminated from the playoffs by the New York Islanders in 1993. In frustration, I hit Pierre Turgeon from behind after he scored a decisive goal in the last game of the series. I received a 21-game suspension to start the 1993-94 season. Some wondered whether the new NHL Commissioner Gary Bettmann singled me out to send everyone a message, but to me, that's just part of hockey. He also used his office to add me to the roster for the 1996 All-Star game, which was a huge thrill for me.

My type of game doesn't rely on tallying great statistics. Wanting to win keeps me motivated, and I'm not too concerned about my point totals. I used to be more offensive-minded, but now I usually draw the checking assignment against the league's top lines. It's a challenge when you're playing guys like Mark Messier and Eric Lindros, but I enjoy it. Especially when we win!

I didn't say much in the dressing room when I was younger. Now, to a certain extent, it's my job as team captain to pull a guy aside for a talk when necessary, but I've learned most of what I know by watching. I believe that if the younger guys see me enjoy coming to the rink every day and practicing and playing hard, the lesson will be taught. You have to work hard and have fun. That's been part of the reason for my long career. I'm taking each year one at a time now, seeing how I feel and how well I play. Everyone gets older and there's more wear and tear on the body, but the day I retire is going to be tough.

Dale Hunter retired after the 1998-99 season with more than 1,000 career points and over 3,500 penalty minutes. (Opposite) Hunter, a consistent spark plug, was team captain of the Washington Capitals from 1994 until his trade to Colorado late in his final season.

Paul Kariya

I SEE MYSELF AS A STUDENT OF THE GAME. I'VE LEARNED greater patience by watching Wayne Gretzky's ability to hold on to the puck and then hit the late man coming in. I repeatedly watch Brett Hull's quick release, how he gets the shot off hard and at the net almost before anyone sees him getting ready to shoot. But it's not just the superstars I try to learn from. Every night, I watch the highlight reels and any game I can. I invariably see someone do something that I've never thought of before. Sometimes it's a subtle play that is unremarkable in many ways, but I see that if I were to replicate that,

my game would improve; I'd have another tool to use. I'm taking a great deal of satisfaction now in improving my defensive game, trying to become as complete a hockey player as I can.

I was pretty small for my age as I was growing up in North Vancouver, and I often heard that the NHL wouldn't be part of my future because of my size. I set my sights on making the Canadian Olympic team, thinking that could be the pinnacle of my hockey career. Playing on the larger ice surface would be to my advantage, where my skating would make size less of an issue.

Getting to the Olympics was a worthy goal, and I dedicated myself to working as hard as possible to get the chance.

I tasted success and had an experience I'll never forget as part of the World Championship Canadian junior hockey team. Playing for your country is a special honor very few get to feel, and I'll be looking for the chance to wear the Canadian sweater whenever I can. I'm grateful for all of my international experience, including the Olympic Games in 1994, although I still experience some pangs of regret that we lost to Sweden in a shoot-out and settled for the silver medal. The Olympics were everything I dreamed they would be, except for that result!

Missing the first World Cup tournament was another of my biggest disappointments so far. I'm really hoping to be able to help Canada in the 1998 Olympics, but I've learned that any number of circumstances could dash that dream. Life in the rugged hockey world got a little easier when I grew to be 5 foot 11 inches. I've worked hard to build up my strength and intentionally added weight. Still, injuries happen, and the grueling NHL schedule takes its toll. Every guy on the team plays for most of the season hurting in one way or another. There is a little more security for the players now, so few would play with a potentially career-ending injury, but I don't think that much has changed in hockey regarding guys playing with pain.

Wayne Gretzky was the player I, like millions of hockey players, admired the most when I was growing up. He continues to inspire me with his great play. Any expectations that I will reach Wayne's level are ridiculous and unfair. I definitely want to be known as a "smart" hockey player, and winning the Lady Byng trophy and an All-Star berth in 1996 was an acknowledgment that I brought my game up to a high level with a style that relies on finesse and skating. Any comparisons with Wayne have to end there. He's without peer, and I will be satisfied knowing that I have played up to my own potential, not up to anyone else's standards. The pressures I feel come mainly from within, and that's enough to keep me motivated and committed to improving as much as I can.

Scoring 50 goals in my second NHL season felt good, and I'm proud of the recognition I've received, but hockey is a team game. The goal we all share is to win the Stanley Cup, because that is what hockey at its highest level is all about. Individual triumphs are most significant, most satisfying, when they are a contribution to team success. We've got good chemistry on this team now and a desire that unites us in common purpose. That's the only kind of team that I ever want to play on, and I'm confident that we'll reach our goal.

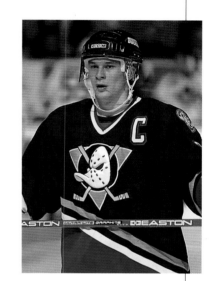

Both of my parents are teachers, so education has always been important in our family and to me. I was glad to have the chance to combine hockey and school at the University of Maine for a couple of years. We had a great team, but my parents were usually more interested in knowing what my grade-point average was than whether I'd scored a goal or if we'd won the game. Of course, they've always been really supportive of my hockey too, spending half of their lives driving me to arenas when I was growing up, but they certainly taught me the value of education. I still fit in a university course when I can, working toward a business degree. I hope that I can have a long NHL career, but anything can happen, and eventually, it will be time to do something else. I plan to be ready.

The first player ever drafted by Anaheim, Paul Kariya won the Lady Byng Trophy twice while becoming a four-time All-Star. (OPPOSITE) Kariya shows the determination that brought him back to All-Star status after a lengthy bout of postconcussion syndrome in 1998.

Red Kelly

My dad lived for hockey and was a big star for the Port Dover, Ontario, team. He taught me how to score on a breakaway—keep your head up, look the goalie in the eye, and never look down at the puck before you shoot.

My brother and I used to ride three miles to hockey practice on our white pony. We'd stable him in the lumber shed next to the rink. We had only natural ice, though, so it wasn't until I got to St. Mike's in Toronto at age 15 that I really got much skating time.

In my first year at St. Mike's, my dad's alma mater, I tried out for the A team, the B team and the midgets and was cut early each time. I was reduced to playing in the schoolyard with the scholastic students, most of whom were there to become priests. Fortunately, I did well enough in the after-school games that the midget team took another look at

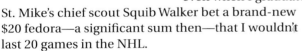

me, and I made the third line as a winger.

Father Flanagan taught me how to skate with speed and power in the legs. When I eventually graduated to the A team, they were short of defensemen, so I was moved back. Coach Joe Primeau showed me some moves, and I played defense for the next 12½ years, moving up to the Detroit Red Wings in 1947. Still, even when I graduated, St. Mike's chief scout Squib Walker bet a brand-new $20 fedora—a significant sum then—that I wouldn't last 20 games in the NHL.

I'd play up to 55 minutes a game. Friends used to warn me that Detroit was playing me too much, they would wear me out, I'd never last. But I was always in great shape, and the more I played, the better shape I was in. When they called me to go on, I went. And I lasted 20 years!

There were injuries, though. I broke a bone in my ankle in 1959. The team was struggling, so management asked whether I might be able to play with the cast removed and the ankle taped. We were brought up to play with injuries, so I tried it. I needed to leave a hole on the only side I could turn to, hoping the opposition would go that way, but managed to keep my vulnerability a secret. We didn't make the playoffs for the first and last time in my career. Reporters wrote for months that my decline had led to our poor season. All that summer, I ran barefoot on the sand and worked with a tennis ball to strengthen my ankle. By training camp

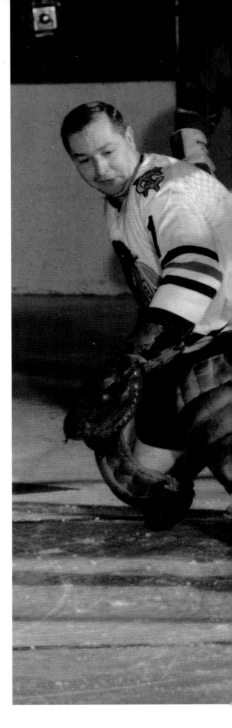

the next season, I was fully recovered.

Near Christmastime, with the team doing well, my game on track and after some serious probing by Toronto reporter Trent Frayne, I decided to tell the story, believing that since my ankle was healed, there would be no harm done. Frayne wrote a good article, but the *Detroit Free Press* ran the story the next day with an enormous headline reading, "Was Red Kelly Forced to Play on a Broken Foot?" After the game that night, Bruce Norris and Jack Adams ordered me to report to Muzz Patrick of New York the next morning. I'd been traded.

I stayed up all night, went to mass in the morning and called my summer employer to see whether I could start work for him right away. I was newly married and needed an income. "Yes" was the welcome reply. I then told Muzz I was retiring from hockey. He tried to talk me out of it, as did league president Clarence Campbell, who threatened that if Jack Adams suspended me, I would be banned for life from any involvement in hockey. I told him I'd given all I had to hockey since I was knee-high to a grasshopper. If they wanted to suspend me, go ahead. I only signed one-year contracts, got no money in advance and didn't think I owed anybody a thing.

In about 10 days, King Clancy called me on behalf of the Maple Leafs, wondering whether I might be interested in playing for Toronto. I was excited about this but needed to talk face to face. We arranged a secret meeting. I disguised myself by wearing a homburg and gloves and carrying a bumbershoot (an umbrella) to avoid looking like a hockey player. King Clancy picked me up at the airport. We came to an agreement, and the Leafs settled a deal with Detroit.

Today, I hear players talk of being traded and not having feelings about their former team. When Toronto played Detroit, I would have gone through a cement wall to stop the Red Wings from winning. I had all kinds of feelings!

Punch Imlach told me of his plan to move me permanently up to center, thinking I could be "the last piece to the puzzle" and help the Leafs beat the Canadiens to win the Stanley Cup. My job would be to check Jean Beliveau. I agreed, because positions didn't matter to me; I loved hockey. As kids on the pond, we'd pick sides and play anywhere. That freedom never changed for me.

"Red Kelly"

Leonard "Red" Kelly was the first Norris Trophy winner in 1954 and was selected as one of the NHL's All-Star defensemen eight times while playing for the Detroit Red Wings. (ABOVE) Kelly won four Stanley Cups as a center with the Leafs, bringing his career total to eight. Here he tries a wraparound against Glenn Hall of the Blackhawks.

Jari Kurri

WHEN I WAS A CHILD IN FINLAND, WE KNEW OF PLAYERS LIKE Mike Bossy and Guy Lafleur, but I didn't really dream of playing in the National Hockey League until I was about 17. I began to realize that it might be possible, because a few of our best players made the jump. I had received national attention in Finland and had some great games there. Playing on the national team is the highest achievement one can reach within Finland, an experience I have enjoyed several times. It is an honor to play for my country, and I've done my best to represent Finland with pride.

At the same time, there is no bigger achievement in hockey than winning the Stanley Cup. I'm grateful that I was drafted by the Edmonton Oilers in 1980. They had a young team, and I got a chance to play a lot right away. I won five Cups with Edmonton, and every one was special. I think I've played some of my best hockey in the NHL playoffs. There's tremendous satisfaction in scoring important goals, and in the playoffs, that's usually the case. I'm proud to share the record with Reggie Leach for the most goals, 19, in one playoff year. Twelve of those goals came in the six-game conference-final series against Chicago, another record. I was a little nervous when Joe Sakic came close to matching the total playoff record when he had 18 goals in the 1996 playoffs. I was helping broadcast the games back home in Finland after the Rangers were eliminated from the running. I'll admit I was glad to see Joe win the Cup and the Conn Smythe Trophy while leaving the record intact! I want to be remembered as a key playoff performer when there's so much on the line.

I've had the opportunity to play with some of the greatest players in the game. I remember, for example, when I first got the chance to play with Wayne Gretzky. The team had lost about nine games in a row, and Glen Sather was juggling lines, trying to find a combination that would help us out of our slump. Eventually it was my turn to play with Wayne. We combined in a totally natural way, anticipating each other's moves without much needing to be said. We never did talk much, but he was obviously as good a center as any winger could dream of playing with. I learned to be a more consistently good player by playing with Wayne. He puts a lot of pressure on himself, and I learned to do that too. You have to go full-out every night; there's never a day off.

Wayne's passing game is so far ahead of others'. One play that comes to mind occurred in a game against the Chicago Blackhawks. We were shorthanded, and Wayne carried the puck up-ice by himself. I was coming late behind him in case he lost it. Wayne made a quick spin, and the defense followed him to keep the pressure on. I saw an opening and took off. Wayne couldn't even see me, but he made a blind pass right onto the tape of my stick that sent me in on a breakaway. I scored, and when I went back to the bench, the whole team was laughing and shaking their heads, asking, "How did he know you were there?"

When Wayne was traded to the Los Angeles Kings, many felt that my career would be badly hurt. I heard stories that I'd never score without Wayne at my side. I felt redeemed when I had a good season without Wayne on the team and was selected to the Second All-Star team for the third time. Winning the Stanley Cup was always an exceptional experience, but perhaps none was sweeter than the last one we won in 1990. There was a tremendous load off the back of the entire team, because we demonstrated that we weren't a one-man show. I think that Wayne was happy for us too, despite being on an opposing team. We were and continue to be friends, and I loved the chance to play with him again in Los Angeles for another five years.

Individual success always comes second, but scoring 50 goals in 50 games still has a nice ring to it, as does scoring 70 goals in a season. I'm looking forward to surpassing the 600-goal milestone, but I know these achievements will be more meaningful after I've retired from the game. The time seems to be going by so quickly, so I'm eager to do all I can while I'm still young enough.

Teemu Selanne and I both played for the Finnish club team Jokerit, together during the NHL lockout in 1994-95 and individually when we were young men. Belonging to a club in Finland is like belonging to a family. There isn't the same dedication to hockey that you see in the NHL, but the loyalty is fierce. Teemu and I have become good friends over the past number of years, so it's somewhat strange to play with him knowing that I was a childhood idol of his. I'm glad to be an inspiration to younger players in Finland, just as other Finnish hockey players showed me that an NHL career was possible.

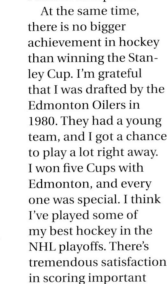

Jari Kurri won five Stanley Cups and five NHL All-Star team selections when he played for the Edmonton Oilers. (OPPOSITE) Kurri spent a season with the Anaheim Mighty Ducks before concluding his career with Colorado, primarily as a defensive specialist, in 1997-98.

Guy Lafleur

I WAS THE ONLY ROOKIE ON THE MONTREAL CANADIENS IN the fall of 1971, and most of the guys had won at least three or four Stanley Cups. Still, there was a lot of pressure on me. Jean Beliveau had retired, and there was an unreasonable and impossible expectation that I would take his place. We had a fantastic team, so I didn't get a lot of ice time. The fans got on me a little in my first three years, but that was hardest on my dad up in the stands. By my fourth year, I was getting a regular shift, and everyone was on my side.

I always felt lucky to be in the NHL. Playing for the Montreal Canadiens made the experience even more special. Despite all that I went through, I've always remained a Canadien at heart. But I wasn't happy about the circumstances surrounding my retirement in 1984. Coach Jacques Lemaire and general manager Serge Savard tried to create an almost exclusively defensive team. Both were former teammates, but relationships change dramatically when a player moves into management. My game was offense, so I sat on the bench most of the time, not even getting on the power play.

When I asked to be traded, I was refused. Since I was a member of the Montreal dynasty that had won so many Cups in the 1970s, Serge felt that the fans would never forgive him. Yet I wasn't as strong a crowd favorite anymore and was hearing some boos again. Serge, Jacques and I had a meeting, and I expressed my frustration at not getting the ice time I needed to play well. I was overjoyed when they promised a dramatic increase in my ice time and even a spot back on the power play.

I arrived at the rink for the next game at three in the afternoon, though the game wasn't starting until eight. I felt great and was ready to show what I could still do, given the chance. I was terribly upset when I got only one shift in the first period and two in the second. I tried to talk to Serge before the third period started, but he couldn't be found. I decided to quit right then. After the game, Serge and Jacques wondered what they should tell the press. I told them I didn't care what they said, and my retirement was announced.

To be elected to the Hockey Hall of Fame in 1988, four years later, made me feel a little like a has-been. Although I was pleased to be named, I felt too young. The only thing on my mind at the induction ceremonies was my goal of making a comeback. A month later, I was at the New York Rangers training camp.

I felt like a rookie all over again in New York. I was nervous, but it felt so good to be back on the ice again. The crowd response was positive all over the league, but I really looked forward to playing in Montreal again. Unfortunately, I had a foot injury the first time the team went to Montreal, so everyone eagerly anticipated our next trip to the Forum.

It was a very strange feeling to come back to Montreal as a Ranger. I still felt like a Montreal Canadien, as if I was on the wrong side of the ice. I wanted to win, of course; to beat Montreal would have pleased me both for personal reasons and for the pride of the team I now played for. I scored twice, and we were leading by several goals, but Montreal ended up winning 7–5. The fans couldn't have been happier, seeing me have a good game but have their team still win.

Coming back after almost four years out of the game was as good a feeling as winning the Stanley Cup. I had thought about it for so long; it was a dream that I had longed to live out almost from the first game I missed after my retirement. I proved to myself that I could have continued to help the Montreal Canadiens. In many ways, I don't feel that I was able to add three years to my career but that four years had been taken away from me.

I would have loved to finish as a Ranger, but because of a management shake-up, I went to Quebec, where I had scored 130 goals in my last year as a junior. Two years there was a nice way to finish. Our last road trip was like a farewell tour for me, with a warm acknowledgment in each city. Even the fans in Boston were kind!

Many people have approached me to say that my comeback was an inspiration to them in their life. I'm glad to hear that, though I did it just for me. There is no point in having a dream if you don't try to make it come true. If you wait too long, age can be a determining factor against you. My son has a dream of playing in the NHL, and though he's 11 and has played only two years, I think that's great. Work toward your dream as hard as you can, I say. Success isn't guaranteed, but you'll know you did all you could and not live with regret.

Guy Lafleur, a member of five Stanley Cup teams, received one of hockey's highest honors when his sweater number 10 was permanently retired by the Montreal Canadiens. (OPPOSITE) "The Flower" excited Montreal fans with his speed and dash during a legendary career that included three scoring championships.

Steve Larmer

I was drafted by the Chicago Blackhawks in 1980 but was sent down from training camp two years in a row, the second time to play for Moncton in the American Hockey League. Things couldn't have turned out any better, though, because my coach in Moncton was Orval Tessier, who was appointed head coach of the Blackhawks in the summer of 1982.

That made a huge difference for me, because the Blackhawks weren't pleased with my play in 1982's training camp. They wondered whether I could play in the NHL, but Orval kept bringing my name up, believing I could play for them. That's how I ended up on a line with Denis Savard and Al Secord. No one could have asked to play with better players, and it was a perfect situation for my rookie year. I got to play a regular shift and even the power play. Winning the Calder Trophy as Rookie of the Year was more of a surprise than anything else. I knew how close I had been to not even making the team.

I played in two All-Star games. The first was in 1990 as a replacement for Denis Savard, who was injured, but I was also invited to play the next year in Chicago. It was a thrill to play on my home rink. I was also scared—being around the best players in the world is intimidating. I was probably more nervous in those two games than I was in any other: on a breakaway, I missed the net by about 30 feet!

When Chicago was eliminated in the first round of the 1992-93 season playoffs, I felt there was nothing more I could do as a Blackhawk. It seemed like a dead-end street to me, and I decided to get back on track with a change of scenery, a different perspective. I asked for a trade, which was promised for that summer, but it didn't come until 13 games into the next season. Waiting was rough. I hadn't missed a single game with Chicago until then: 884 consecutive games.

My teammates knew it had nothing to do with them. We'd been in the trenches together for a long time, and I loved every one of them. It was about me. If I couldn't put all my heart into playing, I didn't think it was fair to the other 20 guys for me to be there. Finally the trade came, and I was on to New York.

Playing for the Rangers was an unbelievably good experience. The script couldn't have been written any better. We had a great year with a talented team, a close team. Still, everywhere we went, we were reminded that the last time New York had won the Cup was in 1940. The playoffs arrived, and we beat the Islanders in four games and Washington in five. In the next series, we were down three games to two against New Jersey, but with especially inspired play from Mark Messier, we tied the series and then won game seven in New York in double overtime. How much more exciting can it get than that?

Our best hockey was probably played in the first game of the final series against Vancouver, but we lost in overtime. We outshot them about 54 to 25 but just couldn't beat Kirk McLean. We won the next three games relatively easily, though the last three were a different story.

It's impossible to reflect on what you're accomplishing when you're involved in playoff hockey. Every game is so intense, you play so frequently, and you have to stay focused on the task before you. Almost before I knew it, we were back in Madison Square Garden for game seven of the Stanley Cup final, which we won 3–2.

I don't know that there's a better city in the world to win in than New York. They gave us a ticker-tape parade, and even teammates who had won the Cup before had never experienced anything like that. Between 1 million and 2 million people lined the streets and hung out of office buildings—it was the most incredible thing I've ever seen. A lot of the guys said they'll remember that more than any hockey game.

As a rookie, I'd been given the opportunity to play each game and probably wouldn't have developed and gained the confidence needed without that chance. Every young player needs the opportunity that I was given. When you get older and aren't capable physically of playing every game, you become a question mark to your teammates and coaching staff. I didn't just want to play *some* games, I wanted to play every night. That became harder to do, and I was taking ice time away from a younger player who could use it to grow and improve.

The lockout of 1994 gave me the opportunity to do "normal" things in the fall and winter. It was a real eye-opener to see what else is out there. My heart was in hockey; on the other hand, the time away planted a seed for retirement. It's time now to be home, see my friends, spend time with my family. That's what's important to me these days.

Steve Larmer played a remarkable string of 884 consecutive games for the Chicago Blackhawks. (Opposite) Larmer unleashes a slap shot while playing for the New York Rangers in their successful bid for the Stanley Cup in 1994.

Brian Leetch

I WAS BORN IN CORPUS CHRISTI, TEXAS, WHEN MY DAD was serving in the navy there. We moved around for a while, but I did most of my growing up in Connecticut. My dad, who played hockey for Boston College, took a job as manager of the first hockey rink ever built in Cheshire, Connecticut. Connecticut youth hockey was certainly good for the number of games we played: 50 or 60 a season. But we never knew where we stood in the spectrum of hockey. No one from Connecticut had ever turned pro.

I played a promising year of local high school hockey, so my parents and I decided that I might have a shot at a college scholarship if I went to a prep school, im-

proved my grades and played a higher level of hockey. I did that for two years, but again, though it seemed to go well, it wasn't until the Central Scouting Bureau published their rankings that I knew my hockey dreams might be realistic. Until I saw that I was ranked to be chosen early in the second round of the NHL draft, I really had no reference points for just how well I might be playing.

When the United States beat the Soviets for the gold medal in the 1980 Olympics, I didn't really understand the full significance of the event. It was exciting to watch it on television and root for the U.S.A., but if the media hadn't built up the game to us, it would have been just another Olympic hockey game. Our underdog status became much clearer when I joined the national junior team at age 16, a stepping-stone toward my goal of making the 1988 Olympic team. We weren't very successful, and I realized what a great accomplishment that gold-medal win was.

I've always loved international hockey, not only for the chance to be on a good team but for the higher level of competition you face. I've seen progress. The U.S. usually tried to throw our most skilled players on the ice with a few guys to go up and down the wing. It was a Canadian style of game, but we usually relied too heavily on our goaltenders to be competitive. It's really only since about 1990 or so that we've felt able to compete more evenly with the strong hockey nations.

But with the young players that we had on the 1996 World Cup team, things changed, and we were fortunate enough to come out on top. There was tremendous excitement entering the tournament when we saw that our big strong wingers also had the skills to score, our

defense was solid and our goaltending was as good as ever. Instead of thinking, "Let's have fun with the guys and do the best we can," we were confident.

In the World Cup tournament, my offensive skills weren't required as much as they are with the Rangers, where I'm frequently expected to participate in the offense. We went with six defensemen pretty regularly and tried to pass the puck up to the wingers and let them go. My greatest strengths are to get involved with the offensive play and try to set things up. If we're down and need a goal or two, I'm looking to get up-ice whenever I can.

It feels like a long season at times. Practicing and going to the rink every day sometimes wears on me, especially when we're not winning. I enjoy the games the most. Playing hockey reminds me of everything I love about competing and being successful and achieving my goals. It's during the tough times—the times that you have to get through—that I think, "Geez, what the heck am I doing out here being booed?" But it's all worth it when you start winning again.

The Calder Trophy in 1989 came to me as a bit of a surprise. Chris Nilan, a teammate and an American like me, approached me about halfway through the season. He said, "Keep working. You could be the Rookie of the Year and win that Calder. I'd really like to see that, and I think you can do it." It hadn't really occurred to me until then, but Chris was dead serious. He got me thinking about it, and the team played better and better as the season went on. It was very exciting to have personal success and have our team do well in my first year in the league.

Receiving the James Norris Trophy in 1992 was an honor, but it comes in the summertime when you're somewhat removed from the game. It's the same with the Conn Smythe Trophy: A small group of guys have the best opportunity to win it, guys with a lot of ice time on a successful team. The Conn Smythe I won in 1994 could easily have gone to several of my teammates. No individual award in any way compares with a Stanley Cup victory, where you get to share the experience with your teammates. There's nothing better than winning, with your friends simultaneously going through exactly the same emotions as you are. Winning the Stanley Cup in 1994 was unbelievable, and I'm most proud to have been on that team.

Brian Leetch won the Conn Smythe Trophy as 1994 playoff MVP when he led all play-off scorers and the New York Rangers to the Stanley Cup. (OPPOSITE) *Leetch, Norris Trophy winner in 1992 and 1997, is quick to jump into the rush and contribute to team offense.*

Mario Lemieux

HOCKEY HAS GIVEN ME EVERYTHING I HAVE, AND I'M GRATEFUL to have been part of the game. It was my life when I was younger, pretty much all I did. I put my skates on after school every day until eight or nine o'clock at night. At a very young age, I decided that I wanted to play hockey for a living. For my first few years, I played with kids two or three years older, and I think that trying to compete with them helped me improve a little faster than the others.

I don't remember learning any particular skills, and I didn't receive any specific coaching; I was just able to do things other kids couldn't. Like most boys, I wanted to go "top shelf" as much as possible, and since I was able to raise the puck better than the other kids, I scored a lot of goals. Hockey was always exciting, especially at the big tournaments, but when you're a kid, you don't realize all that's happening. I'm told that crowds used to come to watch me when I was as young as 8 or 9 years old.

I'm very proud to have played 12 years for the same NHL team. Few players in any sport can say that. I hesitated to join the Penguins at first, but I'm really glad that I made the decision to start my career in Pittsburgh. I believe I've helped build a winning tradition. It was a big challenge the first few years. I knew it would take time, and I gave myself five years for the team to make the playoffs, which is what it took. Good draft picks and some great trades enabled us to build a strong team, allowing me to live out my ultimate dream. Finally lifting that Cup is the best memory I have of the game. Knowing that I'd worked so hard to get to that point brought out indescribable feelings. I feel fortunate to have been part of two Stanley Cup-winning teams.

Winning the Conn Smythe Trophy when we won those Cups added something to the experience. Everything after the Cup is gravy, but those are accomplishments that I'm proud of. The Hart Trophy, which I've won three times, is the most special individual award I've received. I've never tried to win individual recognition, but I've always had a drive for excellence. I believed that if I kept that drive, awards would come. Even as a boy, that desire was in my blood. I grew up wanting to be the best on the ice, the best in the league and then the best in the world.

Scoring the winner in game two and then in game three of the finals of the 1987 Canada Cup tournament are memories I'll cherish for a long time, but that whole tournament turned my career around. I saw what it took to win, to be a championship team. Seeing how talented players who had won the Cup before—guys like Wayne Gretzky, Mark Messier and Paul Coffey—work so hard every day was a true learning experience. Playing with such great players for five or six weeks also gave me a lot of confidence, and my career took off.

The media and the fans make more of the rivalry between Wayne and me than there is. We aren't best friends, but we had a great time together for a couple of days at the 1996 All-Star game. At this stage of our careers, we've both won enough individual awards and Stanley Cups that we don't have to worry about such things as a rivalry. I've enjoyed the few chances I've had to play with him, just as I'm enjoying playing on a line with Jaromir Jagr in the 1996-97 season. Jaromir watches more than he asks questions. When he joined the Penguins in 1990, he asked to see tapes of all my goals and better plays. He might have picked up a few moves by doing that, but he works incredibly hard. He's the first one on the ice and last off at practice, working on his skills. He learns very quickly. Playing with a great player only makes my job easier.

Going through Hodgkin's disease was the most difficult time in my life and in my hockey career. I found out I had cancer in 1993 and had to face it. I truly learned that if you don't have your health, there's not much else to enjoy. I can have the greatest house and the most amazing cars, but they mean nothing without my health.

I've been playing for 13 years now, and I've had many battles with my back in addition to the fight with Hodgkin's disease. That's taken a toll on my body, and I'm starting to look for other things to do with my life. There have been some good times and some tough times throughout my career, but there's nothing that I regret doing or not doing. I have three children, with a fourth on the way, and spending more time with them is important to me now.

I will miss the guys and not being part of a team for eight months of the year, but I'll be glad not to have to go to training camp! I've never enjoyed that part of the routine throughout my career. It's tough to get started, but once that was behind me, hockey has always been fun.

Mario Lemieux captained the Pittsburgh Penguins to two Stanley Cup titles, winning the Conn Smythe Trophy both times. He retired in 1997, became a team owner in 1999, then made a remarkable comeback as a player in December 2000. (OPPOSITE) Lemieux, whose name fittingly means "the best" in French, blasts a shot at the net.

Trevor Linden

Winning the 1988 World Junior Championship at the age of 17 was a great experience. It was a real eye-opener for a Canadian teenager to see the Soviet lifestyle and how things worked there. Winning the championship right in the Soviets' own backyard was a powerful feeling. After we won the gold medal, our whole team walked jubilantly through Red Square. We were so pumped up to be world champions, especially in a country that seemed so foreign. During the 1996 World Cup, I played with three friends from that team: Eric Desjardins, Theo Fleury and Joe Sakic. It was a long time ago, but we still have stories to tell.

That championship was part of an amazing 13 months. Playing for the Medicine Hat junior team, we won the Memorial Cup in May 1987, we won the World Championship for Canada the following January, won another Memorial Cup for Medicine Hat in May 1988, and I was chosen as the second pick in the NHL entry draft in June.

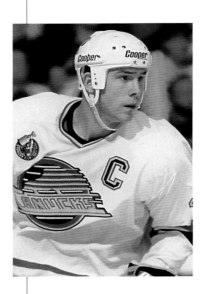

Keep in mind that I was born and raised in Medicine Hat. To rise to national heights while still living in your hometown is a rare and special treat for a junior Canadian hockey player. I grew up in a predominantly rural area. Just to make the Medicine Hat Tigers was a big accomplishment for me. We had a great team—our best team—in 1987. I was only 16, and at the start of the year, I didn't think we even had a realistic shot at the championship. But after I experienced what it was like to win, my teammates and I didn't want to let that feeling go. We really counted on our leadership to pull us through for back-to-back Memorial Cup victories.

I was the youngest guy in the NHL when I first broke in, and the Vancouver Canucks gave me an opportunity to play right away. It could have been overwhelming, but my upbringing prepared me well. I was mature and could handle new situations. My parents know very little about the technical aspects of hockey, which was a real blessing for me. They believed that if you work hard at what you do, you will be successful. They were always supportive of what I did, and instead of teaching hockey skills, they taught me life skills. I learned to work hard, respect the people I work with and maintain proper morals.

A lot of things happened for me at a young age. At 21, I was the youngest captain in the NHL when the Canucks named me to the position for the 1991-92 season. I had shared the job with Dan Quinn and Doug Lidster the previous year. I certainly made some mistakes, but I learned from them, making me a better person, hockey player and captain.

It wasn't difficult to establish myself in the captain's role because of the kind of team we had. There was a good group of guys who had shared their wisdom with me when I first joined the team. Their helpful attitude enabled me to move pretty smoothly into the position.

There's no secret to being a good captain of an NHL team. I try to be fair and be a go-between for the players and the coaches. If there are problems on one side or the other, I help to sort them out. I also try to represent the game the best way possible. I enjoy the role rather than see it as a burden. I've been a team captain since well back in my youth, including with Medicine Hat. I was brought up to be responsible and show leadership qualities. Being a team captain means, above all, being a team player. Even if I wasn't the captain, I think I'd still be the same kind of person.

I look forward to games when there is a lot on the line. Whenever there's an opportunity to get something done and I'm being counted on, that's when hockey's the most fun. Our Stanley Cup run of 1994 showed what can be accomplished when a group of guys come together. Winning the Western Conference final over Toronto was an outstanding feeling. Beating a rival like the Leafs in five games was indescribable. It was almost completely satisfying but even more exciting to be in the Stanley Cup finals against the New York Rangers.

The games went back and forth, and we tied the Rangers after being down three games to one. Most of Canada took us as their team versus New York as representative of the United States. The series was great for hockey, and I'll never forget that season, but there was a bitter feeling that stuck with me for quite a while after. When you dream of winning something all your life and it comes down to one game, it's just crushing to see it slip away. I scored a couple of times in the deciding game in New York, but we fell one goal short. I don't think I said three words on the plane ride home. If you lose in four straight games, you can walk away and say the other team was better. But it really hurts to lose in seven games.

Trevor Linden, runner-up for the Calder Trophy in 1989, became team captain of the Vancouver Canucks in 1991 at age 21. (Opposite) Linden was traded to the New York Islanders in February 1998. He joined the Montreal Canadiens in the summer of 1999 but was dealt to Washington at the 2001 trade deadline.

Eric Lindros

I WAS READING A COLUMN IN A PHILADELPHIA NEWSPAPER the day after we won the 1997 Eastern Conference final, and the columnist mentioned something I had once told him: "All I ever wanted to be was a hockey player."

It's a simple sentence. But obviously, it has taken a lot of hard work and commitment to make it happen, not just from myself but more importantly from coaches, family, friends and other influential people in my life, such as John McCauley (the father of one of my Junior B teammates and a former NHL referee-in-chief). The

long lines of support have extended from my early years in London, Ontario, all the way to Philadelphia and to my life as a National Hockey League player.

While individual successes are nice, being part of a winning program in a team sport carries more clout for me. I've been very fortunate to enjoy that team success at different levels in hockey, including a fun ride through my junior years. As a 15-year-old, I was a member of the St. Michael's Buzzers team that won the Ontario Hockey Association Junior B championship. One of the highlights in my hockey career took place a couple of years later when the Oshawa Generals beat the Kitchener Rangers twice in double overtime to win the Memorial Cup. Fans today still talk about that Canadian junior hockey league tournament providing some of the most exciting hockey at any level.

Less than a year later, I joined a couple of my Oshawa teammates, Mike Craig and Dale Craigwell, to help Canada win the gold medal in Saskatoon. It was my second time to enjoy that gold-medal feeling at the World Junior Championship, but it held extra meaning being able to win on home ice.

Later that year, I was invited to play for Canada in the 1991 Canada Cup tournament—an unbelievable feeling! When I was 15 or 16, I thought that I had a chance to play in the NHL some day, but it was a real rush to be asked to join Canada's best hockey team as an 18-year-old. I first found out about my selection when I opened *The Toronto Star* and saw my name on the list of invited players. That was a big day for me.

I went all out in that Team Canada training camp right from the start. We had a couple of extra players, so the first time I knew I was actually going to be able to play was when coach Mike Keenan wrote out the starting lineup on the blackboard. Names went up quickly,

and I started to think to myself, "Please, please give me a spot on the roster." When Mike wrote the next center's name, it was mine. I felt both lucky and privileged.

We tied Sweden in our first game, and the heat was on. I loved it. We played the U.S.A. next, and there were some underlying tensions. I had been drafted by Quebec that summer, and there was a rumor that my rights were going to be dealt to Chicago, with Jeremy Roenick headed to Quebec. Jeremy and I were mouthing off to each other the whole game, but it's something that we laugh about together now. We beat the Americans in that game and again in the final, thanks to a short-handed breakaway goal by Steve Larmer. I was thrilled to be there, but anything other than victory would have been a disappointment.

I really felt that I had arrived in the NHL after the 1994-95 season. Jaromir Jagr edged me out for the scoring title when we tied on points, but he had more goals. Just to be talked about in the same breath as Jaromir and Dominik Hasek as nominees for the Hart Trophy was exciting. It was a great honor that year to win both the Hart and the Lester B. Pearson Award. I'll always remember the feeling I had when I read on the sides of the trophies the names of the great players who had received those awards ahead of me. I was in awe. It was especially great to win the Pearson, because you are selected by your peers. To be recognized by the guys you go to war against every night is really something. I heard that the Pearson Award is Mark Messier's favorite. That says a lot.

I'm no different that anyone else in that I've dreamed of winning the Stanley Cup. I was brought to Philadelphia for that reason. And while I won't be satisfied until I get the big one, there's an awful lot I appreciate about having the opportunity to play professional hockey. The game has changed in some ways for me. I now do a better job of picking my spots with the physical side of the game. Just because you're throwing a check doesn't mean that your body isn't absorbing a strong percentage of the aftershock. There's pain for both parties. But I still get a kick out of simply being on the ice—staying late after practice with a future superstar like Dainius Zubrus—just doing what I always wanted to do.

Philadelphia's Eric Lindros won the Hart Trophy in 1995, along with the Pearson Award and a First All-Star team selection. (Opposite) Lindros was stripped of the team captaincy after criticizing team doctors during the 2000 playoffs. His trade request went unfulfilled, and he missed the entire 2000-01 season.

Ted Lindsay

I was well established in the NHL and one of the best-paid Red Wings when I decided to form a players' association in the summer of 1956. I had business interests outside hockey, so the association wasn't really for me. It was for the fringe players, the fifteenth or sixteenth guy on the team. We *were* paid better than we would be in any other job, but there were too many things that just weren't right, especially how the NHL wasn't contributing to the pension plan properly. Every player contributed $900 a year, 20 percent of some players' salary. The league was supposed to match that but were putting in only $600. Even much of that was coming from the players' own toil—All-Star game receipts!

Players could be sent down to the minors on a whim. The player would have to move his family and pay his lease in Detroit *and* in his new town. We wanted a vehicle to address these issues and others.

There was a dictatorship. The teams fought each other on the ice, but the owners were united in keeping control over the players. They had a big weapon over us: We loved the game and were blinded by that love. Yet the owners didn't truly appreciate how much we loved it. We never would have done anything to harm hockey. There was no other place to play, and hockey was what we did best.

It was difficult to form a players' association then, because opposing players never spoke to one another. We literally hated each other. If I was walking down the sidewalk and saw an opponent approaching, one of us would cross the street to avoid having to acknowledge each other. One of the wonderful things that came from trying to organize the players' association was that some of my enemies in the league became my closest associates and even friends.

An association wouldn't be credible without Toronto or Montreal, but the Canadiens especially didn't need us. Everyone on their team was a star. My respect for Montreal and Toronto players really grew when they got on board. We formed the association at the All-Star game, which was played in October, before the season started. Then we kept it secret—an extraordinary feat that would have stunned the owners, given that each team had two trainers who almost tripped over each other rushing to management with any information they picked up—until a press conference

was held in January.

The proverbial crap hit the fan the next day. I came into the Detroit dressing room, and no one was getting dressed. Jack Adams looked as if someone had painted him red. I expected that (in fact, I would have been disappointed if that hadn't been the case). He singled out every Red Wing, except me and my business partner, Marty Pavelich, and angrily asked, "Are you for this?" I felt let down by our veterans when no one would even say, "We should take a look at it." That statement would have changed the dynamics greatly.

The next summer, the key organizers—Dollard St. Laurent of Montreal, Jimmy Thompson and Tod Sloan of Toronto, and I—were sent to Chicago. That was exile then. Montreal was smart enough to keep our other organizer, Doug Harvey, for a few more seasons. Detroit also sent Glenn Hall with me, because Glenn was inclined to speak his mind. Jack Adams told Marty Pavelich that he was sending him to the minors. Marty shocked him and retired on the spot.

The owners continued to threaten the individual livelihood of each player. Our lawyers advised us to certify as a union for protection. (The main difference between a union and an association is that in an association, each member negotiates his own salary.) In the fall of 1957, we picked Toronto to certify in Canada, and Detroit in the U.S. The Toronto owner, Conn Smythe, tried to ensure his players wouldn't vote for a union, but the Maple Leafs stood their ground. Sadly, Detroit did not.

I was treated well in Chicago, but in my heart, I was still a Red Wing. I made some friends, but really, I was just existing. My last season in Detroit had been my most productive ever, but I had only one good year out of the next three I spent with the Chicago

Blackhawks. I retired at the end of the 1959-60 season.

In the spring of 1964, I played in an exhibition game between the Red Wings and the Detroit old-timer team. We took Gordie Howe off the Red Wings onto our side. It was the first reunion of our old Production Line—Sid Abel, Gordie and me—since the early 1950s. We gave the Red Wings a heck of a game, losing by a single goal right near the end.

Sid must have seen something in me, because he talked me into playing again. He'd taken over as general manager from Jack Adams a couple of years earlier. It was great to be back with the Wings. Emotionally, I'd never left. We finished first in the league but lost in the playoffs. I hung up my skates again but served the Red Wings in later years as a coach and general manager. I'm proud today to see my sweater number 7 hanging in the rafters with our Stanley Cup banners.

Ted Lindsay

Ted Lindsay captained the Detroit Red Wings for the last two of the four Stanley Cups he won with them in the 1950s. (ABOVE) Lindsay buries the puck behind Toronto's Harry Lumley from low in the slot.

Frank Mahovlich

FIRST IMPRESSIONS ARE LASTING. I SAW MY FIRST HOCKEY game in Timmins, Ontario, at age 4. The McIntyre Arena, built the year I was born, almost became my home. Herbie Carnagie of a team called the Buffalo Anchorite stood out for me at a very young age. Herbie was a smooth hockey player and a beautiful skater. Perhaps more significantly, Barbara Ann Scott, Barbara Wagner, Bob Paul—all the great figure skaters—came up for six weeks in the summer. I think I developed my skating style, with a long, fluid stride, watching those figure skaters. I know that my skating was noticed when I was only in grade three, as I was invited to try out for the school hockey team. The NHL scouts came calling when I was 12.

I came to the Leafs when they were struggling in 1957. King Clancy called me Moses, because he thought I'd lead Toronto out of the wilderness. I scored two hat tricks that year, in Chicago Stadium and then in Maple Leaf Gardens on Christmas Day, 1957, in a win against Jacques Plante and the devastatingly powerful Montreal Canadiens. The crowd response was fantastic. No matter what I did, it was the right thing. Montreal dominated the league then, so beating them in that game really helped me in the quest for the Calder Trophy.

Punch Imlach filled the holes with his knack for picking good talent and recognizing what the team needed. Still, we had no chance of beating Montreal until the early 1960s. We finished first in the regular season in 1961, so we knew we could win it, but we weren't prepared enough for the playoffs. In 1962, we were just sitting there, poised to win, and we won at last, with two more Cups immediately after that. It is truly amazing that we won again in 1967. When I look back at that team, I wonder how the hell we did it. A lot of the players were new to the team since our win in 1964. About eight or nine guys were around 40 years old. You can't find eight players that old in the entire NHL today! It gives you an idea of their talent, and that was in the six-team era.

Frank Selke started trying to get me to Montreal in the 1950s and would tell me this whenever I ran into him. In 1962, Chicago made a bid for me for a million dollars. This was unheard of then, but Conn Smythe stepped in and stopped the deal. Yet Toronto never understood me or my game. I would have been far better off being traded earlier. My career blossomed after I left Toronto. Detroit and Montreal didn't contain me with rules or restraints. They said, "You're talented, go do your thing." Toronto wanted their wingers to go up and down the wing. But if you play only a third of the ice, you're much easier to check.

I was best suited to be a Montreal Canadien. I liked things to happen quickly so that I could let my instincts take over. Montreal had such super teams because they just let the reins go. Of course, they had built a great defense, but that came because they let the young guys like Larry Robinson do what they were good at, let them develop their skills. They had a great organization, going out of their way to do a little extra for the players and the fans.

The 1971 playoffs were the highlight of my career. The record I set for the most points in the playoffs for a Montreal Canadien, 27 points, still stands more than 25 years later. I'd been traded from Detroit in January of that year to a team that would grow to include 12 future Hall of Fame players before I left 3½ years later. A great team is like a great athlete: you prepare yourself to perform to the best of your ability, and you go into the arena with confidence, knowing that nothing is going to go wrong. You've practiced, you feel great, you're prepared. If there was a problem, it was solved before the game started. In Toronto, we always had problems that we couldn't solve.

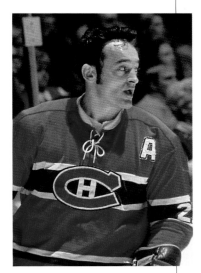

There was always something going on. It's amazing that we won four Stanley Cups when I was there.

As players, we had no control over these problems. Punch Imlach practiced us too hard. We left our game on the practice rink half the time. Despite having great teams, we placed first only once in the regular season. I think that the management orchestrated a lot of the criticism I faced from the fans. I was relieved to be traded from Toronto in 1968, but I always lived there and still do. I wear my Stanley Cup ring from the Maple Leafs every day. Management had a good idea: They made a ring with a quarter-carat diamond and increased the size of the stone every time we won. I think it's one of the most beautiful championship rings I've ever seen, and I'm proud to wear it on one hand, my Hall of Fame ring on the other.

Frank Mahovlich starred for the Toronto Maple Leafs for 10 years, and his deceptive speed, great strength and scoring prowess were major contributions to four Stanley Cup victories. (OPPOSITE) "The Big M" won two more Stanley Cups after joining the Montreal Canadiens in 1971 via the Detroit Red Wings.

Lanny McDonald

NE OF MY MOST EXCITING GOALS CAME WITH THE LEAFS IN
the 1978 Stanley Cup quarterfinals. I broke my nose in
the first round and had to wear a protective shield. We
were playing the formidable New York Islanders, and
Denis Potvin hit me with a hard, clean check that broke
a bone in my wrist. We kept news of that injury quiet,
and our trainer froze my wrist before each game and
taped it rigid.

Our coach, Roger Neilson, had us convinced that we
could beat the Islanders. He gave us a game plan that
we stuck to, and it worked. It was a grueling series that
went into overtime in game seven. I got the puck in the
slot near the Islander net. With my wrist so immobi-
lized, I was really able only to push the puck toward the
goal. I rushed for the rebound and saw the puck lying in
the net. In disbelief, I looked back at our bench as if to
ask, "Can it really be over?" My teammates poured over
the boards in confirmation.

It was a great time to be a Toronto Maple Leaf. There
was a sense that the Leafs "were back" after not having
won the Stanley Cup since 1967. As players, we felt we
were only one or two guys short of being able to win the
whole thing. Unfortunately, management started to dis-
mantle the team through numerous trades. I'd like to
give them the benefit of the doubt and say they were
trying to strengthen the team, but I cannot, and I wonder if my friendship with Darryl Sittler and my involvement with the NHLPA weren't part of the reason for my
trade to the Colorado Rockies in 1979. My family and
I loved Denver, but after being on a team that was a
Stanley Cup contender, it was difficult to play for a team
that was almost mathematically eliminated from the
playoffs in November.

Two years later, the Rockies were on a western
Canada road trip. We arrived in Winnipeg, and I was
pulled aside and told I was going back to Calgary. Because I have a lot of family there, I thought a relative
must be ill. But it was another trade. I wanted to talk to
my teammates, who had boarded the bus to go to the
hotel. I stepped onto the bus and started to explain to
them that a trade had not been my idea at all; I thought
we had a great bunch of guys who were just about
to turn things around. Rob Ramage interrupted me.
"Lanny, get your butt to Calgary. This is a great opportunity for you." But as in my trade from Toronto, my first
reaction was disappointment that my old team didn't
want me anymore.

My first full season with the Flames was my most productive ever. Guy Chouinard was my center, and I'd
never played with such a pure passer. He could send a
puck over four sticks and have it land flat on the ice
right on my stick. "Just go to the net, and I'll find you,"
he said. And he did. I was in a race with Wayne Gretzky
all season for the most goals. What a thrill! I came in
second, with 66 to Wayne's 71.

When I'm asked how many career goals I scored and

I answer "500," the second question is, "How many
exactly?" I tell them, "You need only 500 to join the 500
Goal Club, so why score any more?" I had 489 goals
when I was heading into what I suspected would be
my last season. I hit the 1,000-point milestone early in
March 1989, but I had only four goals. We went on a
five-game road trip, and I finally got on a roll, scoring
six times. There were five home games left in the season, and I needed only one more, but I was anxious. It
was a relief to get the goal in our first game back home.
The Saddledome erupted when I put the puck in on a
wraparound, sliding it past the goalie on the far side.

We concluded that season with a Stanley Cup win, my
first and only one. That
completed a hat trick
for me: 1,000 points, 500
goals and a Stanley Cup.
After 16 years in the
league, it was the per-
fect time to retire. The
Flames permanently
hung up my number
nine the following
March. What an honor!

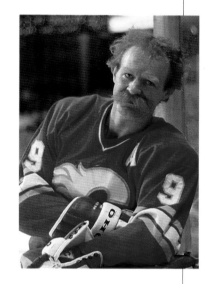

My dream as a child
was to play in the NHL.
Only when that became
a reality did I dare to
dream of winning the
Cup. I enjoyed seeing
my younger teammates
celebrating and jump-
ing around when we won, but people have told me that
I didn't look as excited as they thought I would be. I
was surprised by my own feelings too. I mostly felt
a tremendous peace, deeply satisfied that I'd accomplished what I had set out to do long ago.

My dad once said, "I hope when you're finished,
they'll remember you as Lanny McDonald the man as
much as Lanny McDonald the hockey player." I took
that as advice. I was proud to receive the Bill Masterton
Trophy in 1983 for my dedication to the game and the
King Clancy Trophy in 1988 for my charitable work.
Being a professional hockey player gives you opportunities to give something back to the community. But
regardless of what you do, it is everyone's responsibility
to get involved. Do it from your heart, and make a difference in someone's life!

*Lanny McDonald brought his tremendous strength of
character to Calgary in 1981 and co-captained the Flames
to a Stanley Cup victory in 1989. (OPPOSITE) McDonald
broke into the league with Toronto, where his 1978 overtime heroics are still fondly remembered.*

Rick Middleton

GROWING UP IN TORONTO IN THE 1960S WAS A GREAT TIME to be a hockey fan. How could you not want to grow up to be a hockey player? Once I got hockey in my blood, I played all year long, on the ice and on the street. I learned the stickhandling, the deking, the transferring of the weight on the road with a tennis ball. I believe you can learn everything about the game, besides skating, on the street. I still play street hockey today in a men's league.

While growing up, I was never the best or the biggest or the fastest. I know I had the heart, but anyone who plays the game seriously has the heart. Until I was 14 years old, I was a scrawny little kid who wore ankle sup-

ports in my skates. My coach, a power-skating nut named Frank Miller, showed me some ankle-strengthening exercises. In the span of two years, I changed my skating style dramatically. I didn't have overpowering speed to fly around defensemen, but I wasn't getting hit as much. As a survival technique, I developed an ability to go inside, into the traffic, and go directly to the net.

I'd always have to get in close, because I couldn't score unless I was three feet from the net. I never did develop the big shot from outside. A lot of my friends, including goalies, say that half my goals never hit the back of the net!

But as a teenager, my main concern was my small size. I decided to play a year of Junior B even after being drafted for Junior A hockey by the Oshawa Generals of the Ontario Hockey League. That was one of the smartest things I ever did, and I won Rookie of the Year and felt more prepared for Junior A. I started to get stronger, and my game went to another level while playing two years of Junior A.

I was ecstatic to be chosen in the first round of the 1973 NHL draft by the New York Rangers, but I was in training camp only a few weeks before they sent me to Providence, Rhode Island. I always seemed to take a step backward before I went forward, and I knew how strong the Rangers were (they went to the Stanley Cup final the previous year against Boston). I had a great year in Providence, winning Rookie of the Year in the American Hockey League.

I played for the Rangers the following two years. I was still a young kid, and I didn't handle the pressures of living and playing in New York very well, which is part of what led to my departure. John Ferguson, who traded me to Boston, pulled me over years later and said, "You know, I did it for your own good." John took a lot of flack for that trade because of the way it turned out, but I know he saw potential in me that probably would never have been realized in New York.

Don Cherry was coaching the Boston Bruins then, and he didn't know what to make of me initially. The first day on the ice, we were skating around. I still had my hair long, to my shoulders. Don approached me and said I looked a little bigger and asked if I'd been working out. I said, "No, I just had a good summer, Don," and everyone broke up laughing. But it wasn't the kind of thing to say to Don.

I scored a hat trick in my first game with the Bruins, but he played me on and off for the rest of the year. He said, "You don't know how to check your hat." Over time, I learned to be aware of picking up my check, not getting caught in the offensive zone, mixing up my offensive plays and not trying to beat the whole team every time I got the puck. You had to fit into Don's system, or you didn't play.

At the end of the 1976-77 season, we went into the semifinals against Philadelphia, who were just coming off a couple of Stanley Cup wins. The first game was tied after regulation time. I hadn't played regularly all year or in the playoffs, but Don came to me just before overtime started, leaned over and said, "You're going to get the winner." I looked up at him and said, "So I must be playing, right?"

I did score the winner—against Bernie Parent. I took a knuckler wrist shot that went off Bernie's blocker. Bernie reached for it but knocked it over the line, and the red light went on.

Playing in the Montreal Forum for the Stanley Cup was the ultimate high for me. Even now, I still get goosebumps thinking about it. Of course, Montreal had formidable teams. We lost four straight games in 1977; the next year, we lost four games to two; and the year after that, Montreal beat us in overtime in the seventh game of the semifinals (the famous too-many-men-on-the-ice game).

Even today, I'm disappointed at not winning the Stanley Cup, but looking back, I have nothing but great memories and a lot of pride at being able to play in the NHL for 14 years. I had the time of my life!

Rick Middleton

Rick Middleton was rewarded for his classy play in 1982 when he was awarded the Lady Byng Trophy. He was runner-up to Mike Bossy the following two seasons. (OPPOSITE) Middleton cuts to the net in front of St. Louis goaltender Doug Grant.

tan Mikita

WHEN I WAS 8 YEARS OLD, MY PARENTS DECIDED THAT LIFE would be better for me if I left Czechoslovakia and was adopted by my aunt and uncle in Canada. I arrived in St. Catharines, Ontario, three days before Christmas of 1948. Hockey was the biggest help in making the adjustment to a new life. As the holidays passed, I watched the neighborhood kids playing road hockey. At first, I just looked out at them from behind a curtain. Then I opened the curtain, and they could see me in the window. Before long, I was sitting on the front porch, and eventually, I got enough nerve to go down onto the sidewalk to watch. One day, they were short a guy, so they motioned for me to come and join them.

I had no idea how to play hockey, so the first time a guy went around me, I chopped his legs out from under him. I didn't understand a word of English, but one of the older fellows told me, in sign language, "No, we don't play hockey like that." He showed me how to hold the stick and stickhandle. That was my introduction to hockey *and* where I learned the English language. Needless to say, my vocabulary was limited and included quite a few cusswords.

My new father bought me my first skates. They were about three sizes too big, so I had to jam stuffing in the toe, but in Czechoslovakia, we couldn't even afford boots. The only skating I had done there was on a pond with screw-on skates. They were like the old four-wheel roller skates, with a special key to tighten them to your shoes. A friend and I, both 9 years old, signed up to play hockey in 1949. The league was for 12- and 13-year-olds, but we fibbed and said we were small for our age. We got through tryouts, and by the time they asked for a birth certificate, it was too late to kick us out.

I hadn't completely eliminated the language factor, and kids made fun of me. That made me determined to be better than those kids as a hockey player, but I was also in a lot of scraps. When I got to the NHL in 1959, I was still fighting. My first left-winger was Ted Lindsay, who, at 5 foot 8 inches and 152 pounds, was about my size. (I grew a couple more inches in my rookie year.) I asked Teddy, "You've played 16 years in the league. How did you ever survive?" He answered, "Hit 'em first." I followed that advice and made sure everyone knew that I was tough enough for the NHL.

There were a number of factors involved in my decision to cut my penalties in 1966. Our oldest daughter, who was about 3 at the time, asked me why I had to skate all the way to the other side of the ice and sit by myself. How do you explain that Daddy took a penalty when he shouldn't have and got punished for it?

I also sat down and figured out where all my penalties were coming from. The majority were what I call "lazy" penalties—holding, hooking, tripping. And then I added my misconducts. I made a conscious effort to cut out the lazy penalties and to keep my mouth shut with the referees. It worked. By then, I

had won a couple of scoring championships and felt accepted and secure. I went from a scrapper to Lady Byng winner two years in a row, winning the Art Ross and the Hart Trophy in the same seasons.

I worked on being innovative both in my play on the ice and in improving my equipment for lightness and safety. But my invention of the curved stick came by accident. One day, I cracked my stick in practice, forming an angle in the blade. I was tired and angry at the thought of climbing the 21 stairs to the dressing room to get another stick. I fired a puck in frustration, and the way it left my stick and the sound it made against the boards caught my attention. Before the stick finally broke, I had taken half a dozen shots, and each time, it was the same.

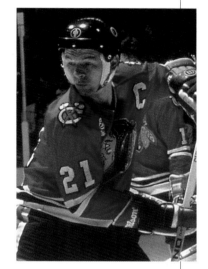

After that, I intentionally bent my stick. I broke a lot before I figured out how to make the wood pliable with heat and soaking. I experimented in practice for a month or two before I used a curved blade in a game. Now sticks are manufactured with a curve, but that was the start of it.

I only played in two games for Team Canada against the Russians in 1972. I was really angry about the Russian invasion of Czechoslovakia in 1968 and thought I'd take it out on their hockey players, but once the puck was dropped, it was just another hockey game. We played the Czechoslovakian national team in Prague after winning the series in Moscow. I was able to spend a few precious days with my mother and relatives before the game. Then our coach Harry Sinden kindly made me team captain. Everyone tried to help me score, but I just couldn't beat Vladimir Dzurilla that night. Phil Esposito scored in the last 30 seconds to tie the game, which felt good, but the welcome I received from the crowd was the proudest moment in my life.

Stan Mikita led the Chicago Blackhawks on and off the ice for 22 NHL seasons. He still holds the franchise records for longevity, assists and points. (OPPOSITE) Mikita parks in front of Montreal goalie Charlie Hodge.

Mike Modano

HOCKEY WASN'T A BIG PART OF MY LIFE AS A KID. WHEN I was growing up, all the neighborhood boys wanted to be Cal Ripken or Joe Montana. I was a hyperactive 8-year-old, and friends of my parents suggested that hockey might be a good outlet for me. Living in Detroit, so close to the Canadian border, we could pick up the *Hockey Night in Canada* telecasts during the Darryl Sittler and Borje Salming era in Toronto. The Maple Leafs became my idols.

The Detroit hockey program for boys took off when I was 11 years old. Little Caesar's and Compuware, a pizza chain and a computer company, sank a lot of money into hockey and even started to recruit players.

We had kids coming from Illinois, Indiana, Ohio—even as far away as California—and billeting with local families, just as junior players in Canada do. As a result, some powerhouse teams were developed.

Hull of the Quebec junior league assured me of their intention to draft me. But the night before the draft, they told me they were going to pick another import instead. I'd already told other teams that I was going to Hull, and with the Ontario draft the same day, I didn't get picked by anyone. I got a call from Rick Wilson in Prince Albert, Saskatchewan, asking if I wanted to come out and see how I liked the city and the idea of playing in the western Canadian junior league. I was 16, and my dad and I agreed that the best thing for my hockey was to move on, so I went and discovered a great organization. The city meant quite a culture shock for a boy from Detroit, but I came to love it, even staying during the summers over my three seasons there. There were only two or three Americans in the whole league, but I was well accepted.

Minnesota picked me first in the 1988 NHL entry draft, but I went back to Prince Albert the next year. I broke my wrist in the midseason All-Star game, so Minnesota called me up to travel with the team and absorb some NHL culture. I did play in a couple of playoff games, but with my cast still on, I wasn't very effective.

I was excited when the team moved from Minnesota to Dallas in the summer of 1993. It gave us a new start and brought us closer together. It was as if the entire team had been traded. All we knew was each other. The move had a lot to do with my 50-goal season. I had a lot of friends in Minnesota, but in Dallas, I had complete focus on hockey. Every puck I touched seemed to find a way through holes and behind goalies. I blew my knee out and missed a couple of weeks and missed some more time with a concussion, but I really think injuries can sometimes be helpful. Mine gave me a chance to rest mentally. Getting away from the game and having the chance to come back fresh kept me positive and confident all season.

Reaching a certain level as a veteran player brings more responsibilities, including playing against the top lines in the league. That's new to me and I love it. We got off to a good start in Dallas, which got people interested, but the honeymoon is over. The pressure to win is building, but after seeing how winning sports teams are treated here, I wouldn't want to be anyplace else. We're already recognized around town more than we ever were in Minnesota.

For a long time, it was tough to play for the United States. I first played for my country when I was a 16-year-old midget. I then played on the U.S. junior team, on a couple of teams that competed for the World Championship and in the Canada Cup of 1991. A lot of players were frustrated with how our teams were run. Canada pushes for champions, but it seemed the U.S. wasn't concerned about being seen as a powerful country in hockey. We didn't have the public backing and encouragement that the Canadians get, and as a result, our best players didn't always show up.

Things have changed. Different people are running things now. We had a great roster for the 1996 World Cup tournament. Once we got to training camp, we realized we had as good a chance of winning as any country. We didn't want to let that opportunity pass us by. We understood what was at stake. Everyone on the team had dreamed of having the chance to beat the Canadians. Our coach, Ron Wilson, gave us a basic plan, opened the doors and let us go.

The best part of the tournament for me was the friendships I developed. We grew close very quickly and were able to celebrate together. Watching the clock count down the final seconds and then being on the ice with the trophy at the end was a big thrill. I went to the finals for the Stanley Cup and the Canada Cup in 1991. Back then, I thought, "I'm only 20. I'll get back again." The first time I was even close since was that tournament. It was so great to finally win something.

Mike Modano

Dallas Stars dynamo Mike Modano won a Stanley Cup ring in 1999, combining strong offense with a commitment to defense. (OPPOSITE) Modano added more grit to his game in 1996. Here, he is determined to get the puck away from Kirk Muller (21) in front of the Maple Leaf net.

Alexander Mogilny

BUFFALO SABRES OWNER SEYMOUR H. KNOX GAVE ME sweater number 89 when I joined his team. I was the 89th pick in the draft, and I came to North America in 1989. Wearing 89 on my back is special to me; it's more than just a number.

I've always had an independent streak, and that was not tolerated by the Soviet authorities. I came to the NHL when I couldn't see any future in the Russian league. So many things were happening politically. Hockey officials could control many aspects of my life

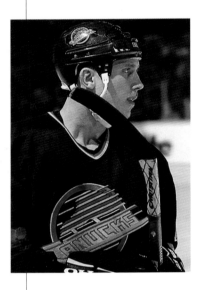

far beyond the ice rink, from what rank I could hold in the army to what kind of apartment I could live in. I thought I had to defect to maintain any hope of extending my hockey career. I left after the 1989 World Championships closed in Stockholm.

It was a huge adjustment to come to the NHL. The language barrier was the toughest part. Lack of communication affected me both on and off the ice. It also took some time to get

used to the airline travel. I had to deal with a fear of flying. I had some decent seasons despite those problems, but it wasn't until Buffalo made a big trade with the New York Islanders in the fall of 1991 that everything really came together for me. Playing with Pat Lafontaine as my center was key to my 76 goals in the 1992-93 season. Our coach, John Muckler, didn't hold us back. He told us to play hard and do whatever worked for us. Offensive hockey is my game, and Pat and I explored a lot of ways to put the puck in the net. It was so enjoyable to play with him. He's such a talented hockey player that he made my job easier. It's tough to repeat a season like that, so there really isn't pressure to match that season's output. Not many players have scored that many goals in a season, but I know I can do it again because I've done it once already. As long as I go out and do my best, anything can happen. You never know.

My trade to Vancouver was good for both teams. Buffalo was rebuilding and trying to cut the payroll, but I also needed a change in my life. I spent six years in Buffalo, but the trade worked out for me. It's great to line up on the same team as Pavel Bure again. We played together for Red Army and in junior. It's a long time ago, but it was exciting to play with Pavel and Sergei Fedorov as linemates in the 1989 World Junior Championship in Anchorage, Alaska. We three will never play together in the NHL because of the large salaries we now get. There

would be too much money involved to reunite us! I'm so glad we had the chance to try that then. It was terrific fun, but that's all just memories now.

I'm paid to score goals and make plays. That's what I do best. I was saddened to see Pavel miss most of the 1995-96 season due to injury, but it was nice to show some of my critics that I could still rack up some points without Pat Lafontaine or Pavel. I proved them wrong. That was the best part of the season for me. We had a lot of injuries on the team, so it was a poor year for the club, but it was a good year, a rebound year, for me.

Being around the locker room is the best part of the game. Ever since I was a kid, I've looked forward to going to the rink and seeing my friends, my teammates. It might be hard for someone who's not a hockey player to understand how good it is. It's like a microclimate. We're together doing what we love. Of course, now we're well paid for it too. It's the best job in the world.

Everyone in the NHL always had the dream of being a good hockey player, or they wouldn't be here. Since I was a kid, I have always been thinking about ways to continue to play the game. The NHL wasn't a part of those thoughts until just before I defected in 1989. But step by step, aspiring to make one team after another, I worked my way here. I'm thankful that I've been able to play this game for so long already.

No particular moment stands out yet as a favorite memory. It's nice anytime you score a winning goal, but I feel I've got a lot to look forward to. So many little things are being done to the game today, arguably for the safety of the players. Tinkering with the rules and the equipment might be signs that the game is moving forward, but if I could change anything, it would be just to let the guys play. I think we would work things out. Everyone wants to win the Stanley Cup—absolutely— but the love of the game itself is why we're here.

Alexander Mogilny's 55-goal 1995-96 season was the highlight of almost five years with the Vancouver Canucks. Traded to New Jersey in March 2000, he helped the Devils win the Stanley Cup that spring. He signed with Toronto in July 2001. (OPPOSITE) Mogilny, who scored just 20 seconds into his first NHL game, notched a remarkable 76 goals in 1992-93 for the Buffalo Sabres.

Larry Murphy

I VIVIDLY REMEMBER MY FIRST DAY PLAYING ORGANIZED hockey. I was 5, growing up in Scarborough, a suburb of Toronto. My dad saw that the local league was accepting younger boys because of a shortage of players. One Saturday morning, he took me downstairs—he hadn't mentioned anything to me before that—dressed me up in hockey equipment and took me to the outdoor rink. There were four teams in the league, and they had a draft of all the kids. Each boy would skate in a circle from the blue line to behind the net, and the coaches would pick players based on their skating ability.

I had been on skates only once before, so while I was excited to be there, I could hardly stand up. The ice was 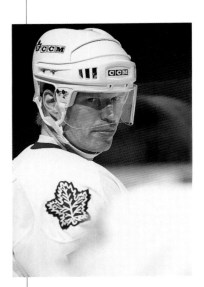 full of kids, and as each was picked, he was pulled out of the group. The numbers dwindled; the group grew smaller and smaller. Eventually it came down to me and one other boy. To avoid labeling one of us as the last pick, they assigned us to teams simultaneously.

In my first year playing, my coach wouldn't let me skate out past our own blue line, because I was on defense and would never be able to get back if I went too far up-ice. My feet got awfully cold on those outdoor rinks, but I looked forward to every game. That first winter, my dad built a rink in our backyard, and I'd be out there every day. By the next year, I could skate and even play forward. Soon I was playing on two teams. I couldn't get enough of it.

When I was 15, our team won the Canadian midget championship and went on a 17-day tour of Czechoslovakia and Russia, playing club teams that fed their elite teams. We sold our jeans for rubles, and I came back loaded up with fur hats and toy bears.

This was a different brand of hockey from anything we'd seen, and I've since come to love international competition, especially on the large ice surface. Wearing the Canadian sweater is like wearing the flag; us against the Soviets was like going to war. Fortunately it was just a hockey game, not a war, and everyone came home more or less in one piece.

Looking back on my own development as a player, I'd say that junior hockey with the Peterborough Petes had a huge impact. Up until that time, I was a middle-of-the-pack player. It was with the Petes that I made the most improvement. I feel fortunate to have played under top-quality coaches like Gary Green and Mike Keenan. We won the Memorial Cup there one year and came second the next, and I would not be in the position I am today without my two years in Peterborough.

The biggest difference in moving up to the NHL from junior is the pace of the game. But if you can keep up, everyone plays his position so well that it can be an easier game to play. I was drafted as fourth pick by Los Angeles, which was great for me, because the Kings were then making big changes on defense. I got the opportunity to play right away without being under the microscope—that's what rookies in Toronto or New York face. I started in the first game the Kings played in the Montreal Forum that season. Standing out on the ice while Roger Doucet sang the national anthem and looking at players such as Guy Lafleur and Larry Robinson had my legs shaking. I was concerned that I might fall down before the game even started.

Playing in the NHL has been wonderful, but it's not all roses. The first time getting traded is the toughest. It was a real confidence shaker for me, wondering why the team didn't want me anymore. I now realize that some trades are made just to shake up the team. Today, the hard part of a trade is uprooting family; the hockey part is easy, because it gives me an opportunity to further my career and to enjoy the benefits of being with a new club.

I'm thankful to have played on two championship teams in Pittsburgh. Anybody who plays in this league and doesn't get his hands on the Stanley Cup misses a lot. While I've never run a marathon, that's what it feels like to win the Cup. The ordeal, the history, the names on that Cup—you know you've really got something special in your hands, you can feel it. I've kept a lot of hockey memorabilia over the years, but the only things I have on display are the miniature replica Cups that the winners get and a picture of my kids with the Stanley Cup. That's how special the Cup is to me, and I'll always be working to get another.

Larry Murphy

*Larry Murphy moved into second place in NHL games played in 1999-2000, trailing only Gordie Howe. He won two more Cup rings with the Detroit Red Wings and sits in third place for career points for a defenseman. (**OPPOSITE**) Murphy, a three-time All-Star who played for the Leafs for two seasons, swings up-ice despite the efforts of St. Louis Blue Peter Zezel.*

Cam Neely

I GREW UP JUST OUTSIDE VANCOUVER, SO IT WAS EXCITING to be drafted by the Canucks in 1983. I had mixed emotions when I was traded to Boston three years later. I hadn't played a lot my last year in Vancouver, and I wondered if I was good enough for the NHL. But the Bruins wanted me, and I hoped that they would give me more of an opportunity to play.

For the most part, I went out to play physically. I liked to take the body, but I also loved to score. Because of my physical play, I was in a position to get more goals. Some have suggested I was born to be a Bruin, and they may be right. Boston fans expect a rugged style from most of their players; it's what the Bruins tradition is all about. Boston management knew what my game was, and they gave me a chance.

1988 was a great year. We beat the Canadiens out for the first time in years and went to the Stanley Cup finals. That period, until 1991 really, was the most exciting time I had in hockey. We had such a great group of guys who were successful on the ice and fun off the ice. We were a real team.

In a game against Pittsburgh in the 1991 conference finals, I got a bad charley horse. A condition developed where part of the muscle turned to bone, and I couldn't play until January of the following year. After only nine games back, I developed a problem with my knee. I needed what I thought was a minor operation, but when I came out of surgery, the doctor told me it could be a career-ending injury. That really threw me for a loop. I was 26 years old, but right then and there, I realized just how much I loved to play hockey. Until then, I had really taken it for granted.

I entered a long rehabilitation program. Immediately after surgery, I had to stay in a continuous-passive-motion machine for three weeks, 23 hours a day. I didn't miss a single minute. The machine slowly raised and lowered my leg thousands of times, which the doctors thought would help my recovery. I was prepared to do whatever was suggested in hope of a chance to play again.

The next season, I played only 13 games before I was down again. Despite all the time off, I had come back too soon. I went back to rehab. Fortunately, I had a great strengthening and conditioning coach in Mike Boyle. When my motivation was down, he picked me up. I give him a lot of credit for my success the following year.

I wasn't practicing and I missed almost every other game, but I played with one of the league's premier centers, Adam Oates. We also had Joe Juneau on our line for a time, another great playmaker. I felt very confident, and it was a fun, fun year. It made all the lonely days in rehab worth it. Fifty goals in a season is always great (and I did it three times), but getting number 50 in only my 44th game of the season *and* in the Boston Garden was special. The fans have always been supportive of me, but they really showed it that night.

When I tore ligaments in my right leg pretty badly with only 13 games left in the season, I was totally frustrated, disappointed and upset. I asked myself whether "someone" might be telling me that I shouldn't be playing. But after a couple of weeks, I calmed down, went back to the gym and started working out again.

I played half the following season, but my groin started to bother me. I treated it like a groin pull, but it nagged at me until a full medical workup revealed the problem as bone spurs in my hip socket. The doctors could only recommend rest. By the end of the following summer, my hip felt fantastic. I started to play, but it was painful again by November. I took time off when I needed to, but the pain got progressively worse until I couldn't skate. I took the rest of the year off, but even over the summer, it didn't get better. I went to see the doctor in late August, and he was really the one who made the decision that my hip would never allow me to play NHL hockey again.

As a player, you hope that you'll be the one to make the decision when your career is over, not the coach, not a doctor. But there it was. My career was successful and lasted as long as it did because of the way I played. On the nights I tried a different style, I was "reminded" by my coaches that I couldn't play that way and be effective. They were right, so I really have no regrets.

Even though I had a strong feeling over the summer of 1996 that I wasn't going to be able to play anymore, it wasn't until I told the public that I realized how difficult it was to say that I was no longer going to be a hockey player or a Boston Bruin. That was tough. I thought I was dealing with it pretty well until that day.

Cam Neely quickly became a fan favorite in Boston with his aggressive play and goal-scoring talent. (OPPOSITE) *Neely, seen here in his familiar spot in front of the net, had an injury-plagued career, and his perseverance was rewarded in 1994 when he received the Bill Masterton Trophy.*

Bernie Nicholls

LOST A BABY BOY WHEN HE WAS JUST SHY OF HIS FIRST birthday. Jack was born deaf and blind. Just after my trade from Edmonton to New Jersey in January 1993, he contracted spinal meningitis. I was traveling back and forth while he was in hospital, and naturally, I struggled on the ice. Such a difficult time puts life into perspective. But many people were writing me off as a hockey player, not understanding what I was going through.

I was in the last year of my contract and worried that I might not have a job the next season. I don't want sympathy in bad times; I want to be alone. But going to the rink, being with the guys, made it easier to forget the bad things that were happening. My family didn't have that luxury. They carried the burden all the time and were looking for help from me. But I was very angry. My wife had to deal with her own grief, hospital visits and looking after our other children by herself. I didn't want kids around and was really hard on them. I couldn't deal with the situation, and my temper started to scare me.

My children mean the world to me. They're life's greatest gift. I just had to deal with too much at once. I have a lot more patience now. It's too bad that people have to go through such times. Above all, I couldn't understand why my little boy had to suffer for so long before he died. It doesn't make sense.

I went to the Blackhawks the following year as a free agent. Chicago is a great organization, and if I could choose one guy to play with, it would be Chris Chelios. He is the nicest guy, so much fun and as good a leader as I've ever had. We went into every game knowing that we were going to win. That is such a great feeling. Early in my career, I had the opposite experience, when we couldn't win no matter who we played.

I was drafted by the Los Angeles Kings in 1980 but went back to junior hockey. I scored more than 150 points for Kingston and was very self-assured, but it still did me a world of good to go to New Haven for 55 games before joining the Kings. The adjustment to the NHL straight from junior is huge. I've seen kids lose their confidence when they don't get the opportunity to play a regular shift, let alone kill penalties or play the power play. Sometimes that confidence never comes back.

It's also imperative for a rookie to get under the wings of older players, veterans who understand that this kid is the future of the team. Rookies are generally too nervous to talk to the coach, and many teammates have a job at stake, so you aren't going to get along with everyone. Charlie Simmer and Dave Taylor, established stars, were there for me. I could talk to them, and they took care of me on and off the ice.

The Kings were at the bottom of the league for years until we got Wayne Gretzky. I was like Wayne's shadow every day in the 1988-89 season, and we had a lot of fun together. Great players bring out the best in everyone, and Wayne did that for me. I also give a lot of credit for my highest-ever point totals to our coach, Robbie Ftorek. I had always believed I was more of a playmaker than a goal scorer. But every time I passed the puck, Robbie was yelling at me, "You've got to shoot! You've got to shoot it!" If he hadn't got on my case so much, I wouldn't have scored 70 goals.

I had been in L.A. nine years and signed a new contract. I went to L.A. owner Bruce McNall for advice on a house I wanted to buy. He advised me to go ahead, telling me I'd be with the club for a long time to come, but my trade to the New York Rangers came three months later. I was incredibly disappointed. I've played long enough to understand that NHL hockey is a business, but hockey will always be a game to me. I hate the business side of sport. People give their hearts and souls for the organization. They play when they're hurt and shouldn't, but when management doesn't want you, you are gone. Loyalty is everything to me.

Life is so fragile that I try to enjoy every part of it. It might look as if I'm not serious at times, but you don't have to have a snarl on your face to be competitive. I've never had trouble with coaches or management about my attitude. I have a strong commitment to winning. When the puck is dropped, I go hard. But when the whistle blows, I relax. Geez, I've played with half the guys in the league now, so I'm always talking to them on the ice and having a ball. I'll have fun until I'm done.

Bernie Nicholls brought his experience and leadership skills back to California when he signed a contract with the San Jose Sharks in 1996. He retired midway through the 1998-99 season. (OPPOSITE) Nicholls, shown pulling away from Bruin All-Star Ray Bourque, set Los Angeles King records when he scored 70 goals and had an eight-point game during the 1988-89 season.

Bobby Orr

SEEING THE FAMOUS PHOTOGRAPH OF ME FLYING THROUGH the air after scoring the overtime goal to give the Boston Bruins the 1970 Stanley Cup brings back a flood of memories. I remember the thrill of getting that goal and the good fortune of being a part of that special team. When I was a boy, I watched in awe as the Stanley Cup was carried high over the shoulders of the winning team, and today, that photograph represents the excitement of realizing that dream. Commenting on the fact that the goal is shown so frequently, Glenn Hall—the great St. Louis goalie I scored on—teases me by asking, "Was that the only goal you ever scored?"

The 1970 Stanley Cup was our first as a team. At the time, the Boston Bruins were a fun-loving and intensely loyal group. In order to win, we recognized that each individual had to do his job. You knew what Phil Esposito, Johnny Bucyk and Gerry Cheevers were going to do, but if we didn't have players such as Don Awrey, Dallas Smith, Ricky Smith or Don Marcotte—names people don't remember right away—playing at the top of their game, we simply would not have been so successful.

I have strong childhood memories of playing ice hockey on the bay in Parry Sound. We played 10 or 12 on a team and skated from dusk to dawn, and if you didn't learn how to skate and handle the puck effectively, you were in big trouble. As I matured, it became apparent that professional hockey scouts, due to the great distance, did not venture to Parry Sound to scout the local talent. Fortunately for me, the Boston Bruins came to scout two players from Gananoque, a team we played in a sectional playoff game. The kids from Gananoque were always talented, but that season, the Bruins found me as well and later invited me to training camp for the new junior team they were forming in Oshawa.

I was 18 years old when I arrived at my first Boston Bruins training camp. I certainly did not expect to make the team and was concerned about how I would be received. After all, I had received a great deal of publicity the prior season with the Oshawa Generals and was being hailed as the savior of the Bruins franchise. As I looked around the locker room and even as I skated during those first few days, I realized that I was different from my teammates in many ways. I was young, and although there had been offensive-minded defensemen before, I played a style that players and coaches were not accustomed to seeing. I was not meant to sit on the blue line and would have suffered if the Bruins had ordered me to sit back. I was told to be careful, but I knew my teammates were there to cover for me. I quickly learned that I was surrounded by players, coaches and front-office personnel who were driven to succeed.

Once I started carrying the puck, there was a good chance I was going to keep going. Given the speed of the game and the reactions of defenders, a player must adjust quickly and instinctively decide what to do with the puck. Today, I think we try to structure our players and the game far too much. Certainly, players have to be aware of their responsibilities in the defensive zone, but so often, we try to make offensive players into defensive players. If a player is creative, let him exploit his talents.

The 1976 Canada Cup tournament, the only time I played for my country, remains one of my most cherished hockey memories. Many experts have stated that the tournament ended my career. That simply is not the case. I was experiencing pain prior to the tournament and felt that this was my final opportunity to represent my country. Based on this experience, I look ahead to the 1998 Olympics in Nagano with great anticipation. We will see the best players in the world, players who have won numerous Stanley Cups and had great personal success, and although many are millionaires, I am confident that playing for their country in the Olympics will be one of their proudest moments.

I took an extended period of time to announce my official retirement. I needed to be certain in my mind that I could no longer play. Following the Canada Cup,

I played a few games for the Chicago Blackhawks, took a year off to recuperate and played a few more games before it was readily apparent that my leg bothered me too much. My game was skating, and my knee would no longer hold up.

Being paid to play a game I loved was a dream. I took great pride in my ability to play the game effectively at both ends of the ice. Unfortunately, between the days on the bay in Parry Sound through "Bobby Orr Night" in 1979, the blocked shots, offensive rushes and other

physical demands caught up to me. I wish I could have played longer, but even though I was in the fray a lot and a reckless player at times—constantly trying to move through tight little spots—I wouldn't change that style for a second. As anyone who knows me would attest, I am always grateful for the opportunity to have played in the NHL and for all the wonderful people I continue to meet.

Bobby Orr

Bobby Orr rewrote much of the record book for defensemen in a legendary career tragically shortened by injury. (ABOVE) *Orr beats Bernie Parent with his patented combination of speed and magic with the puck.*

Bernie Parent

WHEN I WAS 12, I FILLED IN FOR THE REGULAR GOALIE ON A team my older brother was coaching. My parents could not afford skates for me, so I'd never played ice hockey before, although I always played goal in street-hockey games. I was excited to put all the equipment on for the first time. Unfortunately, I let in 21 goals, and my brother didn't invite me back. Despite that disaster, I enjoyed hockey so much that I decided to practice with skates on. A month later, I asked my brother for another chance. We won the game and I was on my way.

Jacques Plante was my idol when I was growing up in Montreal. His sister lived next door, and I got his autograph one day, which made me dream even more of being on a winning team like him and winning the Stanley Cup playoffs. I was so disappointed when I was traded from the Philadelphia Flyers to the Toronto Maple Leafs in 1971. I couldn't foresee that I was going to spend the next year and a half with my hero. That time together with Jacques Plante really turned my game around.

I had been playing in the NHL for a number of years, but I was still very raw when I joined the Leafs. It was so unusual to have a goaltending partner who was willing to share all he knew. I was in a growing stage in my mid-twenties, and Jacques was at the master stage, already in his forties. He taught me a "system" of goaltending, and I grew to understand the game far beyond just playing the angles. A goalie needs to know so many things, such as how to read the opposition—for example, noting whether the puck carrier is a right- or left-handed shot—and how to anticipate where the puck is going.

Going back to Philadelphia for the 1972-73 season with the Blazers of the WHA was a real blessing. I faced about 50 shots a game and was able to put everything I had learned from Jacques into practice. The next year, I rejoined the Flyers, a team on the brink of success. I had watched them when I was playing for the Blazers, and I knew they had what it took to win when they almost upset the Montreal Canadiens in the 1973 semifinals.

The NHL playoffs turned out to be nothing like what I had dreamed about as a kid. Reality is a different ball game. You can't just turn your performance up for the playoffs; it has to carry over from what you've been doing the past seven or eight months. You need discipline and hard work to win, and the system Jacques taught me served me well. He later came to be goaltending coach for the Flyers, and we always remained great friends.

Beating the New York Rangers in the 1974 semifinals means more to me now than winning my first Stanley Cup. When we beat the Rangers, I entered the Stanley Cup finals for the first time. I'll always remember that thrill. The excitement and pressure of playing the final series was so great that I went numb. I don't remember the good feelings around actually winning the Cup. I was strong technically, not just operating on

instinct, yet I was hardly aware of what we had just accomplished. I do remember the zone I was in when we won the final game against the Boston Bruins 1–0. Being in "the zone" is almost like being in the clouds. Everything flows easily around you. There's no nervousness or tightness, and you're able to play your absolute best.

The next year, we beat the Buffalo Sabres for our second Stanley Cup. I was able to savor that victory better. As we flew home to Philadelphia, I just sat back and enjoyed the feeling of winning. I seldom think back on the Conn Smythe trophies I won those years. I'm appreciative, but it's a trophy that can go to a number of players, depending on how fortune happens to fall. I value our team accomplishments most.

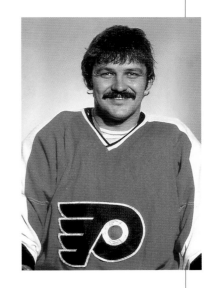

I knew right away that I was in serious trouble when I was injured in 1979. Jim Watson was tying up Don Maloney of the Rangers in front of the net, and they lost their balance. As I turned toward them, a stick flew up and slipped through the eyehole of my mask. There was a sympathetic reaction in my other eye, and I lay in the hospital completely blind for two weeks. The doctors were honest with me and told me they could do very little to restore my sight. Ninety-five percent of the damage could be repaired only by my body's ability to heal itself. I was fearful, but I prayed and hoped for the best, and one morning, I saw a little bit of light.

I knew I was on my way back, but hockey was the last thing on my mind. My vision slowly returned, but because of the nature of the injury, my hockey career was over. Yet hockey helped me build qualities—determination, self-confidence, perseverance—that have helped me set goals and function well in life off the ice. I'm grateful I was able to play the game.

Bernie Parent won the Conn Smythe Trophy for his stellar play in the Philadelphia Flyers' Stanley Cup victories in 1974 and 1975. (OPPOSITE) Parent, wearing what was then a state-of-the-art mask designed by his mentor, friend and former teammate Jacques Plante, suffered a career-ending eye injury in 1979.

Brad Park

I HAD BEEN THE CAPTAIN OF THE RANGERS FOR A COUPLE of years, and we were on a road trip in Oakland. I got called to coach Ron Stewart's room at 7:30 in the morning on November 7, 1975. You don't get called at that time to talk strategy. As soon as Ron opened the door, I said, "Where am I going?" Boston, our archrival, was the last place I would have chosen to go to. I used to get all kinds of hate mail and threatening letters from Boston. At one point, the FBI had to escort me on and off the ice there.

The trade hit me hard, and the first three or four hours were very emotional. Playing in New York had been such a good experience. We had a close team that  was a contender every year. I felt as if I had a Ranger crest tattooed on my heart. I wanted to finish my career there. It was such a buzz to play in Manhattan, the media capital of the world. The pressure to perform was good. Game in, game out, the fans made you rise to the occasion.

We had such an offensive team in New York that I was frequently able to join the rush. When I got to Boston, the Bruins didn't have a club that could play that game. Our coach, Don Cherry, asked me to sit back and concentrate on defense unless I was on the power play or we were behind late in the game. I became less "flashy," and many wondered if I had lost a step.

I was 27 and in my prime when I got to Boston. I was a student of the game, always trying to understand how things worked. I wanted to control the game. I knew where my players were going to be, I just had to be aware of where the other team was. I always looked past the first guy to see where the second and third forecheckers were. You have to know when you have time and when you don't. You have to suck the opponent in by holding the puck longer than most people feel comfortable doing. Once the opponent makes a commitment, you have to know where the out is. I tried not to pass too soon or too late. I always looked one way and passed the other and didn't always pass the puck directly, but put it off the boards or into a hole just before my teammate got there. The toughest thing in hockey was when you had to go back and get the puck with a 6-foot-2-inch so-and-so on your tail with bad intentions. You either panicked or developed patience. Fortunately, I had patience.

Playing for Team Canada in 1972 was the kind of experience that is rare in anyone's life. It was supposed to be fun, but I even got knocked out in training camp by a Dennis Hull slap shot. I moved out of the way, but Yvan Cournoyer got back and deflected it. It caught me on the cheek, and I was unconscious before I hit the ice. I woke up 14 hours later, not knowing where I was.

There were only three of us who played every game of the series. It was very disheartening to lose the first game to the Soviets. We flew back to Toronto the next day, and my wife, who was pregnant, called me to come home quickly. My first child was born early the next morning. That was so exciting, yet as the series continued, the emotional level of the whole team rose incredibly.

We felt great support, but we were so focused on the games that we didn't understand how we were affecting Canada. It was very gratifying to hear the stories later. We built a lot of friendships playing for Canada. When we got back to the NHL, the animosity was not the same. Before the 1972 series, I hated most of those guys. After the series, we'd talk on the ice.

It's hard to take an old warhorse and turn him into a cheerleader. The Bruins had started to phase me out in 1983, so I went to Detroit as a free agent. I didn't want to leave Boston, but Detroit offered me some financial security too. I loved to work with younger players. In some ways, helping my teammates improve served a selfish purpose. It made my job easier. Harry Howell had worked with me when I was a rookie with the Rangers. My dad admired Harry a great deal, and in negotiating my first contract with the Rangers, he got a verbal agreement that I would play with Harry. But Harry went out of his way to make me better, even knowing that someday I might take his job.

It was rewarding to receive the Bill Masterton Trophy —for dedication and perseverance—in 1984. I always loved to compete. There was great pleasure in going one-on-one and coming out on top. In business, it can be a year or two before you get results from your efforts. Hockey brings immediate satisfaction. You win *today*, and you compete again tomorrow.

Brad Park joined the Boston Bruins blue-line corps in the biggest trade of the 1970s. (OPPOSITE) *Park, team captain of the New York Rangers at the time of the trade with Boston, shows some of the skating and stickhandling skills that made him a seven-time All-Star.*

Gilbert Perreault

I WAS LUCKY THAT THE NHL ADDED TWO EXPANSION TEAMS —Buffalo and Vancouver—in 1970. I wanted to play in the NHL right away. That was the first year that the Montreal Canadiens didn't get to choose the top two picks from Quebec. Otherwise, I probably would have been selected by Montreal and spent time on the bench. At the time, it didn't make any difference to me if I was chosen by Buffalo or Vancouver. It was just chance— literally a spin of a roulette wheel—that sent me to Buffalo. I'm glad it worked out the way it did, though, because I had a great career with the Sabres.

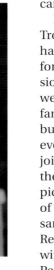

I won the Calder Trophy, and the team had a pretty good year for a first-year expansion team. We almost went to the playoffs. The fans were great, and the building was packed for every game. Rick Martin joined the Sabres as their first-round draft pick in the second year of the franchise. In the same year, Buffalo got Rene Robert in a trade with the Pittsburgh Penguins. We clicked right away, and our line was tagged "The French Connection." I was there to make the plays, Rick was there to score the goals, and Rene did a little bit of both. All three of us were good skaters. Our style was comparable to the European style, frequently crisscrossing with a lot of speed. Rick had a couple of 50-goal seasons, and Rene and I got about 40 two or three times; our line had many good years together. The Sabres have retired all three of our sweaters.

I will always remember my first goal and my 500th. Those goals stand in many ways as bookends on my career. I scored in my first NHL game. It was in Pittsburgh and we won 2–1. I deked one defenseman, and the goalie came out on me. I deked him and put the puck in with one hand on my stick. I got a great pass in the slot from Mike Foligno for number 500. I didn't wait—just hit the puck, and it was in. I had 512 career goals even though I was more a playmaker than a goal scorer. I just had a lot of chances to score.

Most players today drop back to the neutral zone, and the defensemen make a lot of plays at center ice. In my day, offensive players did a lot more skating and stickhandling, changing speed, deking two guys and making plays in the offensive zone. I loved the thrill of beating everyone on the ice, deking through the opposition. When I got the puck, I'd dare them to try to get it away from me. It's rare to see that today, save for a few players like Mark Messier or Jaromir Jagr. You see Wayne Gretzky and Mario Lemieux hanging around the red line. But they are so good offensively that they can play that way. There's also so much hooking and grabbing in the game now. It would be hard to play my game in the NHL today.

It took us only five years to get to the Stanley Cup finals. We built the team up year after year with young players, but we were still startled to make it that far so quickly. We took a lot of people by surprise, but then were favored to beat Philadelphia. The Flyers had a really tough team and beat us in six games. Bernie Parent was unbelievable the first two games in Philadelphia. They beat us 2–1 in the first game and 3–2 in the second.

After eight or nine years in Buffalo, I thought about asking for a trade. I wondered if a change would help my career. I was also curious to see how things were done elsewhere. Even the thought of going to the Canadiens crept into my head. I had grown up being a part of winning teams. I knew it would take a few years to get to that point with Buffalo, but from 1974 to 1979, we had an especially good chance. I can't forget that in 17 years, I went to the finals only once. We had a lot of good years in Buffalo, but every hockey player wants to win the Stanley Cup. You want to play for a good team, and you want to be happy. If you're not happy, it's tough to play NHL hockey. I had that experience when we weren't winning. There was a change in Sabres management in 1979 that revived the team, and my thoughts of moving disappeared. In the end, I was glad to finish with the Sabres.

I'm proud of scoring 500 goals, playing for the same team for 17 years and being elected to the Hockey Hall of Fame. My only regret is not winning the Cup, but what can I do about that? I always try to look on the bright side: I had a good career, I didn't get hurt very badly, I'm still healthy. I play in a lot of old-timer games, and it's still a big thrill to step on the ice. My love of the game has never changed. It's inside me.

Gilbert Perreault played his entire 17-season Hall of Fame career for the Buffalo Sabres. (OPPOSITE) Perreault, who scored more than 500 career goals, sweeps toward the net with his typical speed and flair.

Pierre Pilote

When I was a boy in Kenogami, Quebec, I used to watch the senior league hockey games. I didn't have any money, so I'd arrive very early and would hang around to avoid having to pay admission. The games were outdoors, so I'd just stand on a snowbank. By the end of the game, I'd be almost frozen through. When I got a chance to skate, there would be about 200 kids on the rink. Although I was always interested in sports, I didn't play organized hockey until I was 17.

Our family moved to Fort Erie, Ontario, when I was 13. Unfortunately, the roof of the Fort Erie rink had recently collapsed under a snowfall, so I didn't skate for three years. I did play baseball, and we won three Ontario championships. When the rink was finally rebuilt, I joined an industrial league team, and boy, that was tough hockey.

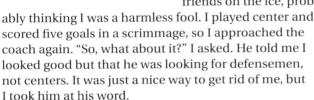

Toward the end of the year, the Niagara Falls Junior B team had to practice in Fort Erie. I was 17 and went to try out for the team. Niagara Falls was already in the playoffs, but that's how little I knew about hockey. Amazingly, the Niagara Falls coach let me and a couple of friends on the ice, probably thinking I was a harmless fool. I played center and scored five goals in a scrimmage, so I approached the coach again. "So, what about it?" I asked. He told me I looked good but that he was looking for defensemen, not centers. It was just a nice way to get rid of me, but I took him at his word.

I was invited back to the industrial league the next season, and I said I'd join only if they'd let me play defense. If there was one thing I could do, it was hit. I started to get some attention as a defenseman, and by the middle of the season, the Junior B teams were scouting me. I graduated to Junior A the next year.

I went to training camp for the St. Catharines Teepees so unpolished. Rudy Pilous, who later coached me on the Chicago Blackhawks, had to argue with the coach even to keep me in training camp. After three weeks, not only did the coach think I'd never make it as a hockey player, I was hurting a lot of his players. He quit over the issue, and Rudy became coach.

I really worked, and although I was still rough around the edges, I made the All-Star team in my second year of Junior A. I hit hard, averaging a "stretcher case" a game. If I didn't, I was upset. I then graduated to Buffalo of the American Hockey League. I had to learn so much, even basics, such as taking a pass and skating backwards. But I was hungry for learning and able to absorb a lot.

I credit the late Frank Eddolls, a former NHL player who was player/coach in Buffalo, for helping me most. I played left defense and so did Frank. He wanted to play with me—I was full of pep and vinegar and would do all the running around—so he talked me into moving over to the right side by telling me how Doug Harvey played right defense. Frank taught me a lot of things, but there was a specific moment on the ice with him when the puck was coming toward me and—out of the blue—I was hit with a realization: This game is easy. A veil was lifted from my eyes. I finally saw the game in simple terms. I even remembered plays I had watched from the snowbanks in Kenogami, and they made sense for the first time. I moved up to the Chicago Blackhawks the following season.

The NHL was a brand-new game, but I shot for the Norris Trophy and the All-Star team every year. That's why those awards are there. You have to work extra-hard to win them. I played a game of intimidation. You had to know who you could intimidate, who you couldn't and who you shouldn't try to intimidate. But before you could sort that out, you had to feel the water, and it took time. I tried to memorize all the moves of every guy in the league. That way, my reactions could be automatic, because if you think on the ice, you're too late. Some guys, such as Jean Beliveau and Gordie Howe, would show me something new every game, but most guys only had a few tricks.

I hit my peak when we won the Stanley Cup in 1961. I led the league in playoff points that year. Everything was coming easily; I hardly sweated. I was so psyched up but was completely relaxed at the same time. Two days after we won the Cup, I realized I'd better start having some fun!

I first met Denis Potvin at the opening of the new Hockey Hall of Fame in 1993. He asked me how big I had been when I played, because he was meeting me for the first time when I was a 60-year-old man. I told him that I had played at 180 pounds, not much more than my weight of today. He shook his head and said, "Pierre, you played a *lot* bigger than that." It was a great compliment.

Pierre Pilote won the Norris Trophy three consecutive years (1963-65) and was runner-up the year previous and the two years following. (**Opposite**) *A strong rushing defenseman, Pilote swings up-ice dogged by Montreal's Henri Richard while his teammates Elmer Vasko (4) and Glenn Hall look on.*

Denis Potvin

I WAS VERY FORTUNATE TO HAVE PLAYED FOR ONLY TWO teams in my hockey career. I have a tough time figuring out whether winning the Stanley Cup as a 27-year-old was as exciting as playing my first junior game at 13½.

I was sitting at home eating a big dinner with my mother and father, and my brother Jean was getting ready for his game with the Ottawa 67s. The phone rang and Jean answered it. I'll never forget the moment he looked around at me and said, "Bill Long is asking if you'd play for us tonight." The next few seconds were possibly the most exhilarating of my life. We played that night against the Niagara Falls Flyers, and to be honest, I don't know whether we won the game or not, but it changed my life. My picture was in the paper the next morning, and the caption read, "Denis Potvin—touted as the next Bobby Orr." From that point on, even my friends in school looked at me differently.

There were a couple of key elements to my game. I worked on passing the puck. That was as important to me as developing my shot and probably became my most valuable asset. I had a good wrist shot, and I was taught that passing and shooting were the same. Passes should be just as hard and accurate. But the most fun I had was hitting. I enjoyed the contact, and hockey provided me with a lot of opportunities—especially with so many of those guys playing with their heads down!

One hit really stands out. Billy Barber and I played together on Team Canada for the 1976 Canada Cup—one of the most exciting events I ever participated in and when I probably reached my highest performance level—but when Billy was playing junior for the Kitchener Rangers, one of his defensemen laid a suicidal pass to him up the middle. The hit I gave him right at center ice was probably the cleanest in terms of timing and execution that I ever made. It was like driving a 300-yard golf ball: The slower you swing, the better the execution, the better the contact, the more it feels as if you're not hitting anything. Billy still reminds me of that hit. His helmet ended up in the third row, but he was madder at the guy who made the pass than he was at me!

The confidence that I displayed was a security blanket. There were a lot of nights when I was scared to death that I wouldn't be able to do what I was supposed to. For a period of time, I couldn't read the newspaper because the stories were either too critical or the expectations were too high and made me nervous. I hated practicing, and I didn't like waiting between games. I was most happy when the puck was dropped and the game started. I only felt comfortable and confident that I'd make the right decisions when I was on the ice.

That lack of confidence always stayed with me to a degree. When I lost that fear of not performing well and started enjoying practice more than games, it became obvious to me that I wasn't going to play very well. I was healthy physically, and I scored 20 goals in my last year, so the tools were there to keep going, but that feeling I'd had throughout my career was gone, and I could never fake it. When it left me, I left the game.

Before I retired, I wondered, "What can motivate me? Is there another record, another Stanley Cup?" I thought the chance of winning another Norris was nil, it looked as if the 1988 New York Islanders were not going to get a lot better quickly and compete with the Oilers for the Cup, and I was 35 years old. I thought of playing somewhere else, but that didn't feel right. I looked for something new and different instead. Now I work as a broadcaster for the Florida Panthers.

Bob Nystrom's goal that won our first Cup was probably the most satisfying moment of my life. The amount of energy we had expended as a team and the fear we had of going back to Philadelphia for the seventh game were both immense. The elation of winning a team championship—I don't think there is anything better.

Our fourth Stanley Cup win is the most memorable, because I kept thinking about my dad sitting up in the stands. He was suffering from cancer, his hair had pretty much gone, and we knew he was going to leave us sometime soon. He said to me, "I know you've got it in you to win another Stanley Cup." At the end of the final game, I held the Cup over my head and turned around and looked up at him. I still frequently see a great picture that was taken at that time. My eyes are up, but I'm not looking at the Cup. I'm looking right past it and handing it to my dad. That felt like a gift to me too, that I was able to give something back for all the hours spent on the sidelines in cold rinks and taking me everywhere with the dream that some day I might be a professional hockey player.

Denis Potvin, three-time Norris Trophy winner, anchored the New York Islanders defense for four consecutive Stanley Cup victories. (**OPPOSITE**) *Hard-hitting Potvin controlled play at both ends of the ice, using his strength and great skating ability.*

Jean Ratelle

THERE WERE INDICATIONS THAT SOMETHING WAS GOING to happen with the Rangers early in the 1975-76 season, but like most players, I never thought it would affect me. We had five centers, and at age 35, I was the oldest. I had been with New York since 1960, so my trade to Boston came as something of a shock. I'm sure it was even more surprising for Phil Esposito to be traded to New York.

We had a great rivalry with Boston while I was a Ranger. There were some excellent games, particularly in the 1972 Stanley Cup finals. Some of my new teammates in Boston weren't too happy with the trade at first. Wayne Cashman was so angry, he destroyed a hotel room with a couple of friends when he heard the news. I couldn't blame him for being mad, because Boston had a close team that had some great success. Yet I was well

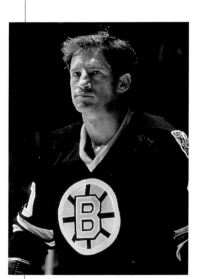

accepted by the players right away. There was never even a hint of animosity expressed toward me.

Going to a good team, an original-six club, and knowing that the Bruins wanted me, made the trade easier to accept. As it turned out, it was a great move for me and my family, because I was able to play six more years in Boston. If Bobby Orr hadn't been injured, we probably would have also won a Stanley Cup or two. Unfortunately, I played only 10 games with Bobby. I sat beside him in the dressing room, and he assisted on my first goal with the Bruins. He's still the best ever, as far as I'm concerned.

A lot of people saw my style as similar to Jean Beliveau's. He was one of my heroes, but everyone is an individual. I don't think you can really copy anyone even if you try. You might pick up a little mannerism when you're a kid, but I didn't do that. My style evolved but never really changed. You have to play your strength, and my game was always to make plays and produce points.

I took a lot of abuse, a lot of hits, when I first came up, even though, at 6-foot-1, I was one of the bigger guys back then. After a while, people respected me for who I was and how I played the game. I worked hard. Not to suggest that I didn't get hit after that, but I saw them coming!

The New York Rangers "GAG" line (for goal-a-game) that I centered between Rod Gilbert and Vic Hadfield played together for 9 or 10 years, possibly the longest any line stayed together in the history of the NHL. Rod and Vic were great players, so it was fun, and we had a lot of success together. I had played with Rod since we were 12-year-old school friends. We complemented each other very well. Rod was a great playmaker who could also score. We played together for so many years that we knew what the other was going to do all the time. It was so easy to play with him. We were predictable in a sense, but with Vic out there too, we always had options when the defense thought they had us figured out. Vic was a top corner-man, a tough left-winger who could score. Before I broke my ankle with 16 games to play in the 1971-72 season, I had 46 goals, Vic had 44, and Rod had 41. We all could have had 50-goal seasons. Of course, to have a year like that, everything had to be clicking without any slumps. The injury was very disappointing; it would have been interesting to see what might have happened. Vic still managed to get his 50 goals, but Rod got hurt near the end and fell short too.

In the NHL, my team worked hard every year and in every playoff series, but I never won the Stanley Cup. For that reason, I can't look back and say that any one year was really satisfying. In the end, we lost.

The Lester Pearson Trophy, awarded to me by the league's players, means the most to me now. The trophy was presented to me in Toronto by Lester Pearson himself, in the last year of his life. That makes it a little more memorable, especially since he presented it at center

ice in Maple Leaf Gardens before the second game of the 1972 Canada-Russia hockey series. That series was one of the biggest surprises in my career.

Our scouting was way off! It was supposed to be easy. The Russians weren't that big, but they were incredibly strong and quick. That was such a sensational series, the most emotional I ever played in, because for the first time, we weren't playing for our team but for our country. We left Canada for the final four games of the series in Russia behind the eight-ball, having won one, tied one and lost two. Those final four games in Russia were incredibly draining, but the rest is history. Playing for Team Canada was great because we won.

Jean Ratelle, a two-time Lady Byng recipient, brought his elegant style to the Boston Bruins in 1975. (ABOVE) *Ratelle uses his size and strength to get an edge over Bob Hess of the St. Louis Blues.*

Henri Richard

HOCKEY WAS ALWAYS A DREAM FOR ME. MY BROTHER PLAYED for the Montreal Canadiens when I was 6 years old. All I wanted to do was play for the Canadiens, with my brother as inspiration. I never missed a game at the Forum until I was 14 years old. I was positive that I, too, was going to play for the team, although I never imagined playing with Maurice. Our age difference was 15 years. I hardly knew him; he married when I was a boy, and then he was so busy with hockey. He was more like an uncle than a brother. It's funny, but Maurice never talked to me about hockey, even when we were teammates. We did our talking on the ice.

Maurice and I had five years on the same team, which was quite a thrill. Mr. Selke asked Maurice to come with me to the office when I signed my first contract. I spoke no English at the time. He asked Maurice if I was good enough to play for the Canadiens. "Definitely good enough," responded Maurice, as he turned and left. In my first game, Bernie Geoffrion got hurt, and they put me on right wing with Jean Beliveau and Bert Olmstead. A few weeks later, I started to play between Maurice and Dickie Moore. We had quite a team and won the Stanley Cup in my first five years. We almost got bored winning. It was better to win after a loss, much more enjoyable.

There must have been a lot of pressure growing up, but I didn't feel it. I always heard stories that I was too small, not tough enough, but I wanted to show everyone that I was good enough to play in the NHL. I wanted it so much. Pressure is an excuse not to perform. You should play better if there's pressure. I was nervous before games, but I don't think that is the same as pressure. I wasn't surprised to make the team, although I wasn't cocky about it. I was the type of player who did my job and whatever happened happened. I played as best I could and expected to have success. Many claimed I got on the team because of Maurice, but I went on to play for 15 years after he retired.

My first goal came after a few games. I got a pretty good shot off and scored on Gump Worsley of the New York Rangers. I didn't have a strong shot as a rule, but I saw that one go in. I was elated and looking for the puck, but I was too shy to go pick it up. Someone else retrieved it for me.

In 1966, I scored an overtime goal against Detroit for the Cup winner. I was rushing to the net and yelled to Dave Balon for the puck. Someone tripped me, and I never even saw the puck come. I went sliding just past the net, and the puck somehow went in off me. Even on the films, no one could see the puck, and though Detroit goalie Roger Crozier claimed I pushed it in with my arm, it was a good goal. If Crozier had stayed on his post, the puck would never have gone in. I'll always remember that goal, but I think the Cup we won in 1971 was the sweetest. I had had a few arguments with coach Al McNeil but went on to score the tying and winning goals in the seventh game. I won 11 Cups in total, a

record that may never be broken. The structure of the league, with the draft and free agency, prevents the creation of dynasties like the one we had in Montreal.

Team captain Jean Beliveau retired in 1971. The oldest player usually got the "C," and at the time, it seemed a normal transition to be voted captain. I never said much to the players, but I had always tried to lead by example. Now that my playing days are over, I see the tradition, the honor, more clearly.

In all my years with the Canadiens, I never played a shift on the power play. With the great teams we had, I couldn't get on that line. I never played as a penalty killer either. That made my job a little easier in ways, although sometimes I wished I could have had a chance to score a few goals on the power play. I might have had that

chance on another team, and though I was tempted by a large contract offer from Houston of the WHA, I'm thankful to have finished as a Montreal Canadien.

I saw the younger guys coming on and retired when I knew I wouldn't play regularly any more. After my retirement, the team went on to win four more Cups in a row. I had declined a contract offer from Montreal for those years. I opened a tavern, and the guys would come for a beer and tease me with, "We really missed you out there, Henri." But I've no regrets.

Henri Richard, younger brother of Maurice and standing only 5 feet 7 inches, was known as "The Pocket Rocket." (OPPOSITE) Richard remained one of the league's more graceful skaters in his 20 years as a Montreal Canadien. He scored a number of important goals in playoff competition and won a record 11 Stanley Cups.

Maurice Richard

I NEVER ACTUALLY SAW THE MONTREAL CANADIENS PLAY until I joined the team in 1942. I had suffered a broken leg playing hockey, so I didn't pass my army examination. It was an easier time to break into the league, with so many away with World War II, and I was fortunate to play with great hockey players like Elmer Lach and Toe Blake. They were excellent at going into the corner and giving me good passes in front of the net, and I scored a lot of goals right from the start. I spoke no English, and they spoke no French, but we knew how to play together in a very natural way.

In our day, every goalie knew the opposing players and had a good idea what most would try to do. I tried to be unpredictable, to keep the goalie guessing when I was in front of the net. I tried all kinds of plays, all kinds of tricks, to score. I'd stay after practice to try different

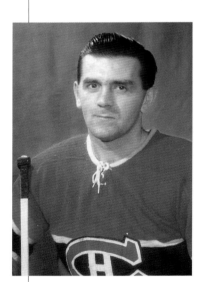

things, to use a surprise move every time I got near the net. In a game, though, everything would happen so quickly that I wouldn't really know what I was going to do until I did it. Most of the time, above all, I just tried to hit the net.

I got my nickname in my second year with the Canadiens. Our line scored a lot of goals in practice, and some teammates started to call me Rocket. The press picked up on it. In truth, I wasn't that fast, not really a good skater. Dick Irvin moved me to right wing from left, because I could not turn to the right very well. I could get around the defense more easily from the right side, and I also had a better angle to shoot from on my forehand. By really working on my backhand shot in practice, in a short while, I could shoot almost as well from that position too.

I had guys covering me pretty closely for 14 or 15 years. No one ever played a weak line against us. We always faced Boston's Kraut Line—Milt Schmidt, Woody Dumart, Bobby Bauer—and Lindsay, Howe and Delvecchio from Detroit. Playing against the top lines on the other teams meant that we had to work hard all the time. A lot of hockey players today seem to think that success will come easily. Hard work every game made me a better hockey player. I wanted to score goals and win all the time; that's all I had on my mind from the time I was a boy of 7 or 8.

If I got a dirty check from someone, I'd get pretty mad and try to get hold of him right away. I didn't want to

wait until the next game. I defended myself too quickly, and sometimes I was right and sometimes I was wrong. Most of my penalties were for retaliation—the referee always sees the second guy who does something illegal.

I was lucky to be on eight Stanley Cup winners, including five with my brother Henri and Dickie Moore as linemates in my last years with Montreal. They did the same for me as Elmer and Toe had. They were hard diggers in the corners and made great passes. Even when Henri went around the defense, he was looking for me. Dickie was the same. As a boy, Henri, 15 years my junior, had always come with my parents to see me play. I watched him from the time he was 6 or 7. He was always the best player on the ice, and I knew he'd eventually make it to the NHL.

At first, Toronto fans would boo me whenever I scored. One of my luckiest nights was the game I scored five goals against Toronto in 1944. I had seven or eight shots on goal, and five went in. Other nights, I could have 11, 12 shots on net and maybe score once. That's the way it goes in hockey. But after my first three years, the people in Toronto would give me a good hand for a goal, even when it was a winner. Toronto was a great town to play hockey in. If I'd been traded, I would have loved to have gone there. Conn Smythe once had a picture made up of me in a Maple Leaf uniform, but it was just a publicity stunt.

I was glad to be able to retire as a Canadien and grate-

ful that many thought I could have still scored goals into the 1960s. Most of the records I set lasted 20 or 25 years but have been surpassed more recently. A few from the playoffs still stand, and I'm thankful to be remembered by hockey fans. I really enjoyed the acknowledgment I received in 1996 during the ceremonies for the closing of the Forum and the opening of the new arena. The

people kept clapping and yelling, and I wished they would stop. I didn't know what to do, but it felt very good. I tried to quiet them, but it was no use. I never thought that something like that could happen to a hockey player.

Maurice Richard

Maurice Richard captured the hearts of Montreal fans forever. His death in 2000 triggered a huge outpouring of public grief and a nationally televised state funeral. (ABOVE) "The Rocket," captain of "Les Canadiens" for his final four seasons, rushes with his typical intensity to beat Maple Leaf Johnny Bower to the puck.

Luc Robitaille

BEING IN THE NHL IS SOMETHING I HAVE NEVER TAKEN for granted. My dream as a rookie was just to make the team. I was a ninth-round draft choice, so I was in heaven once I made the NHL. The draft was held in my hometown of Montreal. It was 1984, the year Mario Lemieux was chosen first by Pittsburgh, and the draft seemed to take forever. It started at one in the afternoon, and I wasn't picked until about seven o'clock that evening. I was waiting anxiously, hoping my name would be called, through every round. When I was

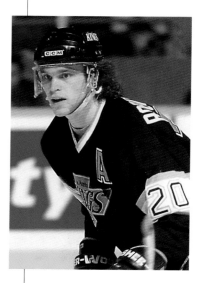

announced as the 171st pick, all I could think was, "I've got a chance, I've got a chance! They *have* to look at me!" So many of my friends never got that opportunity.

When I got to Los Angeles, it was totally different from anything I had ever seen in my life. Hockey was about the sixth most popular sport. Once I was used to being in the big leagues, the game became all about winning, but at first, just to be there was the most incredible thing for me. Some of my best memories are from my years in Los Angeles. I still have good friends there.

It's fun to be playing with Wayne Gretzky again. He's such a great player. I idolized him growing up. Funnily enough, when I played my last year of junior for Hull in the Quebec Major Junior League, he owned the team! I played with Wayne for six years in Los Angeles, and now we're both New York Rangers.

You have to work hard, but you also have to work in a smart way. Sometimes you can try to do too much. I'm not the kind of player who takes shots from the blue line. I have to get open in spots where I can shoot and score. I skate around and try to find openings, playing more around the crease instead of being caught in the corner or behind the net. Wayne is such a good playmaker that he can feather a pass through two or three guys. If I get near the crease and keep moving to get open, he's going to find me.

Going back to your hometown is always special, but playing in the old Montreal Forum put me in touch with cherished memories from childhood. We didn't have a lot of money when I was growing up, but we did get to a few Canadiens games. About once a year, someone would offer us tickets, and though I never saw any team except the cellar-dwelling Capitals or Canucks and our seats were way up high, it was always exciting. My family gets much better seats now!

I'll enjoy sitting down with my kids or grandkids when I retire and talking about winning the Calder Trophy and making the All-Star team, but there's no time for reflecting on any accomplishments right now. It doesn't really matter what I did in the past; I've always got a game tomorrow. Like everyone who hasn't done it yet, I'm really looking forward to seeing what it's like to hold the Stanley Cup. I won a Canada Cup and a World Championship, so I know, and love, the feeling of winning.

Every goal feels good, but if I had to pick one that's meant the most to me, it was the last goal I scored in the 1994 World Championships. Canada hadn't won that tournament in 33 years. In a more personal way, every one of the 20 guys on that team was there because of a disappointing NHL season, out of the play-offs. Here was a chance to turn a bad year into a good one. We got to the finals and were up against Finland, led by my L.A. teammate Jari Kurri. We were tied 1–1 at the end of the game, but instead of overtime, a shoot-out decided the outcome.

Each team got five attempts by five different shooters. I scored and so did Joe Sakic, but we were still only tied 2–2 after the first round of shots. We moved to a sudden-death round, and I was picked to go again. I'd gone low to the stick side on my first try, so I faked the same move the second time, went to the backhand and scored. Our goalie, Bill Ranford, stopped Finland, and we won the gold medal. It was fantastic to be part of that.

The New York Rangers traded Luc Robitaille back to Los Angeles in August 1997. The move revitalized Robitaille's career, and he soon regained his status among the NHL's elite scorers. He signed with Detroit in July 2001. (OPPOSITE) Robitaille, rookie of the year in 1987, scored more than 40 goals in each of his first eight seasons with the Kings.

Jeremy Roenick

I LOVED PREP-SCHOOL HOCKEY. NEW ENGLAND IS A HOCKEY hotbed, and that's where the best high school-age players go. I got to live at home in Boston with my family, which I think is important when you're young. It was so good to get a good education in a college atmosphere while playing a high level of hockey on a championship team. We beat Brian Leetch's number one-ranked team from Connecticut (they had been undefeated all year) for the New England championship, one of the biggest high school tournaments in the country. That kind of experience is a great building block, teaching leadership and what it takes to win.

I was scouted by a number of clubs, and the Hull Olympics gambled by drafting me in case I decided to go to Canada to play junior hockey. Mike Keenan did them a favor by sending me to play for them. He was coaching the Chicago Blackhawks, who had selected me in the 1988 NHL entry draft. I went to the Blackhawk training camp and even played three NHL games, but Mike thought some junior experience was what I needed. I had a great jump-start to junior from playing with NHL players, had some success with Hull and was back to the NHL to stay before the season was out.

Mike Keenan instilled strong physical play into my game. He was a stickler for finishing checks and making the bone-jarring hit, believing that playing as physically as possible added many dimensions to a game. When I first arrived, I immediately had it drilled into me that if I didn't play that way, I wouldn't make the team. I'm a quick learner, and though hitting hard and often was new to me, I wanted to play. It's become an integral part of my game.

I became a popular player in Chicago when the fans saw that I was willing to play aggressive hockey. I energized the crowd and my team with my physical game as much as by making a nice pass or scoring a goal. Hearing the crowd cheer a big hit gave me a big enough rush to keep me going. The big hits *look* more painful than they are, and I've been lucky enough to avoid injuring myself. I have been hurt by hits a few times, but that's come from being on the receiving end.

The best part of playing for an original-six team is its popularity around the league. I'd look into the crowd and see almost as many Blackhawk jerseys as our opponent's, no matter what rink we were in. But the Chicago fans were number one. They light up my face and my thoughts when I talk about Chicago. They support the team with their rowdiness and the aura that they create. Playing in the old Chicago Stadium was without a doubt the site of the biggest thrills I have had playing hockey.

Playing in my first All-Star game was one of the best times. The Gulf War had begun two days before. There was talk of canceling the game, but the fans showed the world their character with thousands of flags. Throughout the game, flags were waving and signs bobbing up in the crowd reading that the Gulf War soldiers were the real All-Stars. It was more of a patriotic day than a spectacle for the NHL All-Stars, and I was proud to be part of it.

I also scored my fiftieth goal in Chicago Stadium, but I hit that milestone for the first time the previous season in the Boston Garden. Most of my family were there to celebrate with me when I banked a fluke shot off Ray Bourque's butt that slipped between Andy Moog's legs into the net. Both times, the setting couldn't have been better for number 50.

Being in the locker room with the guys as part of a team family is what I love most about the game. That atmosphere has been important to me on all of the teams I've played for. The companionship of friends— being with each other, playing for each other, winning with each other—is a great feeling.

A lot of factors came into my decision to leave the Blackhawks, good and bad. In the final analysis, I just had to move on to a different part of my life. You're paid for your talents, but everyone in the league has had to work for so many years to get to this level. The average career lasts only five or six years, so you have to prepare for the future and look after yourself and your family.

We have a big job to do in Phoenix, getting people introduced to hockey and hooked on it. Phoenix is primarily a basketball and football city, but it will come to love hockey. This sport takes a tremendous amount of ability and an array of skills. Unlike other athletes, hockey players have had to learn an entirely new mode of transportation, skating on a millimeter of a blade at terrific speeds with frequent physical contact. There's a lot of excitement in Phoenix already, and it'll only get better when a fuller appreciation of the game comes and the hockey knowledge increases.

Jeremy Roenick brought his rugged brand of hockey to Phoenix in 1996. He was traded to Philadelphia in June 2001. (OPPOSITE) Roenick gets to the net frequently and scored 50 or more goals in two different seasons during his years as a Chicago Blackhawk.

Patrick Roy

When I was a boy, I watched Hockey Night in Canada every Saturday night while using pillows as pads to play hockey in the hall of my parents' house. I became a goaltender because I was really attracted to the goalie pads I saw on TV. I had no particular idol until I got to the peewee and bantam age groups. I first loved to watch Rogie Vachon, but Daniel Bouchard of the Quebec Nordiques quickly became my favorite. I grew up in Quebec City and followed the Nordiques closely. I was never a fan of their archrival, the Montreal Canadiens, until I was drafted by them in 1984.

Montreal always seems to have been able to draft great goaltenders. I look back at Georges Vezina, Bill Durnan, Jacques Plante, Rogie Vachon, Tony Esposito and Ken Dryden. They're all legends of the game now, and though other great goalies have played for Montreal, those men had their first starts in this league with the Montreal Canadiens. I was aware that it was quite remarkable to win the Stanley Cup and the Conn Smythe Trophy as a rookie, but I knew I couldn't stop there. Some drew obvious comparisons between my initial success and that of Ken Dryden. I had a lot of respect for Ken, a great goaltender, not for what he did as a rookie but for his consistency. I'd played just one season, and I was only 20 years old. I'd have to keep working.

I am an emotional person, and I bring my emotions to the game. I simply let it go. I find it easy to get involved in games, to get pumped up, because I love to compete. Competition helps me to perform. I'll do everything possible to get a victory.

My preparations for a game are primarily mental. I really like to look back on goals I gave up against that team in past games. In reviewing the goal, I see that I did this or that and try to understand what I could have done to stop the puck. If there is a question about my positioning or how I reacted, I imagine the situation changed and I'm making the save. In my visualizations, I'm focusing mostly on myself and what I'm going to do, but sometimes, I focus on specific players on the other team. I visualize the opponent and try to foresee situations that might arise. Players like Mario Lemieux and Wayne Gretzky usually have an impact on the game, so I'll see myself facing them and making some saves. Just before the game, I like to look at the net and imagine the goalposts shrinking, the net grown smaller. Hockey is a physical sport, but the mental and emotional sides of the game are important too.

One of my close friends, Bob Sauve, put a little note on the back of my blocker when I first came to play in Colorado. It said: "Be a Warrior." Bob played net for 12 years in the NHL, so he knows what it's like. In the tough times, I look at that advice. You have to be known as a fighter in the NHL. I have a lot of confidence in myself, but there's so much talent in the league that you have to be at your best at all times. I have to keep hungry, renew my commitment to stay tough, in order to play as well as I can.

There was a lot of pride at stake when I left the Canadiens partway through the 1995-96 season. Although I had many great years in Montreal, it was honor that caused me to leave in the end. But the trade that brought me to the Colorado Avalanche was only a function of their desire for the Stanley Cup. That was clear right off the bat. I wanted to show the Avalanche that they'd made a good deal. I hope the people in Montreal feel they also got what they wanted.

I was proud to help Colorado win the Stanley Cup that year. It was a great team effort. Sure, the goalie has to make the save, but he needs the defensemen to be sharp and the forwards to do their jobs. Hockey is a team game. The guys in Colorado were great about easing my transition from Montreal. I just tried to fit in, not to change the routine of the other guys but to adjust to their club. I would say that we were successful.

A lot of people have been really helpful to me. My family supported me every step of the way, and now my wife and kids—who are just starting to grasp what I do—help me to keep going. I've won a number of individual awards in my career, but that's not really what hockey is all about for me. My career objective is not to accomplish certain things but to *have* a career. I don't just want to be able to look back at two or three good seasons. I want to look back at every year with pride. Then, at the end, I'll be able to say: "That was a great career."

Colorado Avalanche Patrick Roy posted his 448th victory in 2000-01, passing Terry Sawchuk for the most wins by an NHL goaltender. Roy's fierce competitiveness earned him his third Conn Smythe Trophy and his fourth Stanley Cup ring in June 2001. (Opposite) *In 1986, as a rookie, and in 1993, "Saint Patrick" won both the Smythe and the Cup playing for the Montreal Canadiens.*

Joe Sakic

IN THE 1996 PLAYOFFS, I HAD 18 GOALS, SIX OF THEM GAME-winners, including two in overtime. I felt great doing my part to help the team. I shot the puck more than I do during the regular season, but they were really going into the net for me. It was the perfect time to be on a hot streak. The team was rolling, although every series had its key moments that made for a tough ride. I realized that Stanley Cup winners really pay a price. I got a lot of warm congratulations later in the summer from my 1996 Team Canada teammates, most of whom were past Stanley Cup champions.

It's hard to find words to describe winning the Stanley Cup. It's something I first dreamed of when I was 6 years old. As captain, I briefly lifted the Cup over my head, kissed it and passed it to my teammates. It wasn't so much lifting the Cup but winning the championship and being number one that felt so great. Winning the Conn Smythe was definitely a big bonus. It's an honor. When I look at the names on that trophy, I see that it's an elite group.

It was a short summer because of the World Cup tournament, but I really enjoyed myself. I live in Denver year-round now, so I never really lost the buzz of winning the Stanley Cup until I joined the Canadian training camp for the World Cup. The Avalanche celebrated as a team for a few days, I took about 10 days off, and then I began training again. You have to take care of your body.

At first, Denver was quite a contrast to Quebec, where everyone recognized us wherever we went. That changed over the course of the season. The city embraced us as their own. I know that the disappointment in Quebec over our leaving was magnified when we won the Stanley Cup in Colorado, but if we had stayed in Quebec, we wouldn't have had the same team. Montreal would not have traded Patrick Roy to their Quebec rival.

It was easy to keep my spirits up in my first couple of years in Quebec, despite the team's poor record. I don't like to lose, but I was just happy to be in the NHL. I love to play the game, and I love to play in front of big crowds. I worked hard and had pretty good point totals. But the defeats took their toll as the years went on. We kept getting a little bit better, but it took a long time.

Everything really turned around with the Eric Lindros trade. We got great players from the Philadelphia Flyers and became a good team. Our morale and confidence picked up right away. The dominant feeling of frustration turned to anticipation. We expected to win.

I was really glad to hit the 50-goal-season milestone late in the 1995-96 season. I'd had 48-goal seasons a couple of times, so it was nice to finally reach 50. It felt as if I had achieved something, but it was more than a personal accomplishment. It helped the team. We get along well, which contributes to our success. When you like your teammates, you play for one another, you give a little extra. We're dedicated but we have a lot of laughs.

Winning the gold medal in the 1988 World Junior Championship was unbelievable. That was the first time I got to play for my country. It was such a good feeling to win a gold medal, to hear the Canadian national anthem played in Russia. It was hard to believe it was happening. So many feelings rushed through me.

I was part of the 1994 World Championship team, but it wasn't the same at the start. I went with a bitter feeling, because it's the guys who don't make the Stanley Cup playoffs who have to play. Once we got going, though, a lot of excitement built up in Canada because we hadn't won that tournament in so many years. We pulled together as a team and had a great finish to a poor year.

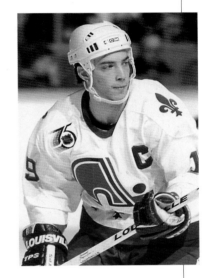

I really enjoyed playing for Canada in the 1996 World Cup. You see the different things that players do. That's the best part. You play with so many stars, and each has a skill that he does best. Especially in practice, you learn different guys' work habits and see what they do to help better themselves as players.

I learned a lot and my confidence was raised. Still, I had to pick up my game immediately. The competition in the tournament was outstanding. The NHL felt a lot slower once I was back with Colorado for exhibition games. Every World Cup game was like a Stanley Cup final; the intensity was incredible. Losing to the Americans was a disappointment, but I'm still thankful for the experience. If you can't get better playing with Team Canada, you have a problem.

Joe Sakic moved into the NHL's upper echelon of scorers while playing for the Quebec Nordiques. (OPPOSITE) Sakic won the Conn Smythe Trophy and a Stanley Cup in 1996 with the Colorado Avalanche, but his 2000-01 season went even better. Sakic made the First All-Star team and won the Hart and Byng trophies, the Pearson Award and a second Stanley Cup ring.

Derek Sanderson

I REMEMBER PLAYING MY FIRST EXHIBITION GAME AGAINST Gordie Howe. My dad was there, and he told me, "Don't take any crap from Howe." Just before the opening face-off, I skated over to Gordie, who was leaning on his stick. I told him that if he messed with me, I'd hurt him. The puck was dropped, it was in my feet, and the next thing I knew, I was getting smelling salts on the bench. I didn't know what happened until John McKenzie, sitting beside me, said, "Number nine, kid. Number nine," and patted his elbow. I couldn't believe it.

My head cleared, and the next shift, I skated up to Gordie and said, "I guess you didn't hear me, old man. I'm gonna get you." Gordie didn't say a word, but the puck was dropped, and again, boom, I'm out cold. I was looking for him, and I still didn't see how he did it! I never did scare him, and we've laughed about it since retiring, but we went at it every game.

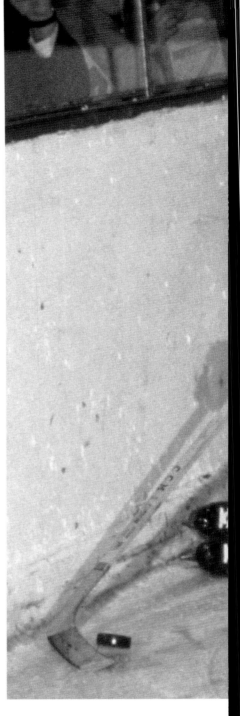

My dad was my hero and my best teacher, but playing five years of junior hockey for Hap Emms and Bill Long was a blessing for me. Bill was a very caring man and had a steadying influence. Hap taught me discipline and the importance of teamwork. I once got a hat trick in a big game and was still completely pumped up and showing off in practice the next day. Hap blew the whistle and called the team together at center ice. He told the team how lucky they were to play with me. "Derek is so good," he said, "that he doesn't need his teammates. He's going to revolutionize what used to be a team game." He made me scrimmage alone against a full lineup. My tongue was hanging out after two shifts, and the message came through loud and clear.

I won the Rookie of the Year award with the Bruins, but when I went to training camp for my second season, our coach, Harry Sinden, approached me with what many players would have seen as a demotion. Recognizing that I had some offensive skills, he told me my real strength was on defense. He asked me to give up my power-play time, center the third line and kill penalties with Ed Westfall. I quickly agreed to do whatever was best for the team, and Ed and I became very successful. Of course, we did have Bobby Orr on the ice with us too.

My dad taught me the sweep check when I was a boy. It was a disruptive forechecking technique that helped kill a lot of penalties and got me quite a few points. All it took was a little courage to get my face down near some skates. The opponent would think I was going to hit him and leave the puck unguarded for a moment. I'd quickly drop to one knee and hook the puck onto my stick.

My dad also had me work on face-offs by watching Teeder Kennedy and Red Kelly take the draw on *Hockey Night in Canada*. I tried never to show an opponent the same move twice. I kept track of wins and losses, and if a guy beat me a couple of times, I'd have Eddie Westfall take the draw. I could see what a guy was doing better from the wing. Once I understood his technique, I owned him. If I won too many in a row, I figured the other guy would be studying me too, so I'd intentionally lose some. I'd tell my wingers that I was going to let the opposing center pull the puck back, so they could anticipate it and we'd still get possession of the puck.

A teammate offered me a beer at my rookie training camp. I declined, telling him I didn't drink. He laughed and said I'd never be able to handle the pressure if I didn't drink, and I wanted to belong, so I said okay. Phil Esposito was there and he stepped in. "Derek, if you don't drink, don't start. You make your own pressure in this league, and alcohol won't help." So I had a choice, but I chose to learn to drink.

Hockey eventually started to get in the way of my social life, and I lost some of my competitiveness. I have a lot of respect for athletes who get big money and live sensible lives. It takes a lot of character to keep the same work ethic. I lived hard and paid the price. Bobby Orr, Phil Esposito, Ken Harrellson of the Boston Red Sox and

Joe Namath all tried to help me, but I wouldn't listen. I'm lucky to have come out the other side.

I wrote a great book in 1983, but it didn't have an ending then. I had just got sober, but since then, I've been to more than 1,200 schools to raise awareness about alcohol. Now I'm a director of an institution that gives financial advice to many current NHL players, and I work as a broadcaster for Boston Bruins games.

Being accepted, just making it to the NHL and be-coming a Boston Bruin, left the biggest impression on me. All the work and the sweat and the bleeding finally made sense. Winning the Stanley Cup was great, but the best part was getting there. It wasn't the victory, it was doing battle.

Derek Sanderson was an important member of Boston's Stanley Cup victories in 1970 and 1972. (ABOVE) Sanderson, a defensive specialist, forechecks successfully, and Maple Leaf Mike Pelyk loses control of the puck behind the net.

Denis Savard

I WENT TO THE MONTREAL JUNIOR CANADIENS' TRAINING camp with my two best friends. Amazingly, all three of us were named Denis, and we had the exact same birthday. We went to school and played minor hockey together from the time we were little boys and lived within a half-mile of one another. Our new team kept us together at training camp, and we all signed contracts. We became known as "Les Trois Denis" and had great success together in the Quebec Major Junior League.

We're still great friends. Denis Tremblay is now a 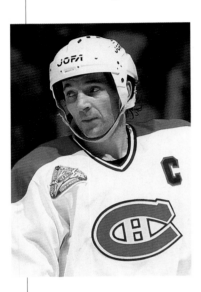 postman in Montreal, and Denis Cyr, who played six NHL seasons, is in Peoria. We obviously dreamed of playing in the NHL together, but I honestly thought I had a chance of making it only in our last year of junior. I was having a lot of fun playing hockey and didn't take it too seriously until just before that season began. My dad told me, "This is a big year for you if you want to become a professional hockey player." I was surprised, because I had heard so often that I was too small to make it. That criticism had always motivated me to prove people wrong, but it obviously had sunk in a little bit too.

The Montreal Canadiens had their eyes on a big center named Doug Wickenheiser, which was just as well for me, because I thought I'd have to spend a lot of time on the bench with them. I thought I would either make the NHL immediately or not at all. Chicago drafted me the same year Stan Mikita retired. I wanted to play right away, and there was a spot for me in the lineup.

I had great years in Chicago. We had a number of shots at winning the Stanley Cup in my first 10 years, but we lost in the semifinals five times. The Edmonton Oilers—by far the best team in hockey at the time—stopped us from getting the job done, but getting that far was still a great thrill.

I had a tough time pleasing Mike Keenan as coach, so despite my desires, I was traded. Yet I had always dreamed of playing for the Montreal Canadiens as a kid, so I feel fortunate to have done that. I enjoyed three years there, capped by winning a Stanley Cup championship in 1993. I'll never forget that. I used to stop in almost every day to say hello to the general manager of the Montreal Forum, who had a big picture of a Canadiens victory parade on his wall. I always looked at it and thought of how nice that would be. When I got to

experience that myself, I was almost sad when the three days of parties and celebration were over. They went by too quickly! I wished it could have lasted a month, but it was soon time to turn a new page.

Montreal is a first-class organization, but they started to play me less. It felt like a good break to sign with the Tampa Bay Lightning. Being on an expansion team created different challenges, which were good for me, but after a season and a half, I was able to get back to where I really belong.

I wasn't playing as much as I would have liked, but a month prior to the trading deadline for the 1994-95 season, I thought that I'd better get in the best shape possible in case there was a team shopping for a third-line center to help a Stanley Cup drive. Several weeks later, Phil Esposito, the Tampa Bay general manager, called me into his office and gave me a choice. Chicago wanted me back, or I could stay with the Lightning. To be polite, I said I'd think about it, but my mind was made up immediately. My wife agreed, and I headed back to the Blackhawks.

My former teammate Darryl Sutter was coaching the team by then, and he gave me a chance to be the player I can be. I got lots of ice time in situations I like, and I was so motivated not to let people down. Everything went well except that we didn't go as far in the playoffs as we wanted. I had the same excitement starting the next season, but as you get older, it gets tougher. Those kids are bigger, stronger and faster than ever. I can still compete, but my body doesn't recover as well.

People reminded me as I started the 1996-97 season that I needed only 36 more goals to reach the 500 mark, but I think I'll have to count the ones I score in practice if I'm going to make it. We met with some of the Blackhawks alumni recently, and Keith Magnuson remarked on how close I was. I jokingly asked him if I could have his goals, and he said, "You still won't have enough." He played 11 seasons on defense and scored 14 goals. Even though my totals are high, numbers are really not important to me. As Keith did, I bring more than that to my team.

I am having more fun now than I ever did. I'm not playing every game, and each time I put on my jersey, I think it might be the last time. I'm savoring every moment.

Denis Savard, seen here serving as interim captain, lived out a dream when his hometown Montreal Canadiens won the Stanley Cup in 1993. (OPPOSITE) Dazzling playmaker Savard, holder of several Chicago scoring records, hung up his skates in 1997. The Hawks retired his sweater number 18 a year later, and he entered the Hockey Hall of Fame in 2000.

Teemu Selanne

GROWING UP IN FINLAND GAVE ME THE OPPORTUNITY TO play a lot of sports at a high level. As a teenager, I was a member of the national junior hockey, soccer and ice-bandy teams at the same time. I loved each sport, but at age 16, I decided to focus on hockey. My parents agreed that I could quit school and see how far I might be able to go in the game. I was moving up the ladder, playing for the Jokerit club team in several levels, so it seemed a safe move at the time. If I didn't do very well, I thought I'd still be young enough to start my studies again.

My twin brother was a goalie, so we had lots of opportunity to practice together. He was pretty good but didn't completely share my drive in athletics. He was a much better student than I, though, and now he is a teacher. It's not really possible to have a hockey "career" in Finland, although the players do get paid a nominal sum. On the other hand, the schedule is relatively light, so I also worked part-time as a teacher of small children. I loved the job, and the combination was ideal for me. I'd teach from nine until one, have lunch and an afternoon nap and get to the arena for five o'clock. I'm able to have some contact with kids now by doing a lot of fundraising in Finland for the children's hospitals. There's no doubt in my mind that, but for hockey, I, too, would choose to be a teacher.

I'm told that the first time being traded is the hardest. I was really upset and disappointed when the Winnipeg Jets traded me to Anaheim. I felt a strong connection to the team, to the city and to the guys I played with. Trading players is unheard-of in Finnish hockey. Once you are on a club, you're there until the end of your career. The trade really brought home the reality that the NHL is a business. Management rarely takes a player's feelings into consideration, which is the aspect of North American hockey that I hate the most. I especially can't understand how even junior clubs are permitted to trade players. That seems terrible to me.

I adjusted to being a Mighty Duck quickly enough, and I'm now really glad to be part of the team. We've got a lot of young guys, some solid veterans and a good attitude. I'm especially excited to be playing with Jari Kurri, a fellow Finn whom I idolized for years. He was starring in the NHL when I was just a boy, and his success helped me to make the decision to concentrate on hockey. I started working with him at his hockey school in Finland in 1991, which was a real thrill, and we've become close friends. We see each other frequently in the off-season, playing a lot of tennis, working out together, doing a lot of charity work and just having fun.

Jari was really helpful when I was deciding whether to try to join the NHL. I did attend a couple of training camps and thought I could play the NHL game, but Jari and others warned me that the differences in language, food and culture, with the added demands of travel and about twice as many games in a season, can really be a drain. If a European player doesn't feel fully prepared, he should wait. I was drafted by Winnipeg in 1988, but I didn't feel ready to make the jump until 1992. I was 22 years old when I joined the NHL. It was the right time for me.

I thought if I could score 30 goals, it would be a great start to an NHL career. I knew that if I worked hard, I would do all right, but scoring 76 goals in my rookie year took me completely by surprise. Breaking Mike Bossy's record never entered my mind until well into the season. Knowing that European rookies are usually scrutinized more closely for toughness and character probably helped me a lot. I was hungry for success, ready to prove that I was good enough. I scored in my second game, and the season unfolded in a marvelous way. The biggest hurdle proved to be the travel. Just to get through the season is an accomplishment that every player can feel proud of. It may look glamorous, but it is a rigorous and exhausting pace. At the same time, I have no complaints. I feel so lucky to have a job that is so much fun and pays so well.

I really enjoyed meeting Paul Kariya at the 1996 All-Star game. Both of us were in awe of the skills you see shown there. "Look at his shot!" I would say. "Can you believe his speed?" It's an amazing atmosphere to be in. Paul and I didn't get much of an opportunity to play together then, but we spent a lot of time together off the ice. I know that he had some influence on my trade to Anaheim. We've become great friends now that we're teammates, and I hope that we have many good years together.

Teemu Selanne

*Teemu Selanne, inaugural winner of the Maurice "Rocket" Richard Trophy in 1998-99 when he potted 47 goals for Anaheim, was traded to San Jose in March 2001. (**OPPOSITE**) "The Finnish Flash," who shattered the rookie scoring record with 76 goals for Winnipeg in 1992-93, cuts sharply in front of Sylvain Lefebvre in a move toward the Toronto net.*

Eddie Shack

I WAS NEVER AFRAID OF ANYBODY. I'VE BEEN CALLED RECK-
less, and I guess it's true. My lack of fear made some
players nervous, because I could be a bit of a rough cus-
tomer. In the corners, in front of the net, even in a fight
I was sure to lose, I never backed down, and I'd be used
against the toughest guys on every team. Gordie Howe
and I made a deal one summer in the early 1960s. I'd
knocked him out a couple of times, and he'd got back at
me as he always did. I agreed not to hit him if he agreed
not to hit me. We never broke that agreement, because
we were both afraid we might not live long without it.

I played junior at the same time as Frank Mahovlich
and Bobby Hull, and I scored just as many goals as they
did. Yet when I graduated from the Guelph Biltmores
to the New York Rangers, Muzz Patrick and Phil Watson
turned me into a checker. I was mad, but I realized
something that made a big difference in my career.
When you're known as a goal scorer, there is tremendous pressure on you to deliver every game. Once that
expectation was taken away, I was able to enjoy the
game a lot more. I liked that and decided that having
fun was going to be my priority. I scored 20 goals a

season for five different clubs in my career, but more important, I left the fans in every city with some Eddie Shack stories to tell.

Despite having good talent, the Rangers did very poorly. I acted up a lot because the poor coaching made me miserable. The Rangers sent me to the Red Wings as part of a deal for Red Kelly, but Red managed to nix the trade. Unfortunately, I had really let management know what I thought of them, with what I believed were parting words. As the trade quickly unraveled, I had the awkward job of walking back on the Rangers bus.

After a particularly long losing spell, management called a meeting to seek player input. We were told to say whatever we wanted, that nothing would be held against us, that we should speak our minds. We took turns talking. Most said something safe about needing to work a little harder, but when my turn came, I let everyone know that any advice I got from management went in one ear and out the other. At the end of the meeting, I was angrily pulled aside and told to pack my bags for Springfield to play for Eddie Shore.

Eddie had a reputation for his harsh treatment of players, but I loved it there. After two weeks, the Rangers had to call me back up or put me on waivers. I got the call but told them I was staying. They *demanded* that I come back, but it took one of my teammates to convince me to return. The Rangers eventually traded me to Toronto, where I was on four Stanley Cup winners in seven years.

I have no formal education but had my butcher's license when I was 13 and drove a truck at 14. I put all I had into hockey when I saw the chance I had as a teenager. Once I became a Maple Leaf, I really knuckled down again and got a lot more serious. Toronto was a good place to be for the hockey and other profitable opportunities (I once filled a truck with Biltmore hats in Guelph and sold them in Toronto). I could get away with anything when we won the Stanley Cup. I'd drive my car on the sidewalk, and the police would just say, "Hi, Ed!"

Many fans remember the "We want Shack" chant that used to ring through the Gardens when I hadn't played much or things were a little dull. Punch Imlach, the coach, would say, "If they want you that badly, why don't you go sit with them?" But he usually relented and sent me on the ice to a nice cheer. Late in my career, I sometimes turned and lifted my arms to entice the crowd to raise the volume. I've heard that chant even after I retired.

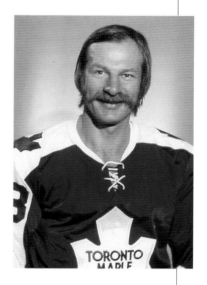

Foster Hewitt picked the three stars for each game in Toronto, but he didn't like me and I was never chosen. I dreamed of the night that I'd hear the roar of the crowd and had a plan that I didn't get to use until I was playing in Buffalo. The three stars would skate out in turn from a gate in the boards behind the net. As my name was announced, I grabbed the hat off a cop standing beside the glass. I skated as hard as I could in my usual enthusiastic style all the way to center ice, pirouetted and skated just as hard back off the ice. I didn't care whether I fell or not, because I knew the crowd would love it regardless. The cop was mad, though, because his hat flew off and was lying out on the ice. I asked Roger Crozier, the next star of the game, if he'd get it for him. I got to do that pirouette a few more times in my career, even in Maple Leaf Gardens on *Hockey Night in Canada*, and I enjoyed it as much as anyone.

Eddie "The Entertainer" Shack won four Stanley Cups in his first stint with the Leafs. He is pictured here late in his career with his trademark handlebar moustache. (**Opposite**) *Shack played with a reckless abandon and enthusiasm that made him a fan favorite. The Bruins' Joe Watson doesn't dare try to keep up.*

Brendan Shanahan

As a 17-year-old junior, I had an unusual responsibility. I was team captain for the London Knights. Wayne Maxner, our coach, would call me into his office after school and tell me to take the guys out for a warm-up. Because we had no assistant coaches, I learned that it actually meant to take the team out for a practice. Some of the older guys didn't like having a much younger captain, especially one who was telling them to put the pucks away and skate. Fortunately, the best and most experienced players were hard workers. After I led an hour-and-a-half practice, Wayne would come out and blow the whistle, and we'd scrimmage. That was just the way it was.

The New Jersey Devils were good about not putting a lot of pressure on me right away, though I didn't really appreciate it at the time. Prior to stepping into the NHL at age 18, I had always competed at a level where I was one of the better players. When the game was on the line, I was used to going over the boards, being relied upon. The players that get to this level like that feeling, they want that feeling, and that's what makes them the players they are. It's tough to resign yourself to sitting out some games, being tutored and not really being one of the main guys. Most players go through that experience. The question is this: Do you resign yourself to being a player who's in and out of the lineup, or are you just waiting for your opportunity?

In my second year, a chance came for me to play on the first line with John MacLean and Patrik Sundstrom. It was just the moment I was waiting for, and I jumped on it. I felt awkward at first, because that was my first time playing left wing. I grew up as a center or on right, but I've played on the left side ever since. Those two guys generated a lot of offense on their own, so it was my job to go to the net, cause screens and pick up rebounds.

I was in the crease so much in our first game together that Mike Liut, the Hartford goalie, eventually stepped on my face. I got my nose a little dirty, literally, with a big gash across the bridge of my nose. More important, I also got four points. Hoping that I'd found my niche and liking the game I played, I tried to bottle that energy. I got 10 points in our first three games together. That's as many as I had gathered in the entire first half of the season. I don't think that there was a shift for the rest of the season that John and Patrik didn't have something to say to me after we got off the ice. They'd tell me ways I could improve, even demand changes and reinforce—with praise and congratulations—the positive things I was doing. They were a constant support.

There was tremendous controversy over NHL free-agency rules when I signed with the St. Louis Blues in 1991. The Blues and Devils each had to present a compensation plan. Judge Houston took a lot of grief for siding with the Devils and awarding Scott Stevens to New Jersey. The judge is an honest fan, and he's called me a few times since. I think he was the happiest person in the world when I first scored 50 goals. He felt it justified his ruling that Scott was fair compensation. He'd call and say, "See? See? I told them it was a fair decision!"

I had great years with the Blues, but no one felt secure when Mike Keenan arrived. Curtis Joseph had a career season and was traded. Other good young players had been dealt away during the season, so I didn't take it personally when my trade to Hartford came in the summer of 1995. Even the owner got fired!

The Hartford organization was great to me, but the prospects for the team looked very uncertain. At this stage in my career, I want to stay focused on the season at hand and not worry too much about the future. The club has given notice that they'll be leaving Hartford. General Manager Jim Rutherford painted the picture that the team wasn't making a lot of money. I had a large salary, and he asked whether I wanted a trade. I said yes.

I've met very few people in hockey who weren't good people. There are a lot of guys here in Detroit I hated playing against. As usual, I've discovered that they're the ones I now like the most. Being in Detroit reminds me every day that I'm in the NHL. This franchise is rooted here; it has a tradition. We see the past great players' names on the walls, so when we play, there's an extra incentive not to draw any shame to the Red Wings sweater.

Brendan Shanahan brought his intense brand of hockey to St. Louis in 1991 and quickly became a fan favorite. (**Opposite**) *Shanahan, an important ingredient in Detroit's two Stanley Cup victories in 1997 and 1998, gets to the net in front of Toronto's Felix Potvin.*

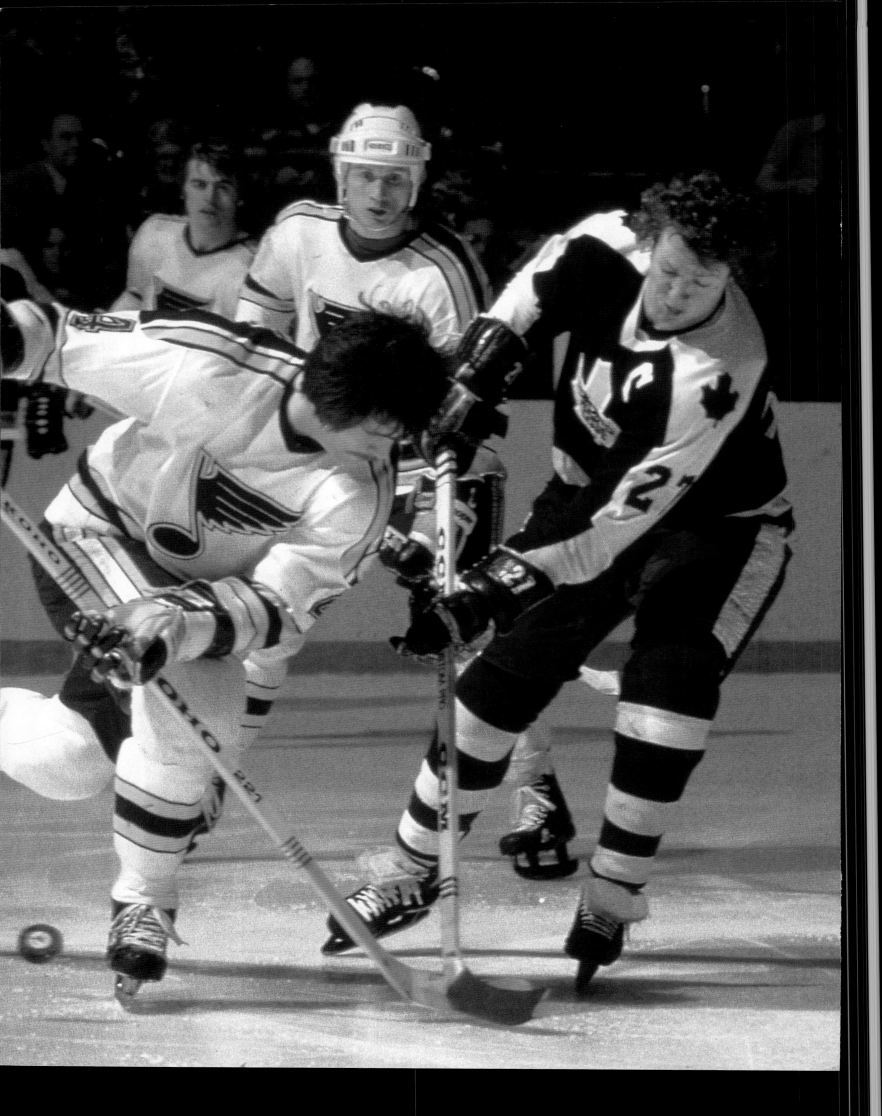

Darryl Sittler

IT'S MORE THAN 20 YEARS AGO NOW, BUT PEOPLE STILL remember the 10-point game I had against the Boston Bruins in 1976. I have a tape of that game, and I play it every once in a while. The feelings and memories all come back to me when I watch it. There was a lot of electricity, a lot of emotion, in the building that night. I had seven points after two periods. Stan Obodiak, the team statistician and public relations rep, came into the dressing room at that point and told the team that Rocket Richard held the then-record of eight points in a game. So I was aware of the potential to make history when I went back on the ice. Within three or four minutes, I had tied the record. I was ecstatic, but it wasn't over yet. I had 10 shots on goal in that game, and six of them went in. With four assists as well, the 10 points in one game is a record that will be hard to break.

The same season, I had five goals in one playoff game against the Philadelphia Flyers, which tied the record. I then went on to score the winning goal for Canada in the 1976 Canada Cup tournament. That year was the highlight of my career.

There was no assurance of even making Team Canada then, with more players invited than could play. My good friend Lanny McDonald and I were given a defensive role on a line with Bob Gainey. We were happy to be there, to contribute in whatever way was asked of us. I feel fortunate to have been able to score the overtime goal to win the tournament over Czechoslovakia. That, too, was an emotional night. Pierre Elliott Trudeau presented us with the trophy in the Montreal Forum. We had a lot of respect for the Czechoslovakian team, and warm feelings were expressed with an exchange of sweaters after the game. It was a moment of pride for our country, and unless you've been in a tournament like that, it's hard to describe the significance of wearing your country's sweater in international competition, let alone the feeling of scoring an overtime goal. When I got back to Toronto, I discovered that Harold Ballard had instructed the Maple Leaf Gardens telephone receptionists to answer, "Hello from the home of Darryl Sittler." I appreciated the gesture very much.

I feel thankful to still be around the game as a consultant to the Toronto Maple Leafs. I talk to a lot of guys who've gone on to successful careers after playing hockey, but many express a sadness at not being involved in the game. The training can be an outlet for stress, and outside of sport, it can be difficult for people to understand a former athlete's competitiveness and drive for success. It's hardest to replace the camaraderie, that feeling of being part of a fraternity, that we've experienced since we were boys.

I always thought of the Hall of Fame as a place for older people, so I was a bit surprised to be inducted in 1989 at the age of 39. The 15 years I had as a player went by very quickly. I never set targets, like scoring 40 goals in a season, but I did set standards for a work ethic, atti-tude and conditioning. What I learned, what I tried to pass on to my children and now to the players on the Leafs, is to get up in the morning with a good attitude and give an honest effort. You will enjoy yourself more, you will improve at what you do, and though everything won't always go your way, giving your best each day brings its own rewards.

As a boy, I always tried to emulate Jean Beliveau. I opened a Christmas gift one year, and it was a Montreal Canadiens sweater. I wore it to bed that night and to school every day. As a rookie with the Leafs, I got to face-off against my childhood hero in the Montreal Forum. I looked up at Jean and got a flashback to my childhood. But here in front of me was the man, not a dream. I didn't say anything, and obviously he had no idea of the feelings that were rushing through me. It was a special moment. I've been lucky to have a lot of contact with Jean since then, and I still have great respect for him.

I try to remind myself now of the feelings I had when I was a youngster. I think it's important that players recall their youth and remember what it meant getting an autograph, standing outside a rink meeting a player for the first time. Once you reach the NHL, it can be easy to forget and not take the time to relate to the kids and the fans in little ways that can really bring happiness to people.

Darryl Sittler, a hard-skating center with a scoring touch, entered the NHL record books with a 10-point game against the Boston Bruins on February 7, 1976. (OPPOSITE) Sittler was an important member of the Toronto Maple Leafs for 12 seasons. Here he battles for the puck with Bruce Affleck of the St. Louis Blues.

Billy Smith

MY NICKNAME, "BATTLING BILLY," FIRST APPEARED IN THE newspaper after a game that included several brawls. I was in a few fights, and there were some incidents around the net. A goalie really had to protect himself in my day. Opposing players would come into the crease, bump me and try to take my feet out, and they rarely drew a penalty for it. No amount of my yelling and screaming at the referee would cause him to take his eyes off the puck. I'm a fan of the video replay. It gives the goalie more of a chance when the referee doesn't have to see everything at once.

I also believe in a goalie spending some time in the minor leagues. It allows him to come along at his own rate instead of being thrown into the NHL before he is fundamentally sound. There's no such thing as "jumping" from junior. Sooner or later, no matter how good a goalie is, there will be problems. A few guys have come right in, but they'll have one good year and then three mediocre ones. The team counts on them to repeat that first season, but they *have* to go through the learning period. The pressure when you're doing that in the NHL is immense. I hit my peak when I was 28 or 29. I was comfortable and had my game under control. When I was younger, I was feistier and tried to do too much. A lot of times when I was poking guys or trying to push them out of my crease, I'd be scored on. I couldn't take control of my opponent *and* stop the puck at the same time.

My advice to young kids is not to worry too much about making the NHL. If it's meant to be, it will be. I wasn't concerned about playing NHL hockey even after I was drafted by the Los Angeles Kings in 1970. I was having too much fun as a junior. I spent two more enjoyable years with Springfield of the American Hockey League. The Kings hadn't given me a real chance at the NHL, so I was glad to be drafted by the New York Islanders when they came into the league through expansion in 1972. They let me play.

I rarely played more than 40 games in a season, rotating with Chico Resch, Rollie Melanson or Kelly Hrudey. I didn't mind that at all. Chico and, later, Kelly and I were great friends. You can't do your job *and* keep an eye on the other guy, so the most help you can give another goalie is to get along as partners.

When I won a championship in the AHL, I thought it was the greatest thing that could ever happen. I never dreamed of holding the Stanley Cup, let alone winning it four times. I've been accused of being too competitive, but I've always loved to win. I get the same thrill in any competition, whether it's a local tennis tournament or the Stanley Cup playoffs. But when it came to the playoffs, I always seemed to get on a roll. There was more pressure, which helped my concentration, and the game seemed a little easier.

I've seen goalies play a great game and make no mistakes, and yet the puck somehow squeezes through. Sometimes these things just happen. In one of my best games—a seventh-game overtime win against the New York Rangers—the Rangers' Donny Maloney scored the tying goal with a high stick to send the game into overtime. Big goals are not always good goals.

Just to get out of our own division was always a battle. Many series went to seven games. The first and the fourth Stanley Cups were probably the most satisfying. The first was special because we didn't know yet if we were capable of winning. The fourth was great because of the aggravation that came with the hype over the Edmonton Oilers. The Islanders were three-time champions but got little respect. We won the first game against Edmonton 2–0, probably the finest game I ever played. Even though the series ended in four games, it was far from a sweep. Every game was do-or-die, and it was great hockey. To top things off for me personally, I also won the Conn Smythe award.

As a goalie coach for the Florida Panthers, my job now is to stand back and watch. I'm not going to approach Mark Fitzpatrick or John Vanbiesbrouck and tell them how to challenge a shooter. I'm there to offer encouragement and quickly bring to their attention anything they might be doing out of the ordinary. Everybody has a different style; if it's working, you shouldn't tamper with it. Patrick Roy stays deep in his net and plays a style that I would never teach anyone else. But he's the best goalie in the NHL because his method is perfect for him.

I had fun even when the Islanders had losing seasons. I could hardly wait to get to the rink every day, not so much to practice but to *play*. But I knew when it was time to quit. I don't miss a thing now. I enjoy coaching and teaching young kids. Seeing a junior goalie pick up some of the things that I did well is a meaningful reward.

Bill Smith

Billy Smith was a fierce competitor and backstopped the New York Islanders to four consecutive Stanley Cups in the early 1980s. (OPPOSITE) "Battling Billy" was strong with his stick and the first NHL goalie credited with scoring a goal (he was the last Islander to touch the puck before the opposition put it in their own net with an errant pass).

Peter Stastny

MY BROTHERS MARIAN AND ANTON AND I ALWAYS PLAYED for our hometown team in Bratislava, the capital city of Slovakia. Until we came, a Slovak team had never won the Czechoslovakian championship; the Czechs had dominated. But as juniors, we won three times in a row and five out of six years. We then won the senior elite-level championship. That brought an increase in the political interference that we had felt for years. Important members of our roster were deemed "unworthy" of playing on our team and traded for cash. We lost at least five men a season and ran out of younger replacements.

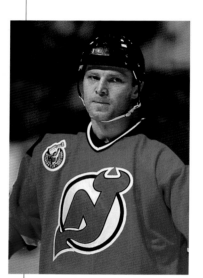

When we finished in third place, our team unanimously demanded a change in the management of our club. That brought increased political pressure, and Marian, Anton and I were targeted as team leaders. We were told if we didn't stay quiet, we would never play for the national team again. That was like an arrow through my heart. I'd received some interest from North American teams after the 1976 Canada Cup tournament, but our dream always was to play for the national team. I most deeply experienced my love of the game playing in the World Championships. I knew that I had no future in Czechoslovakia.

We went to Innsbruck, Austria, to play for the 1980 European championship. Anton and I planned to defect, but Marian couldn't join us. He had three children. A husband and wife could travel together, but the authorities would never allow an entire family to go. When we got to Innsbruck, we called the Quebec Nordiques to see whether they were still interested in us. They were at our hotel early the next morning.

We plotted Marian's escape for an entire year. He was under 24-hour surveillance and lost all his friends because they were routinely interrogated after visiting him. The regime had its ways of making life very difficult. We got him some money, and he managed to get his family to Austria. I was the happiest man in the world. I felt responsible for the hardships he had endured.

There was no better constellation than two of my brothers and I playing on a line together. Each of us was different in skills and personality. We complemented each other, creating a synergy that we used to our advantage. With no disrespect to anyone who played with us, when one of us was injured, it was like a handicap. What we developed over time—reading each other and the situation, the timing of our passing, combined with what we naturally had as brothers—was irreplaceable. Hockey at a high level becomes the management of time and space. We could *create* more time or space because we could see so clearly when the other was getting into trouble, what his way out was and where he *needed* us to be.

When we won the Czechoslovakian championship, we three scored 103 goals in 43 games. One of our most important goals came near the end of the season. A loss or tie against our closest opponent would have given them a good chance of beating us for first place. The game was tied with less than a minute left. Marian corralled a man in the corner and got the puck loose for a couple of seconds, allowing me to pick it up. I was challenged by the other defenseman, so I flipped the puck high into the slot, where I expected Anton to be. He *was* there, and I can still hear the roar of the crowd when he whipped the puck through the goalie's legs. We won 2–1, and that victory broke our opponent's back. It wasn't a championship game, but the other team didn't win again that season.

In my first NHL season, the long schedule, the travel, the physical aspect of the game and the high tempo of the daily practices had me drained mentally and physically by January. The Nordiques started to give Anton and me an occasional day off. After the All-Star game break in February, we went on a tough road trip. Anton and I each got a hat trick and three assists against Vancouver, and the next night against Washington, I got four goals and four assists and Anton got a hat trick and five assists. We scored 28 points between us in two games! We got a standing ovation when we stepped on the ice for our first home game back in Quebec. It seemed as if the people were more than celebrating that achievement, that they felt for us being so far from home. I'd been on a point-per-game pace, but I doubled that for the last 30 games and won Rookie of the Year.

I was disappointed that I didn't get to play with my brothers in the NHL more than we did, but we had some wonderful years together. I have so many good memories of the NHL. The Velvet Revolution allowed me to return to my homeland, and I feel blessed to have lived in such times. I was flag-bearer and captain of the Slovakian hockey team in the 1994 Olympics. It's been like a fairy tale to see Slovakia an independent country for the first time in 1,000 years.

Peter Stastny joined the New Jersey Devils in 1990 and rounded out a long NHL career with the St. Louis Blues. (Opposite) Stastny, who centered a potent line between his brothers Anton and Marian in Czechoslovakia and for Quebec, pulls away from Boston's Mike Milbury.

Mats Sundin

Hockey is the number-one sport—the national sport—in Sweden. Five, ten years ago, the dream for Swedish kids was to make it to the Swedish Elite League and hope to make the national team and play in the big international tournaments. That dream has changed, because the NHL is an international league now. I still take a lot of pride in playing for Sweden when I can, but at age 17, my new goal was to be a successful NHL player.

I give Sweden a lot of credit for bringing out a large number of good athletes for a small country of only 8 million people. I don't know the secret, but I do know that parents are very involved with their children's

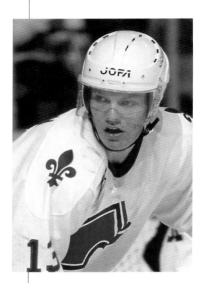

sports from a young age. I first skated when I was 5 years old and started hockey school at age 7.

Growing up in a suburb of Stockholm, we mostly played hockey, soccer and bandy. Bandy is like field hockey on skates, played on a large outdoor sheet of ice. There's no hitting, so you wear only kneepads. You shoot a small orange ball at an oversize hockey net, and the goalies don't use sticks. The game is fast, because the players are unbelievable skaters. I credit mixing sports with some of my success in hockey. My parents let me do whatever I had fun with. I realized myself that I might be able to do well in hockey, and at age 17, it was my decision to drop some of my other activities.

I was aware that I was probably going to go in the top four in the 1989 NHL draft, and my agent told me (quite accurately) I might even go as number one to the Quebec Nordiques. My dad and I went to the draft in Minneapolis but had no idea what it was really all about. We were amazed at the media interest. The Swedish media came over too, which was new for them. I visited Quebec on the same trip. I was overwhelmed by the fans' and media interest in me there. It was a lot of fun for an 18-year-old.

After playing another season in Sweden, I joined the Nordiques in 1990. I was supposed to play another year in Sweden, but I had a contract dispute there and came to Quebec early. I knew that the Nordiques had finished last the previous year, but I had no clue about what lay ahead. Our Djurgarden team had won the Swedish Elite League, and our national team won a silver medal in the World Championships in 1989. It was tough-going in Quebec. My first NHL season was the most frustrating in my hockey career.

Pressure is a good thing. When people expect a lot, I play better, which I think is true for most NHL players. But I hadn't even stopped growing, and there was an expectation that I was one of the players who were going to carry the Nordiques. I wasn't at all ready for that. I didn't have a bad year myself, but we were out of the playoffs by January.

The whole Quebec experience was good for me as a person as much as a hockey player. I learned that if I'm not having fun, hockey is hard for me. I had to learn a lot about myself and discover ways to stay motivated. As a professional, you have to be developing yourself as a player even if the team is not competitive. You always have to try to win and do your best every game.

The team had a strong regular season in my third year, but then had another poor one. My trade to Toronto didn't surprise me, but I just happened to be at Borje Salming's hockey school in Sweden when the trade occurred. We sat down together, and Borje told me all about Toronto. He was very positive and assured me that if I gave my best, there wasn't a better city to play in. That renewed my confidence, and my spirits were high coming to another city that cares so much about hockey. The Maple Leafs are also one of the most popular teams in Sweden because of all the years Borje played there.

Winning the World Championship, the World Cup and the Olympics are all great achievements, but the Stanley Cup is the ultimate goal for all hockey players. This is the best league in the world, and it's a long way

to the Cup. It's still the toughest thing to win. You need more than a great team. Every club is strong, so you need every guy going at the same time. A little luck, like hitting a post-in versus a post-out, also helps.

Playing in Toronto in the playoffs is totally different from the regular season. I haven't seen anything like it anywhere else. For the first period, I run almost completely on adrenaline. I got an overtime goal against St. Louis in the 1996 playoffs, which was such a great feeling. I'm looking forward to seeing a lot more of that kind of hockey in Toronto.

Mats Sundin was the first European to be the number-one pick in an NHL entry draft when the Quebec Nordiques made him their first choice in 1989. (Above) Sundin, captain of the Toronto Maple Leafs since 1997-98, swirls to the front of the net against goaltender Kelly Hrudey of the San Jose Sharks.

Brent Sutter

Hockey was the center of life in Viking, Alberta. I was raised on a farm with six brothers; all our spare time was spent playing hockey at the local rink, on the pond at home or, during the summer, in the hayloft of the barn. Like all Canadian kids, our dream was to play in the NHL. We all had our favorite teams and players. I liked the Boston Bruins and Bobby Orr, and my oldest brother, Gary, loved the Toronto Maple Leafs and Dave Keon. Brian cheered for the Detroit Red Wings and Gordie Howe. Darryl and Duane liked the Chicago

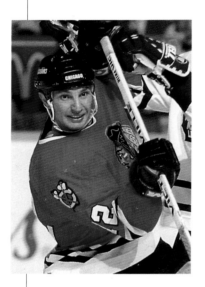

Blackhawks and Bobby Hull. The twins, Richie and Ronnie, cheered for different teams and players. We all kept scrapbooks of our teams and players, and they're still at Mom and Dad's to this day.

I left home when I was 15 to play on a Tier Two junior team, where my older brothers Brian, Darryl and Duane played. Gary, the oldest, decided against moving away from home and didn't go any further in hockey. I played one year with Duane at the Tier Two level before he moved on to Tier One. A year later, Richie and Ronnie came to play, and we were teammates for a year in Tier Two before we moved up to Tier One together. We played together for another year and a half before I was called up to the NHL, where I've played ever since.

I played with Duane for six years in New York for the Islanders before he was traded to Chicago. After 10 years with the Islanders, I, too, was traded to Chicago, where Darryl was assistant coach. He became head coach the next year, and a year later, Richie came to play in Chicago for a year and a half. Looking back, it was awfully nice to have had the opportunity to play with my brothers and play for Darryl when he was head coach. People always ask about my relationship with Darryl when he was coach. To be honest, we both handled it strictly on a professional basis. He was my coach and I was his player, and we treated it that way.

It was a great confidence builder for the rest of us when Brian first made it to the NHL. We saw how hard he had worked to get there, and we knew that we were going to have to do the same. I was the fourth one in the family to make it, which was like a dream come true, but I knew that my work had just begun. The best advice I ever received was, "You worked really hard to get to this level, and now you have to work twice as hard to stay."

I was fortunate to play with the Islanders. To learn and play with the best team in hockey at the time was unbelievable. They had already won two Stanley Cups and were going for their third in a row. They had a great general manager in Bill Torrey, an outstanding coach in Al Arbour and an awful lot of amazing players. They all taught me so much about what it took to be a professional and how to be successful at this level. We won the Stanley Cup that year and the next.

It wasn't easy on Mom and Dad when we were playing against each other. They wanted all the games to end in a tie and hoped that nobody got hurt. Richie and Ronnie were in Philadelphia playing for the Flyers—big rivals of the Islanders—so we had our run-ins with each other. Sometimes it even got to the point where players from both teams had to jump in to separate us. That's a part of the game that we all expected to see, because first and foremost, we have always wanted to win. That has never changed.

None of us are among the greatest skilled players in the world, but we relied on hard work and on being team players, a lesson we learned at a young age growing up on the farm. A lot of credit for our success has to go to Mom and Dad. There were so many of us in the family that we had to work hard together, for each other. Two or three of us would do the farm chores while the others were shoveling snow off the pond so that we could play hockey. We never thought of the things we had to do on the farm as work. They were just part of what we had to do to be successful on the farm. That relates back to the game of hockey, because it's a team game. It might be an old cliché, but you play for the front of the jersey, not the back.

The ultimate success for me was winning the Stanley Cup and the Canada Cup in 1984, 1987 and 1991. The dedication and commitment that has to be felt by everyone, making whatever sacrifice is needed to win and doing it together, is really what the game is all about. Team goals and accomplishments will always be the most important to me. My brothers may not have won the Stanley Cup like Duane and I or the Canada Cups that I won, but I'm darn proud of all of them because I know they've been a big part of any success I've had.

*Brent Sutter, one of six Sutter brothers to play in the NHL, mixes it up in front of the net. He retired after the 1997-98 season. (**Opposite**) Sutter works for position in the slot against Chicago defenders Adam Creighton (22) and Doug Wilson during his tenure as captain of the New York Islanders in the late 1980s.*

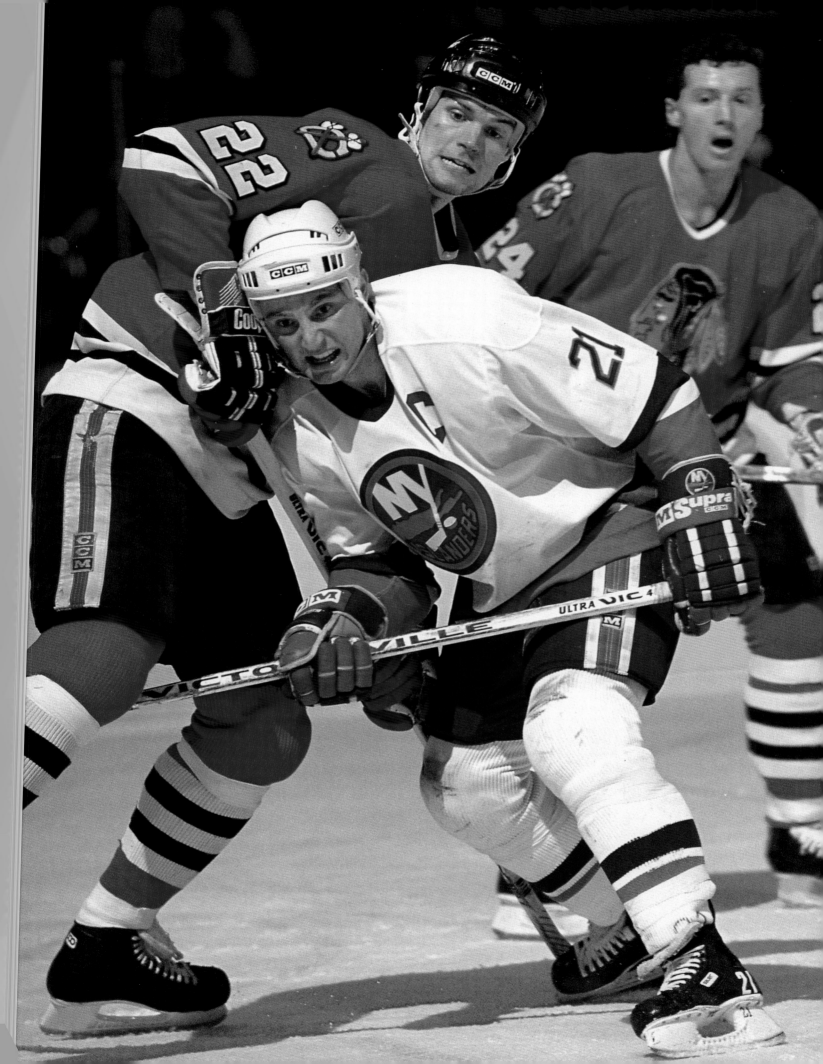

Keith Tkachuk

I WENT TO BOSTON UNIVERSITY, A GREAT SCHOOL, AND THEY developed me into a better hockey player. After my first year, I decided to live out a dream and try out for the U.S. national team. I was surprised to make it, but it was the best experience I've ever had. Wearing the U.S.A. jersey is every American kid's dream. After watching the 1980 Olympic team and seeing Mike Eruzione score the winning goal, every kid playing hockey in the U.S. said, "I want to play on the Olympic team."

Anytime you can play for your country, wherever you're from, pride is a huge factor. I got to play in the 1992 Olympic games, which few people can claim. That was absolutely unreal. What made it even better was to have my family come over to Albertville, France, and experience the same things I was. The skiing and ski-jumping slopes were right next to the rink. It was a great atmosphere. We did pretty well and finished in fourth place. No one predicted we'd be in the top five in that tournament.

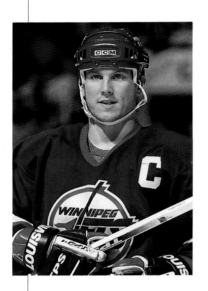

The World Cup of 1996 had the same type of feeling. We were playing with the best in the world. To go out and win against talent like that—and to do it against Canada in Montreal—that was a dynamite feeling. I made a lot of friends too. We bonded together for a month and jelled well. Each line had a different job. That's why we won—because everybody played as a team and we accepted our roles. We all pulled the rope together.

We wanted to play Canada. We wanted to *beat* Canada. I don't think it would have been the same if Sweden had defeated Canada or if we beat Sweden. That was the most satisfying part of the tournament. Those final three games were the best anybody's ever watched. It was an awful feeling when Canada scored to go ahead in the third period of the final game, but then we pulled together and scored two big goals. When Derian Hatcher scored an empty-netter, it was probably the best feeling I've ever had in my entire life, and I speak for everyone on my team. It was a tough day for Canada. It was pretty quiet outside that Molson Centre.

One minute you're hugging everybody because you've won a World Cup with them, and the next week you're playing against them. But business is business. That's what the game of hockey is all about now. What I love most is waking up every day and going to the rink. That will never change. You have your family at home, but being with your teammates so much forms a tight bond. There's not a greater feeling in the world than being with your friends every day.

I was at 49 goals late in the 1995-96 season, squeezing my stick so hard because I wanted number 50 so badly and couldn't get it. I had an open net when Los Angeles pulled their goalie near the end of our second-last season game. I did not want to miss that! I enjoyed the fiftieth goal for that night, but more important, we were in the playoffs. The ultimate goal in hockey is always the Stanley Cup, so you put all of your individual awards aside. It's nice to be remembered as a 50-goal scorer, but it would be much nicer to be remembered as a Stanley Cup champion.

I play with a lot of intensity because that's how I'm successful—when I'm playing hard and with the body. That's the way I grew up playing in Medford, Massachusetts. My brother Kevin and I were only 11 months apart in age. We played all sorts of sports—football, baseball, soccer, hockey. I liked football best until I got to high school and started taking hockey seriously when I was 16. Watching the Bruins over the years helped. They always had a big, rough team. I want to be known as a player who works hard and hits hard every night. Those are the guys everybody remembers.

I got my NHL start in Winnipeg and played there for five years. People were very good to me. Who knows, I could have started somewhere else and not be enjoying the success I am today. We had some ups and downs, but I'm going to miss the city and some good people. I met my fiancée there. The weather wasn't too great, but it was a good hockey town. People cared.

Phoenix has a great climate, and we're playing in front of a sold-out crowd every night. We wear shorts to the rink and have the opportunity to play golf every day. A lot of people are new to the game, and it's up to us to educate them. You can actually tell they're learning, because they're starting to boo a little bit. That's not great to hear, but it is a good sign. People are starting to love the game.

Keith Tkachuk was chosen team captain in only his second full season with the Winnipeg Jets. He resumed the post when the team moved to its new home in Phoenix. (OPPOSITE) *Tkachuk adds a fiery combativeness to his high skill level, a potent combination that led to 50 goals in the 1995-96 and 1996-97 seasons.*

Bryan Trottier

I'VE NEVER LOOKED AT EITHER MY CAREER OR MY LIFE AS A progression. There are, however, stages, and I was a hockey player for a while. After winning two Stanley Cups in Pittsburgh, I spent a year in sales with the New York Islanders, my first NHL club, where we won four Stanley Cups in the 1980s. The job wasn't as close to hockey as I thought it would be, so when the Penguins called, we discussed player/coach possibilities—which got me back playing for a season and allowed for a nice transition from being a player to full-time coaching.

When I was with the Islanders, I was always described as one of the leaders, so when I first went to the Pittsburgh Penguins as a free agent in the summer of 1990, I didn't really see my role much differently. I knew what I was capable of doing. I still wanted to contribute offensively and play the defensive side of the game when called upon. Maybe I didn't have the same recklessness that I had when I was 20, but I certainly had more guile.

I wasn't highly touted before being drafted by the New York Islanders in 1974. I had a great season for the Lethbridge Broncos in the Western Hockey League *after* being chosen, but I played in relative obscurity until then. I wasn't 18 yet, but the NHL allowed underage players to be selected in the first two rounds to prevent the WHA from signing everyone. The 1974 draft was held by telephone, so it wasn't the big public event that it is today. I was still very excited to be drafted by the NHL Islanders in spite of the lack of media attention, and as it turned out, the money, the opportunity and the guarantees the Islanders offered were better and more secure than those I received from the WHA's Cincinnati Stingers. Plus, I had always dreamed of playing in the NHL—the Montreal Forum, Maple Leaf Gardens—so I was genuinely committed to New York from the moment I was drafted.

I had no preconceived notions about the NHL and took nothing for granted. Basic hard work, combined with the chance to play with great players, led to a good rookie season. The system of our coach, Al Arbour, was strict but basic—aggressive forechecking, puck pursuit and defensive positioning—and complemented my style. I played most of my first season with Billy Harris and Clark Gillies. We started off quickly, and their scoring abilities plus a strong power play helped me set rookie scoring records that year for points (95) and assists (63), and I won the Calder Trophy. I took success in stride. Playing in the All-Star game that year was a tremendous compliment. Billy and Clark are down-to-earth guys who helped keep my feet on the ground. Our success was a team success. Good things happen when players want to do well for each other. We were young, eager and pretty talented, and we wanted to win.

I was most fortunate to play with Mike Bossy for almost 10 years. Mike knew how to score and was underrated for his playmaking skills. We had a certain chemistry. We shared the same expectations, and our friendship and desire to do well for one another created a nice push-and-pull kind of relationship. It was no coincidence that my point totals went up with Mike's arrival. I think we both would have done well without each other, but he was the most significant individual player who contributed to the bulk of my successes. I can't thank Mike enough for all the great plays he made, the beautiful goals he scored, how hard he worked and what he meant to my career.

We didn't tag ourselves as a dynasty, but we felt like one! It was a tremendously proud group of guys that won four consecutive Stanley Cups in Long Island. We wanted to strut and feel like champions every year. We never wanted to take that for granted, because it is a great feeling. Playing with those guys made every day a highlight. When Bobby Nystrom scored in overtime to make us Stanley Cup champions for the very first time, every dream I'd had as a kid became a reality. All the dedication, all the practices, became worthwhile. The realization—Wow, I'm a Stanley Cup champion! —what a proud and special feeling!

External acknowledgments are great. When someone hands me an award, I say, "Thank you very much. I appreciate it," but that's not why I want to win. It's for the feeling! The joy is in the self-esteem and the team pride that come with winning a championship. Just the fact that they paid me to have that much fun made every payday like an award.

There's a camaraderie and respect among all hockey players, but there's no fooling your teammates when you're victorious. Everyone knows what every player meant to the winning of the Stanley Cup. The relationship between teammates is different from the one between a player and management. I still have to do what I need to do as a coach, but the players understand this. The bond created when you win a championship, with the same players you're now coaching, makes for a respectful and unique situation.

Bryan Trottier was a team leader for 15 seasons with the New York Islanders. (OPPOSITE) Trottier earned two more Stanley Cup rings with the Pittsburgh Penguins.

Norm Ullman

DESIRE IS LIKE TALENT: IT'S BRED INTO YOU, AND EITHER you have it or you don't. I credit desire and determination as keys to my long career, along with the good fortune that none of my many injuries kept me out of the lineup for too long.

Growing up in Edmonton in the 1940s and 1950s meant growing up in the Detroit Red Wings organization. In my second year in the NHL, I was placed at center between Howe and Lindsay, giving me a great boost in getting established. Every player in his early years

had to show he couldn't be run out of the rink. Without team "enforcers," you had to fend for yourself. We kept the sticks down, but I once got into a stick-swinging fight with Rocket Richard. We had collided accidentally when the play turned up-ice, and perhaps he thought I had intended to hurt him. I got up and went after the puck, but before I knew it, he gave me a terrible whack with his stick and opened a huge gash on the back of my head. I chased after him, absolutely livid, and took a couple of swings with my own stick before dropping it and hauling him down to the ice. That was the most upset I ever got.

In 1965, I was selected to the First All-Star team and led the league in goals scored. I was only a couple of points away from winning the scoring championship and was runner-up in the voting for league MVP. That was the most gratifying year out of my 20. Everything seemed to jell for me and the team, and we finished in first place.

Montreal always had strong teams in those days, and I'd be up against big and talented Jean Beliveau or Henri Richard, who was quick and always on top of things like Dave Keon of the Leafs. Against Chicago, I always played opposite Stan Mikita. He was smart, very shifty, a playmaker who could score goals. Still, we had a lot of good playoff series against Chicago in the mid-1960s, and I had my share of success. One highlight for me was setting the record, which still stands, for the fastest two goals in a playoff game.

Funnily, both goals were scored on almost identical shots. We were playing Chicago in 1965. For the first goal, I came in on two defensemen, on the right side. I cut across, away from one defender, but was immediately confronted by the other defenseman. Using him as a screen, I shot the puck hard but right

along the ice. It went in just inside the right goalpost.

After the face-off at center, the puck went just inside the Chicago blue line. I believe it was Eric Nesterenko who picked up the puck, and I raced toward him. I saw him peek over his shoulder to a defenseman, so I immediately changed course. Sure enough, he passed it back and I got my stick on the puck. Again, I took a couple of strides until the defenseman was close enough to be a screen and fired a wrist shot right along the ice. It went just inside the post on the other side. The two goals came only five seconds apart. It was a wonderful feeling, not only because both goals were scored on Glenn Hall—who I considered to be the best ever along with Terry Sawchuk—but because they put us in the lead and we won the game 4–2. It was particularly satisfying to beat Chicago, who were heavily favored to win the Cup.

Unfortunately, we always lost the finals. I had five tries, and we should have won a couple of times. We once had Toronto down 3–2 in games and were winning for most of game six. The Leafs tied the game late, and Bob Baun scored a bizarre goal in overtime. The shot wasn't that hard, but it hit a bump on the ice, struck the top of Bill Gadsby's stick blade and deflected over Terry Sawchuk's shoulder. But we lost the next game and the Cup.

A couple of years later, we beat the Canadiens in the first two games of the final, right in Montreal. But we lost the series 4–2, after a controversial overtime goal in game six by Henri Richard. He'd been knocked down about 20 feet from the net, but he slid into the net with the puck under his arm for the winning goal. For years I thought I *had* to win a Stanley Cup, but I came to believe that fate was just not on our side. In my first 15 seasons, Chicago won the Cup once. Toronto and Montreal won all the rest.

The most disappointing part of my career came after a great start in my second last year in Toronto. I was about fifth in the league in scoring and played in the All-Star game, but I spent most of the next year and a half on the bench without explanation. I could have stayed in the NHL with Kansas City, but Edmonton in the WHA gave me an offer to play back in my hometown. A lot of family were still there, and I really enjoyed rounding out my professional career where it started.

Elected to the Hockey Hall of Fame in 1982, Norm Ullman notched his thousandth career point as a Toronto Maple Leaf in 1971. (OPPOSITE) Ullman, an elegant skater who played for the Red Wings for 12 seasons, looks for a steal from the Leafs' George Armstrong in front of goaltender Bruce Gamble.

John Vanbiesbrouck

ONE OF THE MOST VALUABLE PIECES OF ADVICE I EVER GOT was from my midget coach. He urged me to go as a walk-on to Sault Ste. Marie and try to play junior hockey. Many people would disagree with him, but he said, "You can always get an education, but you don't always get the chance to become a professional hockey player." It was what I needed to hear, and I thank him. You can't be committed to more than one thing and expect that they're all going to work.

I was disappointed when the New York Rangers decided that I was no longer part of their future. They traded me to Vancouver, who were very up-front in telling me that they were going to expose me in the 1993 expansion draft later that week. I had expected something to change, but to be out in limbo was terrible. It said to me that I was no longer an impact player and that my value had decreased.

It was an unusual draft in that a lot of quality players were exposed. I remembered Phil Esposito in New York telling me, "In order to be successful in anything you do, you have to be able to adapt to the situation. If you resent it or try to do anything else, it's not going to work." The draft took place in June, so I had some time to adapt to being a Florida Panther.

I didn't know what to expect of a first-year expansion club. I tried to talk to people who'd had similar experiences. I ran into Chico Resch, who had gone from the Stanley Cup-winning New York Islanders to an expansion team in Colorado. His team had fared poorly, yet Chico had personally done quite well. I asked him what it would be like. He told me, "There will be a lot of nights when the game will be close, but your team will not have the skill or the ability to muster up the tying or winning goals." I anticipated a frustrating time.

When the Florida team first got together, I was surprised to lose my sense that it was going to be a bad situation. The expansion draft hurt a lot of teams, and we were the benefactor. Maybe I was naive, but right from the outset, I thought, "We're going to accomplish something down here." We performed admirably right from the word "go." We went into Chicago for our first game, one of the toughest buildings in the NHL, and got a 4–4 tie. Our confidence was high, and we held the .500 mark for a long time.

You have to believe in yourself before anyone else will. I got to know myself better by being called upon to reach deep for my teammates. That was true for all of us and made us a good team. I could pick moments from my career that I was happy with, but one save or game is a temporary satisfaction. Consistency is most meaningful. After the 1995-96 season, I could honestly look at myself in the mirror and say that I'm proud of what I did.

My oldest brother Frank was my first inspiration. He was a goalie and six years older. Another brother, Julian, was a shooter, and I stopped a lot of pucks in the basement or the backyard. What really drew me to the net was always being in on the play. And the position never grows old.

Goaltending is constantly being developed. It's never stale. Tony Esposito was an innovative guy. He invented the "cheater," the extension from the thumbpiece to the collar roll of the catching glove. It changed goaltending. I take a piece of his history into the net with me. A modern example of innovation is how Ron Hextall first moved the puck in the mid-1980s. I had always tried to play the puck, but Ron turned handling the puck into a send-a-guy-in-on-a-breakaway, kill-a-penalty, score-a-goal escapade. Goalies started to curve their sticks when we realized that we, too, could really launch the puck.

Eddie Giacomin and Billy Smith have touched my life as a goaltender. I picture them in my mind when I'm on the ice. Sometimes I even hear their voices in my head in an internal conversation, offering me support or giving me technical advice, such as reminding me not to drift off the post. Billy is goaltending coach for the Panthers now, helping me refine my game in the flesh, but his and Eddie's past accomplishments have been the inspiration for so much of my game.

My style is a combination of influences, ranging from watching Bernie Parent, Tony Esposito and Eddie Giacomin handle the puck, Billy Smith's tenacity, Ken Dryden's stand-up style and Grant Fuhr's athletic ability to witnessing Mike Richter's contribution to the evolution of goaltender fitness. I've *tried* to learn from every goaltender I see, especially watching the championship goalies every year. Patrick Roy stands out for me in the modern age. You have to admire these people and learn from them in order to improve.

John Vanbiesbrouck is shown above in his 1996 All-Star game sweater. (OPPOSITE) *"Beezer" was the cornerstone of the Florida Panthers franchise for five seasons. After stints with the Flyers and the Islanders, he joined the Devils for a Stanley Cup run before retiring in June 2001.*

Pat Verbeek

My dad and I took a train from Sarnia to Montreal for the 1982 NHL entry draft. I knew that, at 5-foot-9, I had a height disadvantage, but I was ranked to be chosen in the first few rounds. I had grown accustomed to concerns over my height and had worked hard to prove that I was physically strong and tough enough to make it. I'm a pretty emotional person, with a passion for winning. When my emotions get stirred up, I don't find it hard to play a more aggressive and meaner style of game than many people are willing to play. The New Jersey Devils picked me in the third round.

The Devils called me up for my first NHL game late in the 1982-83 season. We were playing our biggest rival, the New York Rangers. I didn't get a shift on the ice until late in the third period. We were killing a penalty, and I chased a puck down the ice. When Dave Maloney tried to cut back into me, I ended up hitting him pretty hard into the boards. He was knocked unconscious, and a brawl ensued. I emerged unscathed, and that was my welcome into the league.

I spent six full seasons with New Jersey. Then I heard rumors that my name was circulating in trade talk, but

I didn't believe them. Even though I'd seen teammates traded, I never thought it would happen to me. I was in the woods in northern Ontario on a fishing trip when my trade was made. I called home after the trip, and my sister told me I was a Hartford Whaler. It was a real surprise and a very weird feeling. It took time to get used to the idea, but I looked forward to getting to Hartford.

I was captain for my last three of the six seasons I played for the Whalers. Being captain of a team brings some pressure, but I loved the feeling of responsibility. You have to lead on and off the ice. I was honored by, and enjoyed having, the captaincy, but being on a team that was struggling to win games made a hard job more difficult. In hindsight, there were situations I could have handled better. I learned a lot when I was traded to the Rangers and saw how Mark Messier served as captain. Mark is able to give his team a kick in the butt without belittling anyone. He keeps everyone feeling part of the team—that they are being counted upon for the group's success. I give my best every shift, and in Hartford when I saw someone who wasn't doing the same, I came down on him. I can be very intense and was probably too harsh at times. Mark showed me another way to handle those situations.

Hartford and New York are close geographically, but playing for the Rangers is a whole different ball game. New Yorkers take their sports seriously, and I came in when the Rangers were trying to defend their Stanley Cup. I enjoyed being in the media spotlight in front of fans who went crazy when we were winning and loudly let us know when they didn't like what we were doing. I'll likely never play in that kind of atmosphere again, because New York is unique in the NHL in that respect. At times, it felt as if the fans were pour-ing salt into our wounds, but despite that adversity, I loved being a Ranger.

To be able to select the team that you want to go to is an empowering experience. Free agency is no different than an average person being able to choose which city he wants to work in, but until recently, professional hockey players were never able to make that decision. Being free to sign a contract with the Dallas Stars was very satisfying for me. Dallas is a heavy contrast to New York in that hockey is only beginning to grow in popularity there, but it's no hockey wilderness either. The Dallas Cowboys garner most of the media attention, but we're still always on the front page of the sports section.

Perhaps like most Canadian boys, I knew I wanted to be a professional hockey player when I was 7 years old. The most exciting aspect of joining the NHL was realizing that I'd accomplished what I had so long wanted to do. That realization also meant I needed to set some new goals. I've continually done that, but looking for a Stanley Cup ring is a driving force in me. I also just love to go to the rink in the morning. After talking with retired players, I know I'll miss being in a team atmosphere. I love jousting with my teammates in ways you just can't get away with in the company of other people. Being part of a team is the kind of fun you can't have anywhere else.

*Pat Verbeek took on a leadership role in his six seasons with the Hartford Whalers, serving three years as team captain. (**Opposite**) Verbeek won a Stanley Cup ring with the Dallas Stars in 1999. Here, he winds up for a shot on net before Toronto's Mark Kolesar reaches the puck. Verbeek's teammate Todd Harvey looks on.*

Doug Wilson

I scored the tying goal against Russia to send the last game of the 1984 Canada Cup tournament into overtime. Wayne Gretzky gave me a great pass from the corner, and Bobby Bourne screened the goalie as I rushed into the slot and fired the puck at the net. That tournament was hockey at its highest level, and every athlete loves when the best play the best. We had so many great players on our team, and it was about the last time the Russians played us with their famous KLM line—Vladimir Krutov, Igor Larionov and Sergei

Makarov. To play for my country, score that goal and go on to win in overtime was as good as it gets. The memories and friendships from going through that kind of experience will last a lifetime.

My brother Murray and I spent countless summer hours as boys shooting pucks off a piece of plywood against the side of our house. The only problem was that the house had aluminum siding about halfway up. We'd run when we hit it, although my mom obviously knew who did it! I loved to shoot, and it became an important tool for me. Murray was a natural athlete who did the decathlon, and he included me in his activities from the time I was a little boy. I can never repay him for what he gave me.

He joined the Montreal Canadiens five years before I graduated to the Blackhawks, and I was able to spend time with him and his teammates. You learn by osmosis when you spend time with men such as Henri Richard, Yvan Cournoyer, Larry Robinson and Bob Gainey, not so much *about* the game but about the commitment and passion you need to bring to the game. The Montreal Canadiens scouts always had opinions on how I was doing as a junior, so Murray would phone me and pass on helpful information. I was fortunate to play for the finest junior coach in Canada, Brian Kilrea, but when my hockey season finished, I'd go to Montreal, take in a lot of games and hang around the locker room. I idolized my brother anyway, but to be in that atmosphere with him was tremendous. There seemed to be a Stanley Cup victory almost every year—Murray won four of them—and I got to take part in the celebrations. The Montreal Canadiens are known as a classy operation with a great tradition, and there was no inconsistency seeing them behind closed doors.

My first roommate when I joined the Chicago Black-

hawks was Stan Mikita, and Bobby Orr was one of my early defense partners. They weren't just superstar players, they were superstars as people, and along with men such as Keith Magnuson and Cliff Koroll, they had a big impact on my life. Both exemplified a saying I first learned from my father and have tried to live my life by: "You make a living by what you get, and you make a life by what you give." Stan was always incredibly giving, not only to charity events but to the people he interacted with on a daily basis. Bobby Orr was the same way.

Bobby told me, "Go with what you have. If you can skate and make plays, jump up there." He had so much talent, vision and genius that no one could emulate what he did exactly, but I watched him closely and learned more about timing and reading situations.

Winning the Norris Trophy in 1982 meant a lot to me, because it was one of the last things my father saw me accomplish. He passed away from cancer shortly after. The award was a great honor, but to have him able to attend the presentation ceremony and share that moment made it even more special. He was one of the great givers of all time.

Everything had fallen into place that year, although I broke my jaw and played six weeks with it wired shut. I lost 25 pounds, so I guess I was extra-fast! I scored 39 goals and 46 assists, but I still think I had my best season the following year. My numbers weren't quite as high, but my defensive game was stronger. The Norris Trophy gave me a level to strive for and gave my career another kick-start.

I had a no-trade clause in my contract with the Blackhawks, but I received an unusual offer to be involved in orchestrating my own trade in 1991. My choices boiled down to the New York Rangers or the new San Jose Sharks. The opportunity to be in on the ground floor of an NHL team was an exciting challenge. My wife Kathy and I researched the San Jose area and concluded the move would be good for our family too. It was the best decision we've ever made. I captained the first-year Sharks, and it was one of the closest teams I ever played on.

My thousandth career game was coincidentally but fittingly played against the Chicago Blackhawks. The Sharks brought in all my friends and family and started a scholarship fund in my name to mark the occasion. I had similar feelings of appreciation when I served as an honorary team captain at the 1997 NHL All-Star game in San Jose. It felt like a reward for being a pioneer.

Doug Wilson was captain of the San Jose Sharks in the team's first two seasons of operation. (**Opposite**) *Wilson was also a three-time All-Star in his 14 seasons on defense for the Chicago Blackhawks.*

Lorne "Gump" Worsley

HOCKEY BROUGHT ME UPS AND DOWNS, BUT I ALWAYS MANaged to have some fun. We played for the love of the game and the sweater we were wearing. I still live in the house that my wife and I put a down payment on with the $1,000 award I received for winning the Calder Trophy for best rookie in 1953.

Montreal can be a difficult place to be if you're not winning. I lost old friends, and my wife would have "Your husband stinks!" shouted at her in the grocery store. My son was told he wouldn't pass if I didn't get his teacher playoff tickets. I had to go raise hell at the

school! When I was 40 years old, I had some arguments with management and wondered whether it was worth continuing. I phoned my wife and she said, "Come on home." I went to see general manager Sam Pollock and told him I was quitting. "No one quits the Montreal Canadiens," he said. I told him that I just had.

Wren Blair called me a month or so later, and I went to play for Minnesota. I loved it there, and Cesare Maniago and I became a "Mutt and Jeff" goaltending tandem. Cesare eventually convinced me to have a mask made, and I tried it in practice but couldn't get

used to it. I found it very warm and couldn't see the puck between my feet. I only wore a mask for the last six games of my career. I was 45 years old, knew I was retiring, and Minnesota was mathematically eliminated from the playoffs. Wren Blair said, "Save your eyes, Gump. Put it on." But I didn't like it.

I grew up in Quebec, but I played for Rangers-sponsored teams. I was allowed to attend New York's training camps, which were a month long, and Charlie Rayner tutored me on how to play goal. I had some of the basics, but he taught me most of what I know. I did that for three years. Charlie was very good to me, staying after practice and getting a couple of guys to shoot on us. He showed me how to cut the angles and play the position. He was coming to the end of his career, and I eventually took his spot on the Rangers when he retired.

Facing a lot of shots was an occupational hazard in New York. Our team wasn't that bad— four of us are now in the Hall of Fame—but we had poor coaching. One coach of many, Phil Watson, always took the credit for wins and blamed the players for losses. He had coached me on the New York Rovers before I turned pro, and he felt he could pick on me. It got so bad that one day I told him, "I was here when you arrived, and I'll be here when you leave." He was gone the next year.

I was traded to Montreal halfway through my career, and I've yet to be informed by the Rangers. Frank Selke, Sr., called to welcome me to Montreal, but Muzz Patrick had told me the night before the trade that I'd be a Ranger for the rest of my career. I had grown accustomed to facing 50-shot games in New York. When I got to Montreal, I generally only got about 20 shots a game, which in truth was harder. Not only was the expectation of winning strong, I wasn't in the game as much and really had to concentrate.

Shortly after I arrived in Montreal, I was sent down to Quebec. I was 34 years old and thought it was the end of my career. I didn't get the callback for a year, but I came up and won my first Stanley Cup. The last five minutes of the seventh game seemed to last five years. I kept looking at the clock, and the hands never seemed to move. We were leading 4–0, and I was sure I'd never let *five* goals in, but I was incredibly nervous. I was 13 years in the league by then. I can't really put the feeling in words, but I could have walked home without my feet touching the ground. Every Cup win was the same, and I won four over the next five years.

Concentration, never taking my eye off the puck even if it was in the other end, was critical. I also had the habit of always knowing when the big guns were on the ice. Then I'd be ready. George Armstrong would shoot for the far side 99 percent of the time. Howe was unpredictable, but Delvecchio usually shot high. Hull would try to shake the goalies up by talking of firing his first shot at the goalie's head, but then he'd put it around our knees. Of course, when the curved stick came out, no one knew where the puck was going. The people in the fifteenth row were in more trouble than I was, and I had no mask on!

Being selected to the Hall of Fame in 1980 was like winning the Stanley Cup all over again. It's a marvelous feeling to be a member, the icing on the cake of my career.

Lorne Gump Worsley

Lorne "Gump" Worsley backstopped four Stanley Cup victories for the Montreal Canadiens in the 1960s.
(Opposite) *Worsley makes a save against Gary Sabourin and the St. Louis Blues and clears the puck to Minnesota North Stars teammate Barry Gibbs.*

Alexei Yashin

WHEN I WAS GROWING UP IN RUSSIA, GETTING TO THE WORLD Championships and the Olympics were the highest achievements. I won two gold medals in the World Championships, one with Russia's junior team in 1992, one with the national team in 1993. Both were wonderful, fulfilling dreams I'd had since I was a boy. Winning a championship creates a special feeling, but it can pass rather quickly. I was the happiest person in the world for 15 or 20 minutes after winning, but then I started to think about the future and what might come next.

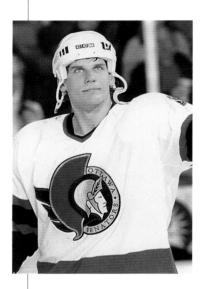

Some good friends came to the NHL the year before I did. Alexei Kovalev, Igor Korolev and Darius Kasparaitis tried to tell me about what life is like here, but it's really hard to understand until you come over. There was no real surprise, but I was most struck by how the different cultures have produced different mentalities. I'm not talking about hockey; I'm talking about the general culture. I find that North Americans work very hard, maybe because it's so hard to find employment. They're very happy just to have a job. In Russia, a job was guaranteed and everyone got the same salary, but there was no real incentive to improve yourself. In the North American system, you have to be learning something new all the time.

I have played professional hockey both in Russia and in North America, and one thing is constant: When I get involved in the game, my results are better. I try to do the best I can, whether it's killing a penalty or trying to score a goal. I get worried and disappointed only if I'm not getting chances to score. I take nothing for granted—in the NHL, anytime you put the puck in the net, it is a pleasant surprise.

Along with a few other young Russian players, I came to the 1992 NHL entry draft, but I didn't fully realize what the event was all about. I hadn't paid much attention to the previous drafts, only observing that some guys from Russia had been chosen and then played in the NHL. It wasn't really until a couple of months after the draft that I understood that it was a great honor to be chosen second overall.

I enjoy playing against my old Russian friends, because there is an extra element of competition there. I want to do well against them, so there's no joking around—it's as intense as playing against Mark Messier or Mario Lemieux—but as professionals, we do the best possible for our own teams while remaining good friends off the ice. I really like that about the NHL.

It's part of the business of hockey that sometimes there are difficult negotiations. I've had some contract disputes that have kept me out of the lineup, but I was always supportive of my teammates. It didn't matter where I was—in Russia or Ottawa—I was happy for them when they won and sad when they lost. It was tough to be away from the game. I worked out with the Red Army team in Moscow, practicing hard while waiting for decisions to be made, but that was not nearly the same. Once everything got resolved, I was happy to get back.

Playing on a team like the Ottawa Senators forces you to look down the road. The future is bright, because we have so many young players who are gaining valuable experience. We're working together, improving as a unit.

I've had a couple of five-point games and was selected the NHL Player of the Week once. That happens to someone every week, but it was a big event for me. Still, my greatest moment in the NHL was participating in the 1994 All-Star game. I had played *against* the greatest players, but I had never really associated with most of them. It was pretty scary to be the only rookie around so many superstars. Alex Mogilny sat beside me in the dressing room and was very helpful, but it seems to be a tradition that everyone introduces themselves. I liked the atmosphere, where everyone treated everyone else like an equal. It was a great celebration of hockey.

I was happy with the game I played. Lines were frequently mixed because the coach tried to give everybody ice time, but I played most of the game with Joe Sakic and Pierre Turgeon. I'll remember all my life the goals I scored. I had a two-on-one with Joe. He hit the post, and the puck landed right on my stick. I had an open net to shoot at. On my second goal, I didn't even see the puck go in right away. I fired a shot that glanced off the goalie's stick and went top-shelf. With less than four minutes left in the match, that goal made it 9–8 and turned out to be the game-winner. That was a great feeling.

Alexei Yashin is the Ottawa Senators' career leader in goals, assists and points. However, several contractual disputes, including one that cost him the entire 1999-2000 season, prompted his June 2001 trade to the New York Islanders. (OPPOSITE) Yashin shows great balance and stickhandling ability behind the opposition net.

Steve Yzerman

My rookie year in Detroit was a lot of fun for me. For the most part, I was on a line with Ron Duguay and John Ogrodnick, both great skaters and goal scorers. Many other strong veterans were on the team. I learned a lot, especially from Brad Park and Danny Gare. It was a real thrill to play in the All-Star game that year. I was a late addition and was called just a few days prior to the game. It was quite intimidating to meet most of the league's best players for the first time, and I was a bit overwhelmed by the whole experience.

The Red Wings had indicated their interest in me at the end of my last junior season with Peterborough but only said that I was one of the players they were considering. I was not surprised to go so high in the draft, as I had a very successful junior career, but when Detroit selected me fourth overall, I don't think there were high expectations for me to play right away. As a result, I came in pretty quietly and was able to develop without a lot of pressure.

I was only 21 but starting my fourth year with the Red Wings in the fall of 1986. Jacques Demers was named coach, and a lot of player changes were made. In short order, I had become one of the longest-serving veterans on the team. Jacques called me into his office and surprised me with the news that I was the new captain. It's a role I take as seriously now as I did then. I've always tried to do the little things well. On the ice, I strive to be strong and solid defensively and play my position well. Off the ice, I work hard to be well conditioned. There are occasions when I have to talk to one of the guys, but we have a conscientious group of players here who work very hard.

I really got on a roll in the 1988-89 season. We had a competitive team, and I got a lot of ice time. I was very pleased with my production; my total of 65 goals and 90 assists might have won a scoring championship in another era, but it doesn't work that way. Mario Lemieux had about 200 points, and Wayne Gretzky almost as many. Those two guys are among the best of all time, and I was honored to be closest to them in the scoring race.

It seems a long time ago now, but I'll always treasure receiving the Lester Pearson Award in 1989. I haven't won a whole lot of individual awards over my career, and to be voted as the league's outstanding player by the players themselves was certainly an honor.

Hockey takes on a different meaning when you play for your country. I don't feel any extra pressure—at least, no more than when I'm playing in Detroit. It's just the type of competition that brings out the best in everyone. I first played for Canada on our World Junior team in 1983. We finished third, but I really enjoyed the experience.

I was just as glad to participate in the World Cup last year, even though we didn't win. I will always remember the overtime goal I scored. The goal turned out to have been offside, but the linesman missed the call. I came down the left side and was going wide. I shot the puck at the net but fanned on it a little. I think the puck was going wide, but it hit the goalie in a funny spot. I didn't even see it go into the net. I was taken out into the corner and assumed that the puck had gone back into the slot and someone had banged in the rebound.

I was a Bruins and Islanders fan when I was growing up, but with 14 seasons in Detroit, I've got Red Wings blood in me now. The past few years have been really enjoyable. We've had a good team that's gone as far as the Stanley Cup finals. That's a lot of fun. There are high expectations for us now, and we share them. This is a good situation to be in. There is a lot of excitement around town and in the locker room. Setting high goals helps me to be sharp and play well. And my goal, our goal, is, of course, to win the Stanley Cup.

I'm playing a little different style of game for the Red Wings these days, and I've enjoyed the transition. We play a simpler brand of hockey, dumping it out and dumping it in. We're now a more defensive club, and I'm finding it gratifying to win close, low-scoring, hard-fought games. I concentrate on defense but also work hard to get scoring chances. I really bear down when those chances come. I have to produce, because the name of the game is still to put the puck in the net.

Steve Yzerman, team captain since 1986, led Detroit to the Stanley Cup in 1997 and again in 1998, when he won the Conn Smythe Trophy. Yzerman crossed the 600-career-goal mark while making the First All-Star team during the 1999-2000 season. (Opposite) Yzerman snaps a shot at the net before Toronto's Kenny Jonsson can reach the puck.

Appendix

Current as of July 7, 2001.

Abbreviations

CALDER: The Calder Memorial Trophy is an annual award presented to "the player selected as the most proficient in his first year of competition in the NHL," as selected by the Professional Hockey Writers' Association.

1ST ALL-STAR AND 2ND ALL-STAR: A First and Second All-Star team is selected at the end of every season by the Professional Hockey Writers' Association.

ROSS: The Art Ross Trophy is presented annually to "the player who leads the league in scoring points at the end of the regular season."

RICHARD: The Maurice "Rocket" Richard Trophy, inaugurated in 1999, is an annual award presented to "the player who leads the league in goals scored at the end of the regular season."

HART: The Hart Memorial Trophy is an annual award presented to "the player adjudged to be the most valuable to his team," as selected by the Professional Hockey Writers' Association.

BYNG: The Lady Byng Memorial Trophy is an annual award presented to "the player adjudged to have exhibited the best type of sportsmanship and gentlemanly conduct combined with a high standard of playing ability," as selected by the Professional Hockey Writers' Association.

NORRIS: The James Norris Memorial Trophy is an annual award presented to "the defense player who demonstrates throughout the season the greatest all-round ability in the position," as selected by the Professional Hockey Writers' Association.

SELKE: The Frank J. Selke Trophy in an annual award presented to "the forward who best excels in the defensive aspects of the game," as selected by the Professional Hockey Writers' Association.

MASTERTON: The Bill Masterton Memorial Trophy is an annual award presented to "the player who best exemplifies the qualities of perseverance, sportsmanship, and dedication to hockey," as selected by the Professional Hockey Writers' Association.

CLANCY: The King Clancy Memorial Trophy is an annual award presented to "the player who best exemplifies leadership qualities on and off the ice and has made a noteworthy humanitarian contribution in his community," as selected by the Professional Hockey Writers' Association.

JENNINGS: The William M. Jennings Trophy is an annual award presented "to the goalkeeper(s) having played a minimum of 25 games for the team with the fewest goals scored against it."

VEZINA: The Vezina Trophy is an annual award presented to "the goalkeeper adjudged to be the best at his position," as selected by the general managers of each NHL club. Until the 1981-82 season, the Vezina Trophy was awarded to "the goalkeeper(s) of the team with the fewest goals scored against it," which became the criteria for the William M. Jennings Trophy.

PEARSON: The Lester B. Pearson Award is an annual award presented to the NHL's outstanding player, as selected by the National Hockey League Players' Association.

SMYTHE: The Conn Smythe Trophy is an annual award presented to "the most valuable player for his team in the playoffs," as selected by the Professional Hockey Writers' Association.

HOF: Honored member of the Hockey Hall of Fame. The year of induction follows.

rs: regular season
po: playoffs
For forwards and defensemen:
gp: games played; **g:** goals; **a:** assists; **tp:** total points; **pim:** penalties in minutes
For goaltenders:
gp: games played; **m:** minutes; **ga:** goals against; **so:** shutouts; **ave:** goals against per game average

The following is provided for each player:
Name
Birthday
NHL career dates
NHL teams played for
NHL statistics
NHL awards

ANDY BATHGATE
August 28, 1932
NHL Career: 1952–68, 1970–71
NY Rangers, Toronto, Detroit, Pittsburgh

	gp	g	a	tp	pim
rs	1069	349	624	973	624
po	54	21	14	35	76

1st All-Star (2), 2nd All-Star (2), Hart, Stanley Cup, HOF 1978

JEAN BELIVEAU
August 31, 1931
NHL Career: 1950–51, 1952–71
Montreal

	gp	g	a	tp	pim
rs	1125	507	712	1219	1029
po	162	79	97	176	211

1st All-Star (6), 2nd All-Star (4), Ross, Hart (2), Smythe, Stanley Cup (10), HOF 1972

LEO BOIVIN
August 2, 1932
NHL Career: 1951–70
Toronto, Boston, Detroit, Pittsburgh, Minnesota

	gp	g	a	tp	pim
rs	1150	72	250	322	1192
po	54	3	10	13	59

HOF 1986

PETER BONDRA
February 7, 1968
NHL Career: 1990–
Washington

	gp	g	a	tp	pim
rs	754	382	282	664	525
po	67	26	25	51	46

MIKE BOSSY
January 22, 1957
NHL Career: 1977–87
NY Islanders

	gp	g	a	tp	pim
rs	752	573	553	1126	210
po	129	85	75	160	38

Calder, 1st All-Star (5), 2nd All-Star (3), Byng (3), Smythe, Stanley Cup (4), HOF 1991

RAYMOND BOURQUE
December 28, 1960
NHL Career: 1979–2001
Boston, Colorado

	gp	g	a	tp	pim
rs	1612	410	1169	1579	1141
po	214	41	139	180	171

Calder, 1st All-Star (13), 2nd All-Star (6), Norris (5), Clancy, Stanley Cup

JOHNNY BOWER
November 8, 1924
NHL Career: 1953–54, 1958–70
NY Rangers, Toronto

	gp	m	ga	so	ave
rs	552	32016	1340	37	2.51
po	74	4378	180	5	2.47

1st All-Star, Vezina (2), Stanley Cup (4), HOF 1976

JOHNNY BUCYK
May 12, 1935
NHL Career: 1955–78
Detroit, Boston

	gp	g	a	tp	pim
rs	1540	556	813	1369	497
po	124	41	62	103	42

1st All-Star, 2nd All-Star, Byng (2), Stanley Cup (2), HOF 1981

PAVEL BURE
March 31, 1971
NHL Career: 1991–
Vancouver, Florida

	gp	g	a	tp	pim
rs	595	384	296	680	406
po	64	35	35	70	74

Calder, 1st All-Star, 2nd All-Star (2), Richard (2)

JIM CAREY
May 31, 1974
NHL Career: 1995–99
Washington, Boston, St Louis

	gp	m	ga	so	ave
rs	172	9668	416	16	2.58
po	10	455	35	0	4.62

1st All-Star, Vezina

GERRY CHEEVERS
December 2, 1940
NHL Career: 1961–62, 1965–72, 1975–80
Boston

	gp	m	ga	so	ave
rs	418	24394	1174	26	2.89
po	88	5396	242	8	2.69

Stanley Cup (2), HOF 1985

CHRIS CHELIOS
January 25, 1962
NHL Career: 1983–
Montreal, Chicago, Detroit

	gp	g	a	tp	pim
rs	1181	168	667	835	2389
po	187	29	93	122	343

1st All-Star (4), 2nd All-Star (2), Norris (3), Stanley Cup

DINO CICCARELLI
February 8, 1960
NHL Career: 1980–99
Minnesota, Washington, Detroit,
Tampa Bay, Florida

	gp	g	a	tp	pim
rs	1218	602	591	1193	1398
po	141	73	45	118	211

PAUL COFFEY
June 1, 1961
NHL Career: 1980–
Edmonton, Pittsburgh, Los Angeles,
Detroit, Hartford, Philadelphia,
Chicago, Boston

	gp	g	a	tp	pim
rs	1409	396	1135	1531	1802
po	194	59	137	196	264

1st All-Star (4), 2nd All-Star (4),
Norris (3), Stanley Cup (4)

YVAN COURNOYER
November 22, 1943
NHL Career: 1963–79
Montreal

	gp	g	a	tp	pim
rs	968	428	435	863	255
po	147	64	63	127	47

2nd All-Star (4), Smythe,
Stanley Cup (10), HOF 1982

VINCENT DAMPHOUSSE
December 17, 1967
NHL Career: 1986–
Toronto, Edmonton, Montreal,
San Jose

	gp	g	a	tp	pim
rs	1132	377	668	1045	998
po	111	32	50	82	112

Stanley Cup

ALEX DELVECCHIO
December 4, 1931
NHL Career: 1950–74
Detroit

	gp	g	a	tp	pim
rs	1549	456	825	1281	383
po	121	35	69	104	29

2nd All-Star, Byng (3),
Stanley Cup (3), HOF 1977

MARCEL DIONNE
August 3, 1951
NHL Career: 1971–89
Detroit, Los Angeles, NY Rangers

	gp	g	a	tp	pim
rs	1348	731	1040	1771	600
po	49	21	24	45	17

1st All-Star (2), 2nd All-Star (2),
Ross, Byng (2), Pearson (2),
HOF 1992

BERNIE FEDERKO
May 12, 1956
NHL Career: 1976–90
St Louis, Detroit

	gp	g	a	tp	pim
rs	1000	369	761	1130	487
po	91	35	66	101	83

SERGEI FEDOROV
December 13, 1969
NHL Career: 1990–
Detroit

	gp	g	a	tp	pim
rs	747	333	470	803	499
po	135	44	97	141	93

Hart, Selke (2), Pearson,
Stanley Cup (2)

SLAVA FETISOV
April 20, 1958
NHL Career: 1989–98
New Jersey, Detroit

	gp	g	a	tp	pim
rs	546	36	192	228	656
po	116	2	26	28	147

Stanley Cup (2), HOF 2001

THEOREN FLEURY
June 29, 1968
NHL Career: 1988–
Calgary, Colorado, NY Rangers

	gp	g	a	tp	pim
rs	948	419	573	992	1547
po	77	34	45	79	116

2nd All-Star, Stanley Cup

RON FRANCIS
March 1, 1963
NHL Career: 1981–
Hartford, Pittsburgh, Carolina

	gp	g	a	tp	pim
rs	1489	487	1137	1624	917
po	135	40	83	123	87

Selke, Byng (2), Stanley Cup (2)

GRANT FUHR
September 28, 1962
NHL Career: 1981–2000
Edmonton, Toronto, Buffalo, Los
Angeles, St. Louis, Calgary

	gp	m	ga	so	ave
rs	868	48945	2756	25	3.38
po	150	8834	430	6	2.92

1st All-Star, 2nd All-Star, Jennings,
Vezina, Stanley Cup (5)

MIKE GARTNER
October 29, 1959
NHL Career: 1979–98
Washington, Minnesota,
NY Rangers, Toronto, Phoenix

	gp	g	a	tp	pim
rs	1432	708	627	1335	1159
po	122	43	50	93	125

HOF 2001

BERNIE GEOFFRION
February 16, 1931
NHL Career: 1950–64, 1966–68
Montreal, NY Rangers

	gp	g	a	tp	pim
rs	883	393	429	822	689
po	132	58	60	118	88

Calder, 1st All-Star, 2nd All-Star (2),
Ross (2), Hart, Stanley Cup (6),
HOF 1972

ROD GILBERT
July 1, 1941
NHL Career: 1960–78
NY Rangers

	gp	g	a	tp	pim
rs	1065	406	615	1021	508
po	79	34	33	67	43

1st All-Star, 2nd All-Star, Masterton,
HOF 1982

DOUG GILMOUR
June 25, 1963
NHL Career: 1983–
St. Louis, Calgary, Toronto,
New Jersey, Chicago, Buffalo

	gp	g	a	tp	pim
rs	1342	429	914	1343	1207
po	170	56	122	178	219

Selke, Stanley Cup

MICHEL GOULET
April 21, 1960
NHL Career: 1979–94
Quebec, Chicago

	gp	g	a	tp	pim
rs	1089	548	604	1152	825
po	92	39	39	78	110

1st All-Star (3), 2nd All-Star (2),
HOF 1998

WAYNE GRETZKY
January 26, 1961
NHL Career: 1979–99
Edmonton, Los Angeles, St. Louis,
NY Rangers

	gp	g	a	tp	pim
rs	1417	885	1910	2795	563
po	208	122	260	382	66

1st All-Star (8), 2nd All-Star (7),
Ross (10), Hart (9), Byng (4),
Pearson (5), Smythe (2),
Stanley Cup (4), HOF 1999

GLENN HALL
October 3, 1931
NHL Career: 1952–53, 1954–71
Detroit, Chicago, St. Louis

	gp	m	ga	so	ave
rs	906	53484	2222	84	2.49
po	115	6899	320	6	2.78

Calder, 1st All-Star (7),
2nd All-Star (4), Vezina (3), Smythe,
Stanley Cup, HOF 1975

DOMINIK HASEK
January 29, 1965
NHL Career: 1990–
Chicago, Buffalo, Detroit

	gp	m	ga	so	ave
rs	516	29873	1114	56	2.23
po	73	4444	154	6	2.08

1st All-Star (6), Hart (2), Pearson (2),
Jennings (2), Vezina (6)

DALE HAWERCHUK
April 4, 1963
NHL Career: 1981–97
Winnipeg, Buffalo, St. Louis,
Philadelphia

	gp	g	a	tp	pim
rs	1188	518	891	1409	730
po	97	30	69	99	67

Calder, 2nd All-Star, HOF 2001

PAUL HENDERSON
January 28, 1943
NHL Career: 1962–74, 1979–80
Detroit, Toronto, Atlanta

	gp	g	a	tp	pim
rs	707	236	241	477	304
po	56	11	14	25	28

GORDIE HOWE
March 31, 1928
NHL Career: 1946–71, 1979–80
Detroit, Hartford

	gp	g	a	tp	pim
rs	1767	801	1049	1850	1685
po	157	68	92	160	220

1st All-Star (12), 2nd All-Star (9),
Ross (6), Hart (6), Stanley Cup (4),
HOF 1972

HARRY HOWELL
December 28, 1932
NHL Career: 1952–73
NY Rangers, Oakland, California,
Los Angeles

	gp	g	a	tp	pim
rs	1411	94	324	418	1298
po	38	3	3	6	32

1st All-Star, Norris, HOF 1979

BOBBY HULL
January 3, 1939
NHL Career: 1957–72, 1979–80
Chicago, Winnipeg, Hartford

	gp	g	a	tp	pim
rs	1063	610	560	1170	640
po	119	62	67	129	102

1st All-Star (10), 2nd All-Star (2),
Ross (3), Hart (2), Byng, Stanley Cup,
HOF 1983

BRETT HULL
August 9, 1964
NHL Career: 1985–
Calgary, St. Louis, Dallas

	gp	g	a	tp	pim
rs	1019	649	534	1183	389
po	163	90	76	166	65

1st All-Star (3), Hart, Byng, Pearson,
Stanley Cup

DENNIS HULL
November 19, 1944
NHL Career: 1964–78
Chicago, Detroit

	gp	g	a	tp	pim
rs	959	303	351	654	261
po	104	33	34	67	30

2nd All-Star

DALE HUNTER
July 31, 1960
NHL Career: 1980–99
Quebec, Washington, Colorado

	gp	g	a	tp	pim
rs	1345	321	688	1009	3446
po	167	41	73	114	691

PAUL KARIYA
October 16, 1974
NHL Career: 1994–
Anaheim

	gp	g	a	tp	pim
rs	442	243	288	531	137
po	14	8	9	17	4

1st All-Star (3), 2nd All-Star, Byng (2)

RED KELLY
July 9, 1927
NHL Career: 1947–67
Detroit, Toronto

	gp	g	a	tp	pim
rs	1316	281	542	823	327
po	164	33	59	92	51

1st All-Star (6), 2nd All-Star (2),
Norris, Byng (4), Stanley Cup (8),
HOF 1969

JARI KURRI
May 18, 1960
NHL Career: 1980–98
Edmonton, Los Angeles, NY
Rangers, Anaheim, Colorado

	gp	g	a	tp	pim
rs	1251	601	797	1398	545
po	200	106	127	233	123

1st All-Star (2), 2nd All-Star (3),
Byng, Stanley Cup (5), HOF 2001

GUY LAFLEUR
September 20, 1951
NHL Career: 1971–85, 1988–91
Montreal, NY Rangers, Quebec

	gp	g	a	tp	pim
rs	1126	560	793	1353	399
po	128	58	76	134	67

1st All-Star (6), Ross (3), Hart (2),
Pearson (3), Smythe, Stanley Cup (5),
HOF 1988

STEVE LARMER
June 16, 1961
NHL Career: 1980–95
Chicago, NY Rangers

	gp	g	a	tp	pim
rs	1006	441	571	1012	532
po	140	56	75	131	89

Calder, Stanley Cup

BRIAN LEETCH
March 3, 1968
NHL Career: 1987–
NY Rangers

	gp	g	a	tp	pim
rs	939	205	655	860	453
po	82	28	61	89	30

Calder, 1st All-Star (2), 2nd All-Star
(3), Norris (2), Smythe, Stanley Cup

MARIO LEMIEUX
October 5, 1965
NHL Career: 1984–97, 2000–
Pittsburgh

	gp	g	a	tp	pim
rs	788	648	922	1570	755
po	107	76	96	172	87

Calder, 1st All-Star (5), 2nd All-Star
(4), Ross (6), Hart (3), Pearson (4),
Masterton, Smythe (2),
Stanley Cup (2), HOF 1997

TREVOR LINDEN
April 11, 1970
NHL Career: 1988–
Vancouver, NY Islanders, Montreal,
Washington

	gp	g	a	tp	pim
rs	928	303	397	700	704
po	85	30	53	83	82

Clancy

ERIC LINDROS
February 28, 1973
NHL Career: 1992–2000, 2001–
Philadelphia

	gp	g	a	tp	pim
rs	486	290	369	659	946
po	50	24	33	57	118

1st All-Star, 2nd All-Star, Hart,
Pearson

TED LINDSAY
July 29, 1925
NHL Career: 1944–60, 1964–65
Detroit, Chicago

	gp	g	a	tp	pim
rs	1068	379	472	851	1808
po	133	47	49	96	194

1st All-Star (8), 2nd All-Star, Ross,
Stanley Cup (4), HOF 1966

FRANK MAHOVLICH
January 10, 1938
NHL Career: 1956–74
Toronto, Detroit, Montreal

	gp	g	a	tp	pim
rs	1181	533	570	1103	1056
po	137	51	67	118	163

Calder, 1st All-Star (3), 2nd All-Star
(6), Stanley Cup (6), HOF 1981

LANNY McDONALD
February 16, 1953
NHL Career: 1973–89
Toronto, Colorado, Calgary

	gp	g	a	tp	pim
rs	1111	500	506	1006	899
po	117	44	40	84	120

2nd All-Star (2), Clancy, Masterton,
Stanley Cup, HOF 1992

RICK MIDDLETON
December 4, 1953
NHL Career: 1974–88
NY Rangers, Boston

	gp	g	a	tp	pim
rs	1005	448	540	988	157
po	114	45	55	100	19

2nd All-Star, Byng

STAN MIKITA
May 20, 1940
NHL Career: 1958–80
Chicago

	gp	g	a	tp	pim
rs	1394	541	926	1467	1270
po	155	59	91	150	169

1st All-Star (6), 2nd All-Star (2),
Ross (4), Hart (2), Byng (2),
Stanley Cup, HOF 1983

MIKE MODANO
June 7, 1970
NHL Career: 1988–
Minnesota, Dallas

	gp	g	a	tp	pim
rs	868	382	518	900	600
po	127	45	64	109	86

2nd All-Star, Stanley Cup

ALEXANDER MOGILNY
February 18, 1969
NHL Career: 1989–
Buffalo, Vancouver, New Jersey,
Toronto

	gp	g	a	tp	pim
rs	780	396	445	841	394
po	85	24	38	62	38

2nd All-Star (2), Stanley Cup

LARRY MURPHY
March 8, 1961
NHL Career: 1980–
Los Angeles, Washington, Minne-
sota, Pittsburgh, Toronto, Detroit

	gp	g	a	tp	pim
rs	1615	287	929	1216	1084
po	215	37	115	152	201

2nd All-Star (3), Stanley Cup (4)

CAM NEELY
June 6, 1965
NHL Career: 1983–96
Vancouver, Boston

	gp	g	a	tp	pim
rs	726	395	299	694	1241
po	93	57	32	89	168

2nd All-Star (4), Masterton

BERNIE NICHOLLS
June 24, 1961
NHL Career: 1981–99
Los Angeles, NY Rangers, Edmon-
ton, New Jersey, Chicago, San Jose

	gp	g	a	tp	pim
rs	1117	475	732	1207	1288
po	118	42	72	114	164

BOBBY ORR
March 20, 1948
NHL Career: 1966–77, 1978–79
Boston, Chicago

	gp	g	a	tp	pim
rs	657	270	645	915	953
po	74	26	66	92	107

Calder, 1st All-Star (8), 2nd All-Star,
Ross (2), Hart (3), Norris (8),
Pearson, Smythe (2), Stanley Cup (2),
HOF 1979

BERNIE PARENT
April 3, 1945
NHL Career: 1965–72, 1973–79
Boston, Philadelphia, Toronto

	gp	m	ga	so	ave
rs	608	35136	1493	54	2.55
po	71	4302	174	6	2.43

1st All-Star (2), Vezina (2),
Smythe (2), Stanley Cup (2),
HOF 1984

BRAD PARK
July 6, 1948
NHL Career: 1968–85
NY Rangers, Boston, Detroit

	gp	g	a	tp	pim
rs	1113	213	683	896	1429
po	161	35	90	125	217

1st All-Star (5), 2nd All-Star (2),
Masterton, HOF 1988

GILBERT PERREAULT
November 13, 1950
NHL Career: 1970–87
Buffalo

	gp	g	a	tp	pim
rs	1191	512	814	1326	500
po	90	33	70	103	44

Calder, 2nd All-Star (2), Byng,
HOF 1990

PIERRE PILOTE
December 11, 1931
NHL Career: 1955–69
Chicago, Toronto

	gp	g	a	tp	pim
rs	890	80	418	498	1251
po	86	8	53	61	102

1st All-Star (5), 2nd All-Star (3),
Norris (3), Stanley Cup, HOF 1975

DENIS POTVIN
October 29, 1953
NHL Career: 1973–88
NY Islanders

	gp	g	a	tp	pim
rs	1060	310	742	1052	1354
po	185	56	108	164	253

Calder, 1st All-Star (5), 2nd All-Star
(2), Norris (3), Stanley Cup (4),
HOF 1991

JEAN RATELLE
October 3, 1940
NHL Career: 1962–81
NY Rangers, Boston

	gp	g	a	tp	pim
rs	1281	491	776	1267	276
po	123	32	66	98	24

2nd All-Star, Byng (2), Pearson,
Masterton, HOF 1985

HENRI RICHARD
February 29, 1936
NHL Career: 1955–75
Montreal

	gp	g	a	tp	pim
rs	1256	358	688	1046	928
po	180	49	80	129	181

1st All-Star, 2nd All-Star (3),
Masterton, Stanley Cup (11),
HOF 1979

MAURICE RICHARD
August 4, 1921–May 27, 2000
NHL Career: 1942–60
Montreal

	gp	g	a	tp	pim
rs	978	544	421	965	1285
po	133	82	44	126	188

1st All-Star (8), 2nd All-Star (6),
Hart, Stanley Cup (8), HOF 1961

LUC ROBITAILLE
February 17, 1966
NHL Career: 1986–
Los Angeles, Pittsburgh,
NY Rangers, Detroit

	gp	g	a	tp	pim
rs	1124	590	648	1238	981
po	132	53	64	117	162

Calder, 1st All-Star (5),
2nd All-Star (3)

JEREMY ROENICK
January 17, 1970
NHL Career: 1988–
Chicago, Phoenix, Philadelphia

	gp	g	a	tp	pim
rs	908	408	539	947	1134
po	100	44	51	95	71

PATRICK ROY
October 5, 1965
NHL Career: 1985–
Montreal, Colorado

	gp	m	ga	so	ave
rs	903	52693	2287	52	2.60
po	219	13545	516	19	2.29

1st All-Star (3), 2nd All-Star (2),
Jennings (4), Vezina (3), Smythe (3),
Stanley Cup (4)

JOE SAKIC
July 7, 1969
NHL Career: 1988–
Quebec, Colorado

	gp	g	a	tp	pim
rs	934	457	721	1178	398
po	114	56	73	129	58

1st All-Star, Hart, Byng, Pearson,
Smythe, Stanley Cup (2)

DEREK SANDERSON
June 16, 1946
NHL Career: 1965–78
Boston, NY Rangers, St. Louis,
Vancouver, Pittsburgh

	gp	g	a	tp	pim
rs	598	202	250	452	911
po	56	18	12	30	187

Calder, Stanley Cup (2)

DENIS SAVARD
February 4, 1961
NHL Career: 1980–97
Chicago, Montreal, Tampa Bay

	gp	g	a	tp	pim
rs	1196	473	865	1338	1336
po	169	66	109	175	256

2nd All-Star, Stanley Cup, HOF 2000

TEEMU SELANNE
July 3, 1970
NHL Career: 1992–
Winnipeg, Anaheim, San Jose

	gp	g	a	tp	pim
rs	637	379	422	801	233
po	27	13	9	22	10

Calder, 1st All-Star (2),
2nd All-Star (2), Richard

EDDIE SHACK
February 11, 1937
NHL Career: 1958–75
NY Rangers, Toronto, Boston,
Los Angeles, Buffalo, Pittsburgh

	gp	g	a	tp	pim
rs	1047	239	226	465	1437
po	74	6	7	13	151

Stanley Cup (4)

BRENDAN SHANAHAN
January 23, 1969
NHL Career: 1987–
New Jersey, St. Louis, Hartford,
Detroit

	gp	g	a	tp	pim
rs	1028	466	489	955	1935
po	112	42	48	90	207

1st All-Star (2), Stanley Cup (2)

DARRYL SITTLER
September 18, 1950
NHL Career: 1970–85
Toronto, Philadelphia, Detroit

	gp	g	a	tp	pim
rs	1096	484	637	1121	948
po	76	29	45	74	137

2nd All-Star, HOF 1989

BILLY SMITH
December 12, 1950
NHL Career: 1971–89
Los Angeles, NY Islanders

	gp	m	ga	so	ave
rs	680	38431	2031	22	3.17
po	132	7645	348	5	2.73

1st All-Star, Jennings, Vezina,
Smythe, Stanley Cup (4), HOF 1993

PETER STASTNY
September 18, 1956
NHL Career: 1980–95
Quebec, New Jersey, St Louis

	gp	g	a	tp	pim
rs	977	450	789	1239	824
po	93	33	72	105	123

Calder, HOF 1998

MATS SUNDIN
February 13, 1971
NHL Career: 1990–
Quebec, Toronto

	gp	g	a	tp	pim
rs	848	356	506	862	665
po	59	28	26	54	52

BRENT SUTTER
June 10, 1962
NHL Career: 1980–98
NY Islanders, Chicago

	gp	g	a	tp	pim
rs	1111	363	466	829	1054
po	144	30	44	74	164

Stanley Cup (2)

KEITH TKACHUK
March 28, 1972
NHL Career: 1992–
Winnipeg, Phoenix, St Louis

	gp	g	a	tp	pim
rs	652	329	302	631	1512
po	59	21	16	37	120

2nd All-Star (2)

BRYAN TROTTIER
July 17, 1956
NHL Career: 1975–92, 1993–94
NY Islanders, Pittsburgh

	gp	g	a	tp	pim
rs	1279	524	901	1425	912
po	221	71	113	184	277

Calder, 1st All-Star (2),
2nd All-Star (2), Ross, Hart, Clancy,
Smythe, Stanley Cup (6), HOF 1997

NORM ULLMAN
December 26, 1935
NHL Career: 1955–75
Detroit, Toronto

	gp	g	a	tp	pim
rs	1410	490	739	1229	712
po	106	30	53	83	67

1st All-Star, 2nd All-Star, HOF 1982

JOHN VANBIESBROUCK
September 4, 1963
NHL Career: 1981–82, 1983–2001
NY Rangers, Florida, Philadelphia,
NY Islanders, New Jersey

	gp	m	ga	so	ave
rs	877	50175	2493	40	2.98
po	71	3969	177	5	2.68

1st All-Star, 2nd All-Star,
Vezina

PAT VERBEEK
May 24, 1964
NHL Career: 1983–
New Jersey, Hartford, NY Rangers,
Dallas, Detroit

	gp	g	a	tp	pim
rs	1360	515	528	1043	2833
po	117	26	36	62	225

Stanley Cup

DOUG WILSON
July 5, 1957
NHL Career: 1977–93
Chicago, San Jose

	gp	g	a	tp	pim
rs	1024	237	590	827	830
po	95	19	61	80	88

1st All-Star, 2nd All-Star (2), Norris

LORNE WORSLEY
May 14, 1929
NHL Career: 1952–53, 1954–74
New York, Montreal, Minnesota

	gp	m	ga	so	ave
rs	861	50183	2407	43	2.88
po	70	4084	189	5	2.78

Calder, 1st All-Star, 2nd All-Star,
Vezina (2), Stanley Cup (4), HOF 1980

ALEXEI YASHIN
November 5, 1973
NHL Career: 1993–99, 2000–
Ottawa, NY Islanders

	gp	g	a	tp	pim
rs	504	218	273	491	222
po	26	6	9	15	20

2nd All-Star

STEVE YZERMAN
May 9, 1965
NHL Career: 1983–
Detroit

	gp	g	a	tp	pim
rs	1310	645	969	1614	834
po	154	61	91	152	68

1st All-Star, Selke, Pearson, Smythe,
Stanley Cup (2)

Acknowledgments

For the Love of Hockey owes a great deal to Sue Gordon, who supported me throughout a long and, at times, arduous project. This book frequently took me away from my parenting and household responsibilities and left her holding down the fort alone. Our children, Quinn, Tara and Isaac, always remained enthusiastic about the book. Having children changed my life, and I'll be eternally grateful. It was a trip with Quinn to a Leafs game at Maple Leaf Gardens—his birthday request—that led to this book. I hadn't been to the Gardens for more than a decade, but we had so much fun together. Seeing the game through Quinn's eyes helped me remember what I most love about hockey, and on the car ride home, the idea for this book was born.

My family, especially my parents, Alanson and Nora McDonell, were encouraging and offered helpful advice in getting this book through its initial stages. My sisters, brother and in-laws were always supportive, not least with their warm welcome on my road trips. I'd also like to acknowledge the many other friends who opened their homes to me and offered their hospitality.

I'd like to thank Steve McAllister of the National Hockey League Players' Association (NHLPA), one of the most important people in helping this book along from its conception to its birth. Doug Wilson, Lori Radke, Laurel Overland, Ted Saskin, Barb Larcina and Sharon MacFarlane of the NHLPA have also been of invaluable assistance. Doug Wilson and the rest of the Steering Committee of the NHLPA's Alumni Associations (Bob Nystrom, Gerry Sillers, Leo Reise, Andy Bathgate, Keith Magnuson, Tom Reid and Keith McCreary) saw how this book could make a significant contribution to their Players Helping Players Fund, and I thank them for that. I've always respected John Davidson for his work in the goal and in the broadcast booth, so it's an honor to have him write the foreword of this book.

Craig Campbell of the Hockey Hall of Fame spent innumerable hours in the archives selecting photo possibilities for this book, and I am appreciative of his diligence and keen eye. Jane Rodney always made my trips to the Hall more efficient and more enjoyable. Larry Scanlan offered encouragement and guidance and took a gentle but firm hand in helping me with the flow and tone of the text. He was generous in sharing his insight and experience as an editor, writer, interviewer and hockey fan, and I leaned on him frequently. Ulrike Bender, the book's designer, is also Larry's partner, and I trust this is more providential than coincidental. I like what she's done with my idea for this book. Tracy Read and Susan Dickinson of Bookmakers Press and Charlotte DuChene and Catherine DeLury drove us through the home stretch, and I've valued their grace under pressure and attention to detail. Lionel Koffler and Michael Worek of Firefly Books have demonstrated great faith and patience, and I'm beholden to them for both.

Martin Robbert, Claire Astley, Herb Jones, Brian Burt, Alex English, Michael Hayward, Katrin Bergstrome, Therese Conway Killen, Dalla and Jeremy Brown, Pat Pryde, Nancy Macmillan, Michael Hurley, Barb Perry, Gord McDiarmid and Kathrine Christensen—great friends all—have been helpful and strong boosters to Sue and me along the way. Thank you.

I also received tremendous support from the NHL clubs' media and communications personnel, especially Pat Park in Toronto and Frederique Cardinal in Montreal. This book would have been almost impossible to complete without all of them. Susie Mathieu also arranged a number of meetings. Johnny Bucyk of the Boston Bruins was more helpful than I could have dreamed, and taking in a Bruins game beside "The Chief" stands out as some of the most enjoyable time spent on this book.

Vicki Ridout of the Writers' Union of Canada gave me valuable advice, and I thank her for her time. Bob Hilderley and Susan Hannah of Quarry Press in Kingston gave me encouragement, practical suggestions and a publisher's perspective. Therese Conway Killen offered some of her many skills in helping me transcribe stories. Cliff Goff and Mel McNulty of Gananoque All-Sports helped along the way. Don Cherry also offered his assistance without hesitation in the book's early stages, a gesture more important than he likely realized.

I am grateful to all the players who have shared their time with me and their stories and pictures in this book. Perhaps above all, though, I would like to thank the countless unsung hockey players who are not in these pages. *For the Love of Hockey* indirectly tells their stories too, because a passion for hockey itself seems to be almost universal amongst those who have played it. To those who helped develop this beautiful game, dedicated their youth and prime physical years to the pursuit of hockey excellence and entertained and inspired me and millions of other fans go our indebtedness and gratitude.

—*Chris McDonell*

Photo Credits

Steve Babineau, Sports Action Photography: 20, 21, 23, 31, 48, 53, 68, 69, 96, 101, 103, 102, 109, 115, 123, 126, 127, 128, 171

Bruce Bennett Studios: 149, 154, 175, 178

Graphic Artists/Hockey Hall of Fame: 14, 16, 24, 25, 27, 40, 44, 65, 72, 78, 83, 95, 112, 131, 133, 145, 157, 162, 163, 181, 189

Imperial Oil-Turofsky/Hockey Hall of Fame: 17, 63, 73, 80, 111, 147

London Life-Lewis Portnoy/Hockey Hall of Fame: 8, 9, 11, 22, 26, 33, 37, 38, 41, 45, 46, 47, 49, 64, 71, 84, 89, 98, 99, 113, 114, 116, 117, 119, 130, 132, 135, 134, 136, 137, 140, 141, 142, 143, 144, 156, 166, 167, 168, 169, 179, 180, 187, 188

James McCarthy/Hockey Hall of Fame: 12, 81

Doug MacLellan/Hockey Hall of Fame: 18, 19, 28, 29, 30, 34, 35, 36, 39, 42, 43, 50, 51, 52, 54, 55, 56, 57, 58, 59, 60, 61, 66, 67, 70, 74, 75, 77, 86, 87, 90, 91, 93, 97, 100, 102, 104, 105, 106, 107, 108, 120, 121, 122, 124, 125, 129, 148, 151, 150, 152, 153, 155, 158, 159, 160, 161, 164, 165, 170, 172, 173, 174, 176, 177, 182, 183, 184, 185, 186, 190, 191, 192, 193

Mary Jane Mendes/Hockey Hall of Fame: 92

Miles Nadal/Hockey Hall of Fame: 76

Frank Prazak/Hockey Hall of Fame: 13, 15, 32, 62, 79, 82, 85, 88, 94, 118, 110, 139, 138, 146